THE
STRANGERS
NEXT DOOR

◆

THE
STRANGERS
NEXT DOOR

———————◆———————

Edith Iglauer

with a foreword by Allan Fotheringham

HARBOUR PUBLISHING

Published by
HARBOUR PUBLISHING
P.O. Box 219
Madeira Park, BC Canada V0N 2H0

Cover tapestry by Rita Oosuaq; reproduced courtesy of Arctic Co-operatives Ltd.
Cover design by Roger Handling
Many portions of this book originally appeared in *The New Yorker* as "A Reporter at Large" or as "Profiles."
The illustrations in this book by the artists Abe Birnbaum, Tom Funk, Thomas B. Allen and Burt Silverman all appeared originally in *The New Yorker*. The sealskin stencil print by Sheouak, "Men Meeting," appeared on the cover of the program for the First Conference of the Arctic Co-operatives, Frobisher Bay, NWT, March 1963.
Printed and bound in Canada

Canadian Cataloguing in Publication Data

Iglauer, Edith
    The strangers next door

    Essays which originally appeared in various publications.
    ISBN 1-55017-054-6

    I. Title.
PS3517.G43S8 1991   814'.54   C91-091562-8

for Philip and Anna Hamburger

Contents

Foreword

It was a long and weary all-night session in the rotunda of the British Columbia legislature building, filled with reporters who are—contrary to legend—mostly boring people. This would be 1981, the until-dawn drama of the ten provincial premiers hammering out the Victoria Charter, which was to save Canada (once again!) until Robert Bourassa folded his cards and killed the deal.

Throughout the night, as coffee flowed and stale cigarette smoke accumulated, I noticed a most incongruous and indomitable figure: a short and perky white-haired stranger who seemed so out-of-synch with the jaded radio reporters and legislative regulars. Since my sin is that I am attracted to interesting-looking women, I introduced myself and so came into contact with the ineffable Edith Iglauer.

Since that all-night vigil, I have marvelled at her diligence and her remarkable eye for the genius of Canada, which for too long has escaped Canadian journalists. A tremulous product of Manhattan (as she pretends), she has roamed the Canadian North, and in doing so, encountered one Pierre Elliott Trudeau and limned him in a memorable *New Yorker* profile that startled Canadians with its insights. She was one of the first to recognize the master hand of Arthur Erickson, the quirky, brilliant Canadian architect who, in time, will be recognized in this country as Frank Lloyd Wright is in his country.

The lady with the white hair and the infectious smile has extraordinary range: reporting on the watershed historical moment of Marian Anderson's concert in the auditorium of the Daughters of the American Revolution, who had denied the magnificent Miss Anderson the use of that hall for a concert in 1939; covering Eleanor Roosevelt's press conferences at the White House; writing for *Harper's* in the early years of the United Nations; creating a remarkable love story in *Fishing with John*—the Manhattan sophisticate who ended

9

up in Garden Bay, British Columbia, still with the contagious giggle that I love her for, still with the mane of hair.

When Edith Iglauer and I met ten years ago, we became friends within minutes, if not seconds: two souls separated by nationalities, by a continent—joined by wit and irony and love of the language—drawn to one another instantly. And to this day.

ALLAN FOTHERINGHAM

Author's Note

———————— ✦ ————————

I ADDED A NEW ROOM to my house in Garden Bay this year to accommodate writing tools that in my wildest dreams I could never have imagined I would have: a computer and printer first; then a copier, and now an exotic new toy called a fax machine. I softened the impact of this torrent of mechanical equipment by adding an outside deck facing the water, so that when my hands shake and my head spins because my machines misbehave, I can step through my new French doors and pick a rose or a sprig of tarragon or a strawberry from the pots that live there.

I began reading into my past, as I moved my files into my new study, and discovered a lot of old friends in the writing I have done over almost fifty years. It was a strange feeling to wander back over the working life of the person I was, and to speculate on how much of that inquisitive young girl is still with me. As I went along I began to select items from the newspapers, some of which crumbled to pieces when I handled them, and from the war dispatches, magazines and books that I wrote that stirred up memories. This book is a collection from those, along with introductory notes on how they came to be written, or something else about them that I thought readers would enjoy knowing.

While I was in college, I read *The Autobiography of Lincoln Steffens* and decided that I wanted to be a journalist; and that to be one, perseverance was what counted. I was very systematic about trying to get a job as a newspaper reporter. I spent the summer after my graduation sitting on benches outside the editors' offices of the three daily newspapers in Cleveland, Ohio, where I grew up. I allotted the same two hours to each editor every weekday and became a familiar figure, to whom everyone nodded as they arrived and departed. A veteran columnist named Jack Raper, famous for publishing idiotic comments made by public figures and then printing the head of a little bull beside them, would beckon me into his office and cheer me with funny stories. All three editors finally saw me, when it was apparent I wasn't going to vanish, and told me there were no openings for reporters just then.

That fall, I was accepted at the Graduate School of Journalism at Columbia University, which seemed the next best route into the newspaper world. What a great school that was! At that time, there were many magazines and newspapers published in New York, and the faculty consisted almost entirely of writers and editors who were still working journalists themselves.

Walter B. Pitkin, a realist with a store of irreverent anecdotes, who had just had a huge success with his book, *Life Begins at Forty*, taught us feature writing. Douglas Southall Freeman, biographer of Robert E. Lee, rose every Monday morning before five to fly in from Richmond, Virginia to train us in editorial and newswriting. A Monday morning exercise was to write the week's news in an hour, and if Freeman liked our editorials he printed them in *The Richmond News Leader*, which he edited. George Gallup came to tell us about opinion polls, which had just begun to come into style, and Paul White, news editor at the Columbia Broadcasting System, travelled uptown to teach us radio newswriting. Editors from *The New York Times* and Henry Pringle, a well-known writer and historian, managed our newsroom, and we ran all over the city reporting for the School's paper. Our Dean of Women, Eleanor Carroll, sent me to *The Christian Science Monitor*, which was starting a women's page. I began writing for it while I was still at Columbia, and continued for several years thereafter.

At the very end of the school year I thought my dream had come true: I was given a two-week tryout as a reporter on a daily evening newspaper, *The New York Post*.

My first assignment was to interview a charming young movie producer named Arthur Hornblow, Jr., who had just married Myrna Loy, the glamorous film actress. I was to ask him how he liked being married to her. I talked all around the subject and ended up confessing to him that this was my first day as a newspaper reporter. He grinned and said, "*What* did your editor tell you to ask me?"

I blushed and told him my instructions. "How you feel about your marriage is none of my business," I blurted out, and he laughed. He told me he missed his wife and talked to her every morning "across the continent," and after we had gotten that over with, he discussed the American theatre and his own career—he was producing Jack

Benny and Bob Hope movies—all of which appeared in *The Post* as a little story that evening.

My second assignment sent me to a Greenwich Village restaurant whose owner had committed suicide earlier that morning by jumping out of a window. I was instructed to ask the chef, who had worked for the owner for twenty years, how he felt. He was so grief-stricken that I couldn't bring myself to interview him at all. I talked to all the policemen there instead, but that wasn't what the editor wanted. He promptly sent me out to a house in the Bronx to interview the family of a boy who had just been killed riding freight cars. I arrived as the police were breaking the news to the youngster's mother, knowing that if I didn't ask how this poor woman felt I'd be out of a job, but by now I wasn't sure I wanted to keep it anyway.

When I got back to the paper, the editor called me up to the desk. "I couldn't ask your questions at a time like that," I said.

"You shouldn't be in this kind of journalism," the editor replied, and fired me. That's the only time I worked in the newsroom of a daily paper.

I took that editor's advice, and became a free-lance writer, except for a brief period after graduating from Columbia when I had publicity jobs that I detested, and during World War II, when I worked for the government. In that way I was able to choose my own assignments and my own way of working them out. When I finally started writing for *The New Yorker* magazine, in 1958, although I had been a journalist for more than fifteen years I felt as if I were starting all over again, but it was a breathtaking experience. I had the pleasure of knowing the first editor, Harold Ross, but he died before I began to write for the magazine, and the second editor of that great publication, William Shawn, was the person for whom I wrote. In my introductions to the pieces included here that I wrote for *The New Yorker*, I have tried to give an idea of what it was like to work in the free and receptive atmosphere created by an editor as warm and intellectually brilliant as William Shawn.

Whenever I went in to see him, perhaps once or twice a year, either with a new idea, or to discuss what I was working on, I was always tense. I would walk into his office, dropping papers and pencils as I proceeded, and Bill patiently would pick them up and hand them to me when I was safely seated. Once we had started talking, the eager attention with which he listened, interspersed with quick bursts of laughter when he was amused, would make me forget my nervousness, and the words would pour out. When I stopped talking, there would be a few questions, and a quick remark—I never knew anyone who could grasp the essence of an idea and turn it in the right direction so well — and I would rise to go. I would leave, trailing papers and pencils as I departed, and we would both laugh, as he handed them to me once again.

Looking over the pieces I have written, I realize that I have been like someone with family in two countries, attempting to acquaint them with one another. I am not just an American journalist writing about Canada for Americans, but a Canadian journalist writing about America for Canadians as well. Both countries, I have discovered, still regard their neighbors across our common border as "the strangers next door," and like any concerned relative, I want them to know and respect one another as much as I do.

◆

A special note of appreciation to Renée Mead Brown, Jay Hamburger, Philip Hamburger and Franklin White, who were immeasurably helpful; and to my contractors, Don Murray, Rex Baum, Lois Randle and Terry Lindsay, who finished my spacious new study in the nick of time and made it a perfect place for me to work on this book.

E.I.

Part One

◆

EARLY YEARS

Marian Anderson

———————— ✦ ————————

I WROTE SEVERAL ARTICLES in the early forties for the *Christian Science Monitor* about interesting women, most of whom have faded from public memory; but not the unforgettable black singer, Marian Anderson.

One sunny summer afternoon I was sent to interview her at her home in Connecticut. In the article I wrote, published here, she refers to the concert she gave in 1939 on the steps of the Lincoln Memorial before an audience of 75,000. The Daughters of the American Revolution (DAR), an exclusive society whose members trace their forebears back to the American Revolution, had denied Miss Anderson the use of their auditorium because of her race. The words they used were that they were "conforming to local custom in excluding her." The First Lady, Eleanor Roosevelt, then sponsored the free concert at the Lincoln Memorial, and resigned from the DAR.

The following is an excerpt from that article:

———————— ✦ ————————

Marian Anderson opened a new chapter in her life last year when she bought the lovely farm at Hill Plain, Connecticut. Into it went years of planning and dreaming, long years of winter concert tours and briefly snatched holidays. For her it meant, simply a home of her own to return to.

I visited Miss Anderson at her farm, two hours from New York, for this special interview for The Christian Science Monitor. The road suddenly turns up a small hill to a broad gate, with a sign, "Marianna," before it. Beyond is the large white colonial house with green shutters, where she lives. The smaller buildings for livestock are across the road. Hidden deep in a small woods on the side of a slope, is the one-room studio she had built especially for practicing.

She was in that studio when I came — a stately, handsome woman, who rose from the piano with a broad smile of welcome. Wearing a quilted cotton sports jacket over a simple black dress, with an Indian print bandanna around her head and white, flat-heeled sandals on her feet, she appeared completely comfortable and relaxed. She retained the quiet dignity that characterizes her stage presence.

"I love it here. I love to work here," she said softly. "I planned this studio myself, with the help of the architect, a friend of mine." The room was cool and spacious, with an arched roof and a large stone fireplace. As Miss Anderson talked, her eyes lighted appreciatively on objects around the room; on the soft beige walls, the attractive tan and green flowered curtains, the pretty vines in the corners, and the low, long chairs and couches made of bamboo, which she brought back from her tour through Hawaii last year. The green foliage seen through the extra-size windows on three sides fitted perfectly into the fresh, outdoor atmosphere; and the only signs of work were the large grand piano and the recording machine which Miss Anderson uses to check her voice control.

"I don't have any fixed hours for practice each day — except a brief time after breakfast or before lunch, and again two or three hours before dinner," she explained. "Indeed, I often prefer to do most of my work after dinner, with Mr. Franz Rupp, my accompanist, who stays here with his wife four days each week so that we can practice together.

"In town, of course, it's different," she continued. "There I stay at a hotel, and one never knows how one's neighbors may feel about vocal practice." She laughed. "I always have the same room, though; and the people next door fortunately are in the theatre, so they sleep late and work late nights. I never start practicing then before noon."

Her eyes sparkled. "I needed a real home like this," she said, as she led me onto a small porch at the back of the studio, overlooking a long meadow which will soon hold a swimming pool. "During the winter, when one travels so much, one feels 'I am at home' if one is in the same place for three days. Out comes the hot plate and the little cans of soup which always go with us; and we are established.

"I always said that when I did buy a home, it would be on the seashore; and that the house would have high ceilings and a fireplace in every room," she said, laughing. "I guess this pool will have to be my sea. And the ceilings at the house are about as low as they could be, and there's only one fireplace. I bought the place because of the marvellous view of the whole valley from the house." She stood silent for a moment. Then she began to hum in a deep, lovely voice as she turned and walked back into the studio.

Her tone became serious. "Regardless of whether one is an artist or not, one cannot help thinking about the international situation so much of the time now, and being affected by it. Everything reminds one of it. One gives aid where one can, but there is so much to do," she said, sadly.

Miss Anderson indicated that she felt deeply the problem of Negro discrimination in national defense industries. "How would anyone feel?" she asked. "If a fellow is qualified, it is logical that he be accepted for the job. Last spring I sang on a radio program specially designed to bring to the public the realization that here were people asking for the opportunity to help themselves. The program was under the auspices of the National Urban League, and among those who appeared were Canada Lee, Duke Ellington, Joe Louis, and many others.

"One has only one aim," she said in a low voice, as if speaking to herself. "One would like to continue to sing, as long as one can sing well. And what one would like to do is to benefit the group to which one belongs."

She referred to herself in the impersonal sense — simply, unaffectedly, as if she were standing off with the rest of us, looking with wonder at this simple woman, endowed with genius of which she is aware, but which she seems in all her actions and words to consider as the possession of her race, rather than as a personal achievement.

So far this year, the woman whose first music lessons were paid for by a church collection has won the Bok award (in March) of $10,000 as the Philadelphia citizen who accomplished most for the city, and, on June 12th, an honorary doctorate of music from Temple University. While in the same month — June — a biography of her, by her former accompanist, Kosti Vehanen, now on his way to Finland, was published.

"Sometimes one is amazed to find the thing one doesn't think will happen, really coming true," she continued, tucking her legs beneath her and settling back in her chair. "I remember how surprised I was to find the response to the concert in Washington in 1939 so great." She was speaking of the famous concert in the Lincoln Memorial — when 75,000 persons turned out to hear her sing under the auspices of the government after she had been refused the right to have concerts in two Washington buildings because of her race. As she discussed the event, she seemed to relive what was probably the greatest experience of her life, almost as though she could still see the mass of upturned faces.

"It is really a great surprise to a singer to find that she has created such excitement. One gets so thrilled, when singing on such an occasion, that one is completely outside oneself. When you see so many thousands waiting, listening, you have a tremendous feeling of responsibility. Your heart starts pounding, and you are not as steady as usual."

Published in the *Christian Science Monitor*, August 26, 1941.

In 1944, I interviewed Marian Anderson again, this time for the *New York Herald Tribune*. I was married to Philip Hamburger by then, and we were living in New York City, waiting for Phil to go overseas as *The New Yorker*'s war correspondent in the Mediterranean Theatre.

The year before, on January 7, 1943, Phil and I had attended Marian Anderson's second concert in Washington, and this time she sang in the DAR's Constitution Hall, at a gala benefit for United China Relief. It was a first for the DAR, and the first time a black singer gave a concert before an integrated audience in Washington. It was attended by the First Lady, members of the cabinet, the Supreme Court, Congress and the diplomatic corps, and it was sold out.

It is difficult even to imagine now what segregation was like in the United States almost fifty years ago. Washington was similar to most southern cities: there were separate and by no means equal public rest rooms for blacks and whites; the only restaurants where a black person and a white one could eat lunch together were the government cafeterias; hotels did not admit blacks as guests. Northern cities like New York and Cleveland weren't much better. When my mother took Armenia Baker, the beloved black woman who worked for her, to a department store restaurant for a social lunch, it was an Act of Bravery. They could hardly wait to tell me about it, including what they wore and ate, when I arrived several days later from New York.

Marian Anderson, at the height of her career, was stopped from using the front elevator in an elegant New York hotel, when she went there to see her dentist. She refused to use the service elevator to which she was directed, called the dentist, cancelled the appointment, and changed dentists.

In her dignified, quiet way, Marian Anderson, who is eighty-nine and still active, although retired from singing for many years, has been a powerful force for the integration of the races in the United States.

◆

As she looks back over ten years of concert tours, some of which have taken her into the deep South, Marian Anderson, the great Negro singer, feels that there has been considerable improvement in Negro-white relations.

Miss Anderson, who will give her tenth anniversary concert at Carnegie Hall Jan. 7, was interviewed over the holidays, at her peaceful Connecticut farm.

"There are some Negro artists who will not go to the South," she said, in her deep, low voice, as she sat before the fire in her study on "Marianna Farm." "Perhaps they are right, and yet each of us must work in our own way."

For her part, she feels that by singing before white and Negro people in the South, she is helping to bring about an understanding of the Negro.

Last year in Jackson, Miss., which Miss Anderson described as "not a very liberal town," the manager of the city auditorium had been sharply criticized for permitting Negroes to attend her concert. Yet, at the end of her performance, as she put it, "the applause was sufficient to make one feel that the people were pleased." The mixed audience asked for encores and more encores, until finally Miss Anderson suggested that the audience rise and sing "Swanee River" with her. They did, and the next morning an editorial in a local paper said that such a thing had never happened before, and that it had been a great spiritual experience for all to rise above their prejudices.

When Miss Anderson sang in Shreveport, La., in 1941, her accompanist, Franz Rupp, and her traveling manager, Isaac Jofe, who are Europeans, were met at the station by the lady manager of the concert. After rehearsal that afternoon, Miss Anderson noticed that both Rupp and Jofe seemed to be extremely angry about something.

"Anyway," she said, "we had the concert, and there was tremendous applause after each number. At the end, I took Franz by the hand, as I always do, and came out to make a bow. The applause was deafening. When we finally made our train, Franz and Jofe told me what had happened."

The lady manager had drawn Jofe aside while Miss Anderson and Rupp were rehearsing, and had said, "I understand that she takes her white accompanist by the hand, after the encores. She cannot do that here."

To which Jofe had replied, "What Miss Anderson does on the stage is her own business."

The audience, apparently, agreed.

Miss Anderson tours the South every other year. She likes to sing only "where the Negro will certainly have adequate representation, and accommodations equal to the best, if he can pay for the best."

In some cases, Miss Anderson has found that the audience is to be thoroughly segregated too late to pull out, as happened in New Orleans in 1939. But in spite of occasional setbacks Miss Anderson is far from discouraged. "So many people now are trying to learn a little more about race problems," she said, "that surely much good will come of it. Why, just recently, at a concert in Boston, a fourteen-year-old girl came up and asked me what she could do to help the Negroes!"

The most encouraging sign of all, Miss Anderson feels, is the camaraderie being achieved between Negro and white boys in the armed services, and the excellent education many of them are getting.

"When I sing at camps or hospitals," she continued, "the white boys are just as enthusiastic as the Negroes, sometimes more so, as they have had more opportunities with music."

Early in December she opened the "Marian Anderson USO" in Portland, Me. At the request of the Army Signal Corps, she also made a Christmas film with Leopold Stokowski and the Westminster Choir. She wanted to sing a Christmas carol, as the picture was to be used in United States army posts all over the world, but the boys would have nothing but her own favorite, "Ave Maria."

Published in the *New York Herald Tribune*, December 31, 1944.

Mrs. Roosevelt

◆

RIGHT AFTER PEARL HARBOR, December 7, 1941, I went to Washington to look for a job with the war effort. I found one in an exciting place: the radio-newsroom of the Office of War Information. I was the youngest person in the office, so I was put in charge of two desks nobody else seemed to want: religion and Scandinavia.

This was before TV, and radio was the big communicator. We prepared news and other public information that was beamed abroad by shortwave radio to all our allies in countries occupied by the enemy, and to those who were still free. After turning in my copy, I would watch the words I had written click along on the teletype, wondering who would receive it, fearing what the effect might be. I knew from the dispatches that came over my desk, that listening to shortwave radio in some occupied countries, Norway for one, could be punishable by death.

My duties also included obtaining inspirational statements from important individuals, for special anniversaries and for support of victims of the Occupation. I loved the work and soon learned which religious leaders and other important persons would co-operate with our needs.

The First Lady, Eleanor Roosevelt, could be counted on always to grant any reasonable request for a special statement, and she was in steady demand. She was so popular that I suggested to our news desk that her weekly press conference in the White House become a regular feature for shortwave broadcasting overseas, and asked to cover it myself. I was cleared by the Secret Service and joined the circle of White House women journalists, most of whom had covered Mrs. Roosevelt since her husband was governor of New York. They were excellent newswomen, and I felt honored to be one of them.

Her press conference was made up exclusively of women, except on special occasions. When Mrs. Roosevelt returned from a trip to the war zones in the South Pacific, men were present for the first time at her press conference, on September 27, 1943. She opened it by announcing that the only reason she "acceded to the gentlemen's request to be present" was that this trip "had not been purely of interest to the women of the country but to the country as a whole." She added that afterward, she would "go back to the old way of doing things, no more mixed conferences," unless something unusual occurred, which she hoped would not happen.

Several of the women who made up Eleanor Roosevelt's press corps had become her close friends. Among them was Bess Furman, from *The New York Times*, who took me under her wing. When I went off for two days to get married, Bess covered for me, and at the next press conference quietly slipped me my first wedding gift, a Sterling silver serving spoon. Bess told me that "Mrs. R.," as everyone called her, never forgot the birthdays of either Bess or her twin children, and if Bess was in trouble or ill, there would be a call or even a visit from Mrs. R. Thoughtfulness, concern for others, and the strength of her convictions were among the outstanding qualities of this great woman. She was lovely to look at, with beautiful eyes and long-fingered hands filled with rings that each had their own meaning for her. Her beauty came from within, and from the grace and dignity with which she moved. Like her husband, Franklin Delano Roosevelt, she was a symbol of decency and courage, an inspiration for desperate people everywhere.

It was thrilling to walk through the front gate and up the steps of the White House, into the hall, and up the broad staircase to Mrs. Roosevelt's sitting room every week. I never got over that feeling of awe, and wonder at my own good luck.

Following are the notes that I sent around to government officials after the November 23, 1942 press conference, as I did after each one.

———————————— ✦ ————————————

To: George Lyon, Henry Pringle, Irving Pflaum, Matt Gordon, George MacMillan, Leo Pinkus, H. Aronstam.

From: Edith Iglauer

Subject: Mrs. Roosevelt's Press Conference, 11/23/42. At the White House

Note: Mrs. Roosevelt announced that her next press conference will be next Monday, November 30, 1942 at 11 a.m. Please notify me, Room 5439, Extension 2945, if you have any questions for the conference, or statement requests.

Subjects Discussed: (There was no off-the-record comment)

1. Social engagements this week
2. Trip to England
3. Silk stockings
4. $25,000 salary limit
5. Coffee rationing
6. Foster homes for children of war workers
7. Drafting of 18 and 19-year-olds
8. Thanksgiving

1. Social engagements

Today (November 23) Mrs. Roosevelt had the cabinet wives for lunch. This afternoon, the President of Ecuador, the Ecuadorean Ambassador, and his aides are coming to the White House for tea. The President is giving him a formal stag dinner, after which the President of Ecuador and his son will spend the night at the White House.

Tomorrow (November 24) Mrs. Roosevelt is going to Connecticut College to speak, and will be back in Washington Wednesday morning.

Wednesday noon she speaks on the Farm and Home Hour about rural life in England in the war.

Thursday is Thanksgiving. (See Early and President's release) No special guests.

Mrs. R. is going to Hyde Park at the end of the week. She will be back Monday morning, and have her press conference at 11 a.m. Monday noon she will lunch at the Democratic Women's Club.

Mrs. R. made a special note of the fact that tonight (November 23) she is attending the concert given by the United States Air Force Band at Bolling Field. She said she had been asked before she went away, and "tonight seems like a good night to go."

2. Trip to England

"When I went to England, I asked Elmer Davis if there was anything he would like me to do. He has asked me to talk on the Farm and Home Hour, and he and Mrs. Morgenthau asked me to open the Women in War Week Bond Drive in Philadelphia yesterday. He also asked me to make two rather short reports on the situation of women in industry in England. I have been asked by a number of other people to watch out for special things during my trip. This I have done.

"I have also reported back on my trip to Norman Davis, of the Red Cross, to Secretary Knox, and to Secretary Stimson. (I have not seen Mr. McNutt) I have said what my impressions were, and tried to answer questions. I cannot tell you any more than that.

ENTERTAINMENT OF OUR SOLDIERS IN BRITAIN: "The Red Cross is the only agency for US entertainment overseas. It is very well equipped, considering the difficulties of transportation. Occasionally, as a new place opens, someone will see it while it is still ill-equipped, but they are getting whatever they can from the British, and doing a very good job. It seems to me the criterion of a good job is, 'How much is it used?' I never went in a Red Cross recreation center that I didn't find a crowd of boys, which seems to me to be the only way to judge whether it is a good job or not.

WOOLEN SOCKS: "The boys in this country don't like woolen socks, and don't wear them as a rule. After they are over there, they discover that it is very difficult walking there in the mud, and that wet wool is not as bad as wet cotton. Now they will accept wool socks, if offered." (This in regard to a previous discussion in her column on American boys' dislike of wool socks)

IDEAS FROM ENGLAND: "I brought back any number of ideas from England. I don't mean that they are for the United States to copy, but I think it would be interesting for women in the United States to know about them, and perhaps adapt them. Many of course cannot, and should not be developed here now, for we have no use for them.

"It is interesting, however, that in London, a MENDING BUREAU has been opened for American soldiers. Women volunteers do their sewing. This shows a great deal of good will, and adaptability to what is needed.

"Again, the English are using all the material things they have. For instance, they must keep MOBILE CANTEENS on hand for relief after bombing. They have found a way to use these continuously. In shipbuilding districts, the women drive the mobile canteens to the docks, and give the shipbuilders hot meals while they work. One woman told me she had grown to know the men for the first time, and had developed a great respect for them. She had lived in that district for years without ever before becoming acquainted with them. In rural areas, the canteens are used for providing hot school lunches, and to take hot meals to workers in the fields. This shortens their work, and makes it unnecessary for them to go home at noon time.

"We're not so strapped on man power here, for it's different in a country of 130 million people, compared to a country of 46 million. Women are much more needed there, but even in England, they do not encourage women with small children to work unless it is an absolute necessity. Of course many war casualties in families have made it necessary for some women to work to support their families. Besides, theirs is a completely mobilized country, and though there may come a time when we have to become more completely mobilized, that time has not come yet.

POST-WAR INDUSTRIAL PLANNING: "The English have been at war three years, and have had more time to think ahead to what they are going to use later. Mr. Bevin has a wider area of authority than we have here. He told me that he remembered that bad buildings put up in the last war became slum dwellings after the war.

"This time, the buildings here have been put up with the idea that they *will* be lived in. For instance, with a high explosive factory I visited, they have tried to think of how it could be put into a peacetime industry and are planning a new type of training there for workers. It will be very much like our own NYA, but for industrial centers.

YOUNG PEOPLE IN ENGLAND: "You see a fairly large number of young people in the English universities, which are well attended. But remember, they are all doing exactly what the government has asked them to do. Their curriculum is something the government wants them to know, and liberal arts are definitely on the side. Too, some of them are youngsters who can't go back to the fighting forces. You can't always tell by appearance when a man is incapacitated. You never see a young man in civilian defense jobs, or civil service, or in industry, unless he is extraordinarily capable and his place cannot be filled by someone else. You do see boys below draft age helping on the machines. The percentage of men in the fighting forces in England, however, is very much higher than here."

3. Silk Stockings

"I have heard here that in our own shops a service man can go on and buy silk stockings more easily than we can, but I haven't tracked it down."

4. $25,000 salary limit

"I never suggested the $25,000 salary limit. I never heard of it until I saw it in the papers. I had heard that it would not include a person's private income, but I understand now that private incomes have already been taken away in taxes.

"In England, I found that practically nobody has over $21,000 a year after everything has been paid. (Someone asked about the King then, to which Mrs. Roosevelt replied, "I didn't ask the King.") I did ask about a man who is probably the richest in Great Britain, but found out that the bigger your income, the more responsibilities you have to take on. I believe it is hardest for the country person, who has depended for his income on rent from his tenants."

5. Coffee rationing (Is the White House rationed on coffee?)

"We are rationed on coffee. We don't give anyone more than one cup a day. We will give the President of Ecuador after-dinner coffee, but most of us here drink a combination of hot milk with a small amount of coffee anyway. My husband, who thinks he's an expert on coffee, says if you dry out your used grains, and then put in a few teaspoons of fresh, the resulting coffee will be quite good. Franklin himself never has more than a cup in the morning, and a small one after dinner. I myself, wouldn't know the difference, whether I got tea, coffee, or hot water."

6. Foster homes for children of war workers

"Sometimes it works and sometimes it doesn't. The Government is trying to use instead government controlled nurseries, and schools, because it is better to leave the child with its own home and mother."

7. Drafting of 18 and 19 year olds

"If they are very careful about physical and psychiatric examinations, 18 and 19 year olds will fare no worse than the others. It is hard for anyone to go to war. The men who are worst off, and the least good soldiers, the least devil-may-care are those who have established a way of life, a home and family, and are longing to be there all the time. They would ask, 'Are things awfully bad at home?' whenever they saw me. It makes you choke, when you consider that the people back home are certainly better off than they are. The younger ones, on the other hand, have nothing to fall back on, no conscience about whom they go out with, or what they do. They make the better fighting force.

8. Thanksgiving

"We have a great deal to be thankful for this Thanksgiving. I have written more about this in my column for Thanksgiving Day, so I don't think I shall elaborate now. But simply being a citizen of the United States is something to be thankful for." (Note: Mrs. Roosevelt's Thanksgiving Day column might be excellent for short-wave use, and it might be possible to get an advance from United Features for translating.) Material from Mrs. Roosevelt's remarks on England, the President's coffee recipe, her social engagements, and Thanksgiving statement were telephoned from the White House in a brief report, and were transmitted to New York for abroad.

There were always questions about how wartime rationing — shoes, butter, and so on — affected the White House, but the coffee question was perennial. President Roosevelt's coffee drinking habits, which I beamed overseas from the November 23, 1942 press conference, continued to be of interest. At her next press conference on November 30, Mrs. Roosevelt was asked if the President had tried his own recipe for using dried grains. She replied that "the President does his own coffee on his own tray. His theory is that there is no reason why you shouldn't boil it up a second time. I don't know if he's ever done it, but he's going to, I'm sure. He has a Silex, and loves to make his own coffee every morning. I don't really care about coffee so it doesn't matter to me whether I have it or I don't have it"; and in response to a further question: "Yes, he could make it without my knowing. I'm not always at the dinner table."

Then at our January 11, 1943 meeting, Mrs. Roosevelt was asked how the White House coffee ration was lasting, to which she answered, "Very well, so far. We have one cup in the morning, but practically everyone in the White House takes hot milk in it. We have none at lunch, but drink tea instead. We usually have enough then because of the small amount at breakfast for an after-dinner cup in the evening. It seems perfectly adequate to me."

Finally, on March 23 of that year, the subject was laid to rest with Mrs. R's announcement that the President had given up drinking coffee altogether. "He drinks milk in the morning, and says he feels much better," she said. "The President has no coffee at all now." Someone asked if the President had gotten discouraged trying to boil his coffee twice, to which Mrs. Roosevelt replied, "No. He suddenly just decided not to drink any coffee, and he is very proud of himself. I don't know what made him decide but he was very calm about it. I was told he was taking milk, and liked it. Cold milk."

War Correspondent

◆

IN 1945 I WENT ABROAD as a war correspondent for the *Cleveland News*, just at the end of the war. I joined my husband, Philip Hamburger, who was already in the Mediterranean Theatre for *The New Yorker*, and from then on we travelled together. I wrote a series of twenty-six articles for the *News*, and my editor, the late Nathaniel Howard, who did not hand out praise or money lavishly, paid me ten dollars for each article, and a bonus of a hundred dollars when I got home.

Howard was an editor of the old school — tough, conservative but fair, curious about everything, a lot of fun, and a fine writer himself. He also played an impressive jazz piano, but he really excelled in his use of the written word. He wrote a superlative letter, in which he could rip a story apart, or praise it, with perfect syntax and a peppery style that made it a pleasure to read, either way.

I stayed in Cleveland with my family while I was waiting for my accreditation from the War Department. It finally came, together with orders to be at Fort Totten, New York, to fly overseas the following day. I donned my new war correspondent's uniform — complete with khaki skirt, shirt, four-in-hand tie, army jacket, and khaki hat, and departed for the train station. My whole family came along to say goodbye.

Halfway to the station, I made a horrid discovery: I had forgotten to bring my train ticket with me. My brother-in-law, Harold Fallon, and I were travelling in a car behind the rest of the family, and he turned it around and we tore back to the house. My tickets were on the middle of my bed, just where I had left them. Those two speeding trips, back and forth, were the most hair-raising either of us ever made, and I arrived at the station as the train pulled in. All Harold said to me was, "Oh, Edith," but I didn't get off so easily with the rest of my family.

"*Some* war correspondent," they still say, when the subject comes up. "You were lucky you ever got started."

Until Phil and I wrote about Yugoslavia, it was thought that Tito and his partisans had formed what was known as a "Popular Front" government, with a democratic slant. We were among the first American correspondents to go to Belgrade, right after the war ended. The country was suffering acutely from having been bombed by both sides. Food was rationed, there was no hot water, and there was a shortage of everything: medicine, clothing, and freedom.

✦

Great attention is paid by the new Yugoslav government to the development of the minds and the bodies of young people. This attention makes itself felt particularly through the "Pioneer" youth organization in the schools.

At a special meeting in Belgrade not long ago, which was reported in the newspapers, Marshal Tito addressed a group of small children on the subject of "Good." All that is good does not come from God, he told them, and in fact, he said, God is not the one who gives children what is good.

For instance, he explained, when we say, 'God gives us candies,' they don't come. But when we say, 'Tito gives us candies,' they do come.

At this point, according to the report, a woman dressed in white came into the meeting and distributed candy to the children.

✦

Minister of Education Vladislav Ribnikar is publisher of Belgrade's biggest newspaper, *Politika*, and one of the leading lights of the Partisan movement.

The two biggest problems in education now, he told me, are the reconstruction of destroyed schools and obtaining textbooks. He said that in Belgrade, where many schools were burned and the Germans took all mechanical equipment out of those left, the schools are now being rebuilt.

Schools in Zagreb and Lublyana fared much better during the war. In fact, schools are now open every place but in Bosnia, where devastation was greatest.

Textbooks, he added, are now being rewritten. It will be some months before they can be supplied to the schools.

A new feature in the schools is that Russian is obligatory, Mr. Ribnikar said. Children are obliged to take two languages, and for the other, may choose between French and English. The Serbo-Croatian language is also compulsory, though the children are taught in the native languages of their regions.

I asked him about the Pioneer organizations in the schools, which I had been told all children between the ages of 5 and 15 must join if they want to get along well in school, even though technically, membership is voluntary. He raised his eyebrows.

"There is no direct relation between the Pioneer organization and the school," he said. "No real relation, except that the Pioneer organization organizes the conscious discipline and gymnastics."

◆

He said that the children are members of the Pioneer organization, which has replaced the pre-war Sokols, only until they are 12 years old. Then comes another young people's group — also voluntary, he said — the Communist Youth Organization. Another youth organization in the schools, which he said was on a "wider basis," and is called USAOG, has as its aim voluntary aid for the reconstruction of the country, such as woodchopping.

As I was leaving he told me he thought I might want to know that religious education is still given in the schools, but is optional. Parents must request it. Most of the children in Belgrade take religious teaching, he said. Their teachers are priests, paid by the state.

I saw many bands of school children marching through the streets, with banners and pictures of Stalin and Tito, singing and shouting "Zivio Ti–to" with the same regularity as the parading troops of soldiers. The very young children are usually followed by a straggling group of harried looking parents at the end of the line.

One day, a young mother with two boys, aged about six and nine, came and sat down on the park bench beside me. She smiled shyly, and while her sons went off to play, she said in halting English, "This is a sad country. I wish I could send my sons to the United States.

"Perhaps you don't know about our Pioneer organization. All children in the school are supposed to join, even though it is declared to be voluntary. My little one, who has just turned six, even he must join.

"Each school class in the Pioneers has a chief of staff, with uniform and insignia; there is an assistant chief of staff, a sergeant, then a boy in charge of 10 children, and a commissioner, each with his insignia. Last April, all the school children in Belgrade gathered in the Park and swore allegiance to Tito, and swore that they will fight for him and never spare their lives.

✦

"If they don't join, they cannot pass their examinations with best marks."

One of her children came up and she had him sing several Pioneer songs for me. Most had to do with fighting. One went:

> Comrade Tito, blue violet. You are fighting for
>   national rights.
> Comrade Tito, white violet. All the youth comes to
>   you.
> Comrade Tito, when are you going to Russia? Please
>   convey our gratitude to the Red Army
> And tell them all the youth is for them.

"Does he ever learn anything but war songs in school?" I asked.

"I don't think so," his mother replied. She turned to him again. "Sing us some other songs you have learned in school."

He sang:

> Far over there by a seaside
> There is the leader of the workers and the great
>   Comrade Stalin.

His mother said, "That is an old song that used to be sung after the last war by our soldiers on the Salonika front. It used to go: 'Over there by a seaside, there is my dear village, my sister, my love.'"

Published in the *Cleveland News*,
November 26, 1945.

Part Two

NEW YORK

The UN Builds Its Home

———————— ✦ ————————

I RETURNED FROM EUROPE with my husband, Phil, and we settled in New York. In 1946 I started writing free-lance articles for the *Cleveland News* about the newly formed United Nations. At that time, the UN was at Lake Success, Long Island, where it remained until 1952, when it moved into its permanent headquarters in New York City.

In my private life, I was surrounded by the marvelous writers for *The New Yorker*, including my husband, and I didn't have any confidence in my own ability to write well. I was in awe of good writing, as I am today. So I was astonished to hear myself say, when a friend called and asked if I knew someone who could write an article about the UN for *Harper's* magazine, "I can."

I wrote about the UN for *Harper's* for several years. My two sons, Jay and Richard Hamburger, were born during that period, and I could stay home and write. I didn't make much money—just enough to pay for housework and babysitters, but I would rather write than do housework any day.

I was pregnant with Jay, my first son, while I was reporting "The UN Builds Its Home," but I was sure nobody noticed it. Not long ago I mentioned it to Max Abramovitz, the co-ordinating architect for all the UN buildings, and he laughed and said, "We had a betting pool in the office about when that baby would be born. I forget now who won."

This article was the first of three I have written about architects and building: the second was about the foundation of the World Trade Center, and the third was a Profile of the Canadian architect, Arthur Erickson. I don't know why architecture interests me so much, except that I can never pass men digging into a city street without wanting to peer into the excavation, to see what's going on.

───────────── ◆ ─────────────

Wallace K. Harrison, the architect in charge of planning and construction of headquarters for the United Nations, recently received a letter from an old friend, an expert on international affairs. "Speaking frankly, Wally," it said, "there's a fifty-fifty chance of having a UN to put into those beautiful new buildings you are putting up."

These days, Harrison hears a good deal of that sort of talk. It makes him hopping mad. "Dammit, we had the same kind of thing after the first world war," he says. "People got discouraged about an international organization for peace and lost interest. But I refuse to believe human beings are so stupid that they won't back up the one hope we have."

Gloomy predictions about the imminent collapse of the United Nations stimulate Harrison's staff to put on more speed. "The faster we get those buildings up, the better people everywhere will feel about the stability and permanency of UN," one of Harrison's associates has explained. "The sooner UN settles down for good, the more people will be willing to believe in it. An international organization is like everybody else. It won't feel secure until it has a roof over its head."

To this end, some four dozen weary architects, engineers, researchers, and clerks, and a stream of advisers and outside experts, crowded each day for almost a year into a tiny suite of offices on the twenty-seventh floor of the RKO Building at Rockefeller Center in New York. Behind a door marked *United Nations Headquarters Planning*, they designed a world capital to be built on a plot no larger than one thirty-fifth of a square mile along the eastern shore of Manhattan Island. Its seventeen acres comprise six city blocks, running from 42nd to 48th Streets and bounded lengthwise by the East River and First Avenue. On this small parcel of land there must eventually be enough buildings to accommodate a Secretariat of possibly 5,000 workers; a General Assembly of more than 3,000 delegates; the press and public; three large Councils which might meet simultaneously; committees and commissions that require small meeting rooms; delegations from a possible seventy member nations; some half-dozen specialized agencies; and the thousands of spectators who will want to come to see their world organization for themselves.

There has never been an architectural problem quite like this one; these plans must satisfy fifty-five clients. The League of Nations, faced with the same multiple-client handicap, was eleven years putting up its one building in Geneva, from 1926 to 1937. Even before it was completed, it was too small for the League's needs. After an international competition so loaded with politics that the judges never found the courage to pick one plan, three firms of architects, Swiss, French, and Italian, were selected to work together, which they did so badly that a fourth English firm was finally called in to keep the peace.

As Harrison has said, "With the experience of the League of Nations behind us, anything that we do will be better." It was felt by all interested parties that co-operation, not competition, was more in keeping with the spirit of the UN. Harrison, co-designer of Rockefeller Center, was selected as its director. He was to work with an international administrative and technical staff, and receive advice from prominent architects all over the world.

"We expect to order steel for the Secretariat building by the first of the year," Max Abramovitz, Harrison's partner in the architectural firm of Harrison & Abramovitz and his deputy on the UN project, explained, "and we'll start excavating after the close of the current Assembly session."

It will literally be impossible to point to any one architect or designer and say that his scheme was selected as the final one. The buildings that rise on the UN site, their positions, the general contours of the landscaping, even the approaches and exits, will be the product of many minds — testing, revising, improving, discarding, in a process bound to give the world capital a thoroughly international flavor. Approximately fifty different schemes were worked out by members of Harrison's advisory Board of Design for the site as a whole and for the individual buildings planned on it. Some architects submitted as many as six or seven complete plans.

In the beginning, the planners had four distinct architectural points of view. Some favored a monumental, some a functional, design. Some leaned toward replicas of past styles, others belligerently pushed for a new form of expression. Functional design seems to have triumphed over monumental, on the theory that what is best suited to the actual needs of the workers in the buildings will have its own symbolic beauty. Likewise, those seeking a new mode of expression appear definitely to be in the driver's seat. Everyone seems fairly well satisfied with the trend the plans have taken. Perhaps this is because the plans are based essentially on one of the most old-fashioned ideas in the world. In an age when the person gets a good deal less attention than the platypus, the buildings have been planned around one idea: to make the individual happy.

"The fundamental unit in our planning is the human being," Harrison has said. "We find it practical to provide things that will make him content — light, air, even trees and gardens. That way, we think he'll be made more efficient." This goal has necessitated complicated and involved analyses of the site — its topography, subsurface geology, orientation to summer and winter sun, the length and overlapping of shadows, sewer connections, police precincts, and hundreds of minute engineering technicalities.

At first the planners were stunned by the complexity of their task. They had to design structures not only to house thousands of persons carrying out interlocking and separate functions, but to keep them from getting in one another's way. One of the biggest dilemmas, other than moving people through the halls and up and down stairways, was where to park the automobiles of the delegates, Secretariat, and press. Plans call for space to park 2,000 cars beneath the Secretariat building. No building has yet been designed with room underneath for so many vehicles. How to get rid of the toxic fumes from the cars without killing off the people in the building? Harrison consulted his chief mechanical engineer, John Hennessy. Hennessy suggested a vertical shaft to be built through the center of the Secretariat building, probably near the elevators, to carry off the fumes, aided by ventilators and sprinklers. Air-conditioning has been another headache. The overwhelming attitude of Secretariat employees indicated that the only successful international air-conditioning system would have to be controlled largely by the individual. This is the most expensive variety, but obviously the temperature that would most please an Icelander might be murderous for a Brazilian.

Once the buildings are up and the delegates are in them, they must be thoroughly protected. As Frank Begley, the UN Security Chief, sees it, security will be divided into three parts: fire, police, and identification. In building the new headquarters, the latest engineering developments will, of course, be used to keep the UN free from fire hazards. Begley plans to keep a small force on the grounds, probably with its own firefighting jeeps for wastebasket blazes and other minor mishaps. If there's a big fire, the New York Fire Department will come clanging.

As for police protection, Begley feels that the move into New York from the present suburban location, despite the advantage of having the city police close by, will add infinite woes to his job. The UN will unquestionably become part of every sightseeing trip, with public visitors increasing from the current top average of 1,000 to 5,000 daily. It was first thought that a stone wall should be built around the UN grounds, but this was quickly discarded as unsuitable for a world capital. Instead, Begley will add additional plain-clothes men to spot-check within the halls. There will be the same permanent pass identification system as now, but Begley hopes that some kind of landscaped shrubbery on the perimeter will deter people, especially

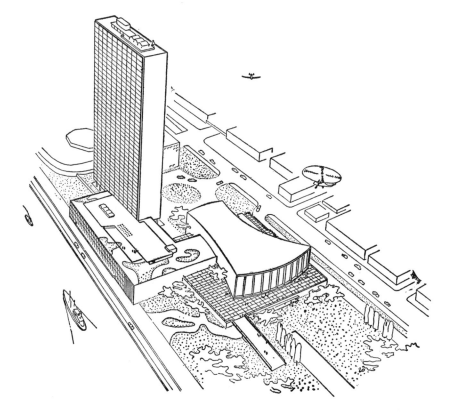

children and panhandlers, from entering the grounds at other than designated points.

To determine what communications would be necessary within the buildings, one of Harrison's researchers prepared a study of every known labor-saving device in the field of a mechanical or electrical nature. Essential communications requirements for the world capital are speed, privacy, and silence. Pneumatic tubes will transfer documents within the buildings and one-way glass will be installed in the broadcasting booths so that broadcasters can see without disturbing the delegates. The Secretary-General will be able to sit at his desk and throw a switch to see what is going on in every conference room and Council chamber.

Visitors to the Planning Office in Rockefeller Center who expected smart, rather cushy surroundings were startled by the plain, drab workrooms, filled with a hodgepodge of architects' paraphernalia. To the left of a tiny waiting room were cubicles where research and administrative work was done. Behind was a long, L-shaped room filled with drafting boards. Almost any time, even over weekends and holidays, from two to twenty-five architect-designers borrowed from Harrison's office and from three other leading New York architectural firms sat on high stools painstakingly translating ideas submitted by Harrison and his top advisers into workable designs. On an average day, draftsmen were considering such dissimilar projects as a circular ramp instead of a staircase for one of the meeting-hall areas; a scaled drawing of the grounds demonstrating the amount of free space around the buildings; a cinema to be placed below the Assembly Hall; the underground garages; a library; and the general structure of the skyscraper Secretariat building.

To the right of the waiting room were two cubbyholes and a conference room. In one of the cubbyholes, architect Hugh Ferris made his "renderings" of the architects' sketches, from which the fifty-five UN clients, to whom the average blueprint is meaningless, could get an idea of what the finished buildings will look like. Ferris, a former president of the Architects' League, is a grizzled, abstracted man who frequently lay on his stomach during Board meetings, a cigarette drooping from one corner of his mouth, and calmly sketched a site model under discussion. The public has seen his work in newspapers and periodicals. There was considerable merriment among the planners when *Life* magazine presented an imaginative "rendering" of its own that bore little resemblance to the authentic, careful Ferris work.

Ferris's drawings have also had particular value for the architects. If, for example, someone suggested that the Secretariat building be placed at right angles to the East River, Ferris would make a quick sketch of a finished building, with a realistic landscaping, to show how it would appear in its final setting.

The other cubbyhole was a child's paradise, filled with green plasticene block models of projected UN buildings. Interiors were also modeled to show table shapes, passageways, and levels for observers, press, and public. Every new drawing from the drafting room pinned up on the conference room walls for the architects to see and discuss was accompanied by a green plasticene model balanced on a flat board set on an upturned wastebasket.

The conference room was the center for UN planning activities. Long and narrow, it was cluttered with drafting tables, site models, and other architectural apparatus. The walls were covered with drawings and in one corner there was a strange object resembling a giant blood pressure gauge with an electric light hovering overhead. This was a heliodon, to measure the light of the sun. Nearby was a glass-topped table, with water floating inside plasticene walls, illuminated from below by an electric light. This was pleasantly called a "ripple tank," used to test the acoustical capacity of projected rooms and meeting halls.

Wandering about in this informal menage were the world-renowned architects selected and called in by Harrison and Lie. They could usually be found bending over a drafting board, talking to one of Harrison's designers, or standing in small groups in the conference room, staring fixedly at a wall drawing. Having no desks of their own, they rarely settled in one spot for more than a few minutes, seeming to be in restless, perpetual consultation.

There are ten members of the Board of Design Consultants, and they shuttle back and forth between New York and such divergent points as Australia, Brazil, Belgium, Canada, China, France, Sweden, the Soviet Union, England, and Uruguay. Technically their appointment was for a four-month period, from February 15 to June 15, 1947, for which they received $5,000 plus traveling expenses. Several were already here when appointed, and others have come back and forth repeatedly, having commitments at home. Probably the majority will continue to be associated in some capacity or other with UN planning at least until the first buildings begin to rise.

In selecting architects for the Board, two types were ruled out. Harrison was anxious to have the services of the famous Finnish architect, Alvar Aalto. Both the Russians and the Poles objected to using any architect from a country that had an enemy status or had been an Axis satellite. As one Pole expressed it, it would be impossible to work with those whose fingers were stained with the blood of his Polish countrymen. The Russians simply said that it would show we didn't have enough talent on our side. The UN, they felt, belongs to its members and should be built by them. In a slightly different category were German émigrés, notably Walter Gropius, now at Harvard. When his name and one or two others were suggested, several UN members gently made it clear that the émigrés have been in the United States long enough to be considered as Americans, and that the United States already had its representative in Harrison.

No one pretends that the Board has functioned with perfect smoothness. Sometimes it has seemed as if Harrison's role has called less for architectural knowledge than for the application of cold towels to aching egos. Even Harrison, certainly one of the most even-tempered and amenable men on the Eastern seaboard, has been known to retire with an attack of nerves after an afternoon's meeting in which the egocentric Le Corbusier has monopolized the discussion with an exposition of his views.

Unquestionably the most colorful member of the Board of Design, Le Corbusier, or Corbu, has belligerently stated on more than one occasion that he was sent by the French government to "defend modern architecture." Virtually all the architects on the Board of Design have been influenced by Corbusier's brilliant designs and views on modern functional building, and another Board member, Oscar Niemeyer of Brazil, is considered one of his most successful disciples. There is thus little argument with Corbusier's point of view, but rather a secretly voiced wish that he would not express it so often and so vehemently, as if he were speaking to a group of high school students. Perhaps Corbusier's experience with the League of Nations, when his plan for the League buildings was chosen over hundreds of others in an international competition, and then ruled out on the maddening technicality that it had been done in printer's ink instead of China ink, has had a good deal to do with his unwillingness to recognize any other architect's ideas for UN unless he is persuaded that they are an adaptation of his own.

Diametrically opposed to Le Corbusier is the forty-six-year-old Soviet member of the Board, a gentle, witty engineer-designer, Nikolai Bassov. A specialist in factory design and construction, Bassov achieved great fame in Russia during the war when he shifted huge industrial plants back of the Ural Mountains. He arrived in the United States in May 1946, to serve as Soviet member of the UN Headquarters Commission in selecting a permanent site. Since he was already in the United States, it was a short step from the Commission to the Planning Office.

Where Le Corbusier has been theoretical and given to flights of fancy, Bassov is thoroughly practical. He is always the first to inquire about costs, elevators, utilities, ramps, widths of halls, and traffic circulation. Engineer rather than architect, he has conducted a running opposition to Corbusier's favorite device, the use of concrete *pilotis*, or stilts, to raise buildings off the ground so that the space underneath can be used for pedestrian traffic. This, Corbu feels, gives the building a light appearance, as though it were floating in the air. Bassov refers to *pilotis* as "chicken legs." "It is unnatural for such a heavy volume to stand on chicken legs," he says, "and what is unnatural is always impractical."

Several Board members do not speak or understand English, which has often made for tough going at meetings. Bassov always uses an interpreter. Corbusier does on occasion, although almost all the architects have enough mastery of French to understand him. The white-haired, portly Uruguayan architect, Julio Vilamajo, designer at Montevideo of some of the finest public buildings in the Western hemisphere, neither speaks nor understands English and has had to depend on the interpreting services of one of Harrison's architects.

Oscar Niemeyer, brilliant modern Brazilian designer who has been one of the most active planners on the Board, is most at home in Portuguese, but tries to limp along with a sketchy knowledge of English.

England is represented on the Board by Howard Robertson, the British architect called in as consultant on the League of Nations Palace. "I was brought in to work on the League of Nations building as a sort of balance of power," he says. "The others were stale, they had been there too long. With the UN it's much better, because the ideas are all coming out in the beginning instead of at the end, as they did at the League, when it was too late."

Robertson's original idea for the UN site was an enclosed, cloistered place, a re-creation of an atmosphere like Oxford's, with the quiet of the courtyard predominant. But he willingly followed along with the final decision to spread the buildings out over the grounds.

Gyle Souilleux of Australia has been particularly useful to the Board because of his specialized knowledge of acoustics. Most of his previous work has been in theatre and auditorium building. He warned the Board, for example, that it would be wise for acoustical reasons to stay away from the domed roofs favored both by Vilamajo and Markelius of Sweden for their symbolic representation of the earth's shape. Souilleux has been studying ways of eliminating foot travel for Secretariat employees inside UN buildings. "I got the impression at Lake Success that people were walking down endless miles of corridors," he recently explained, "and my pet idea is to try by the use of many escalators and elevators to cut down the astounding amount of horizontal travel." Souilleux is firmly convinced that because of the distances, and such other discomforts as poor air-conditioning and fluorescent lighting in place of daylight, no one can work at Lake Success more than two years without cracking up.

Sven Markelius, Swedish member of the Board, has made his special concern the areas surrounding the United Nations headquarters. Just two weeks after his arrival he submitted a report with detailed plans for improving not only the neighborhood immediately around the site, but the area visible directly across the river, in Queens. In the opinion of his colleagues, it was an extraordinary piece of work. "The United Nations Headquarters as the proper center of the whole world's mutual interests must present in itself the dominance and dignity proper for the capital of the world," he said. "The stimulus to the surrounding parts of East Manhattan caused by the arrival of the United Nations Headquarters to this area will cause, if no great efforts are made, an extremely intense development in the very near future. The United Nations site will be enclosed by a gigantic wall of high buildings, which by their compact mass and high dimensions will deprive the United Nations Headquarters of every opportunity for distinction. The whole thing will get the character of a deep box at the bottom of which the United Nations Headquarters will be overshadowed."

To avoid such a catastrophe he made definite zoning suggestions, particularly in reference to the height of buildings on First and Second Avenues, suggested a riverside park belt, and so on. Some of his ideas had a somewhat embarrassing disregard for heavy real-estate interests in the surrounding areas. Although it will take years to achieve anything approaching the Markelius grand concept of appropriate surroundings for UN, definite interest has already been shown by local agencies in making the UN region a cultural center. The New York Public Library has talked of putting a projected branch building nearby. There have been rumors that the Metropolitan Opera Company may someday build its new home in the vicinity. Even the Consolidated Edison Company, which has one of its huge, somber, square-shaped power plants immediately below the site, has been drawing up plans for a more felicitous façade.

New York City's Board of Estimate late last summer turned thumbs down on a redeveloping scheme proposed by the real estate operator, William Zeckendorf, involving widespread condemnation of land around the UN, rezoning, and subsequent sale to private operators, principally Zeckendorf. The private operators would then presumably build cultural, residential, and business structures more suitable to the UN than the present dismal array of warehouses and gas stations.

As for the opposite shoreline, the New York state legislature has passed a law empowering New York City's Board of Estimate to remove at least the advertising signs which dot the Queens shore, although no action has yet been taken. At the moment, an electric *Pepsi-Cola* hits the spot directly across from the projected site.

As Director of this international menagerie, Wallace Harrison is extraordinarily well fitted for his present job. He was born in Worcester, Massachusetts, the son of a machine shop and foundry superintendent. He left school at fourteen, before receiving a high school diploma, and worked as office boy in various architects' offices, first back home, then in New York, where he took night courses at Columbia University. Ten years later he was an associate professor at Columbia's School of Architecture.

His international education began during the first World War, when he commanded a submarine chaser in European waters. Before returning to the United States in 1923, he traveled throughout Europe, studying at various schools of architecture. During the second

World War Harrison succeeded Nelson Rockefeller as chief of the Office on Inter-American affairs. Rockefeller is one of his closest personal friends.

Harrison at fifty-one is known as a visionary planner who has sometimes made rather fantastic experiments. The expenses of some architects are not over forty per cent of their total fee for a job. Harrison's sometimes run over one hundred per cent. Instead of working with one idea from the start, he may call in full-time model makers to study forty or fifty schemes for one building or one set of buildings. This procedure costs money.

One of the juiciest architectural contracts of all times evaporated when Harrison took up with the UN. William Zeckendorf originally had grandiose plans for a tremendous $125,000,000 private project to be built on what is now the UN site. He had lined up Harrison as sole architect for the job, and guaranteed him a rumored six to seven per cent of the $125,000,000 outlay. Harrison stood to make a net profit of almost four million dollars. As Director of the United Nations Headquarters Planning Office, Harrison's office expenses are paid by the UN on a cost basis. His own salary is $12,500, and Abramovitz, as his deputy, is paid slightly less. But the firm of Harrison and Abramovitz still takes in tidy sums from other jobs. It currently is working on a new building for Time, Inc. on Park Avenue in New York, and a building for the Aluminum Company of America.

The role of Harrison's partner, Max Abramovitz, has been deliberately played down to avoid any impression of American over-weighting in the planning. But Abramovitz is the man who frequently fills in the details of Harrison's "visions"; he drew up, as one of his colleagues described it, "practically every design you could think of" for the UN site before the Board of Design met, even designs that were obviously unsuitable but might contain germs of ideas. Abramovitz recently said to a friend: "The United Nations must have a look all its own, with a character and dignity distinct from any other set of buildings. We are not interested in a replica of a past style. We are a diffrent, new, strong generation, and we feel that it is up to the architects to express the age."

The site chosen for the United Nations permanent headquarters was until a short time ago one of the least attractive sections of New York. This was the home of the Slaughter House Gang, named for the slaughter houses that have dotted the east side of First Avenue for the past one hundred years. Long before that era of dives and bawdy-houses a peaceful tobacco farm, established in 1639, was the first settlement in the area. The site of the Wilson Meat Packing plant at 45th Street and First Avenue is said to be the place where Nathan

Hale, the American Revolution patriot, who was hanged by the British as a spy, made his famous last speech, "I only regret that I have but one life to lose for my country."

Ownership of the site was complicated by the fact that Zeckendorf's real-estate firm, Webb & Knapp, owned parcels but not the whole area. There were a number of options to purchase and some syndicate ownerships. A.H. Feller, General Counsel of the UN, likes to lean back in his chair and think about the afternoon of March 25, 1947, when the UN conducted a little ceremony in honor of the final closing of the title. John D. Rockefeller III and Lie were there, and New York's Mayor William O'Dwyer was expected. The only other person who wasn't there was a man from Chicago, who owned 9/300 of the site and had started by plane from Chicago in a blinding snowstorm. His was the only signature missing. "Luckily the Mayor was late," Feller reminisces, "and just in the nick of time, in walked a little man. 'I'm from Chicago,' he said, 'and I've come to sign some sort of a UN paper!'"

Feller laughs about the one speculator who tried to cash in on the site. He had got wind of the negotiations and bought up a lease on a small brick shack at 47th Street. He promptly asked $10,000 from the UN for the rest of the lease, but he didn't know that UN demolition won't reach his shack until after his lease expires. "We're just letting him sit and speculate," Feller says.

Considering the location of the site in crowded Manhattan, there has been relatively little trouble with occupants who must be moved away. The only residential tenants on the site are fifty-one families in an apartment house at the north end. One family bought a house in the country, but the other fifty will cost the United Nations approximately $30,000 to move to apartment houses several blocks away, which are being purchased and reconditioned at UN expense.

Negotiations with the slaughter houses have been both amusing and irritating. The UN was perfectly willing to sign the only restraint put upon it in attaining ownership of the site: it promised never to slaughter cattle in the area. It has already begun filling in the cattle runs below the East River Drive, through which the packers have been driving steers and sheep coming off barges in the East River.

Swift & Company, whose slaughter house occupied two blocks on First Avenue, tried to shift its moving date from July 26 to late fall. "They claimed their meat slaughtering was more important than the United Nations," one harassed negotiator said. Delay would have held up the opening of the site by as much as a year, and Swift & Company was finally persuaded to move on time. To reroute vehicular traffic, as is now planned, under First Avenue between 42nd and 48th

Streets through a tunnel, all the steam, electric power, and water lines must first be taken out and moved, and a temporary road must be made close by. Only then can digging for the tunnel begin. This most complicated of municipal engineering operations takes a good twelve months to complete.

Harrison does not permit these inevitable annoyances to distract him. He is possessed with the grandeur of the vision and the importance of the work in which he and his associates are engaged. "Do you know the mood I want to catch in the UN building?" he often says, glancing from his workroom windows in the direction of the site. "I want people to see those buildings and *feel* their beauty, impressiveness, simplicity, peacefulness, and meaning. Above all, I want them to feel their permanence."

Excerpted from "The UN Builds Its Home," published in *Harper's*, December 1947.

The Mounted Men

◆

WHEN MY SONS WERE LITTLE and I wanted to stay at home with them, I quite often would send in suggestions for the Talk of the Town section of *The New Yorker*, which is made up of anonymous short pieces at the front of the magazine. Somebody else would write the piece, but I got paid for a number of ideas.

My husband urged me to ask to report some of my suggestions myself, and the first set of notes that I sold to the magazine was about fresh raspberries that I bought in the dead of winter. It took me one year to get up the courage to send my finished notes to Bill Shawn. They were turned into a very nice Talk story.

After that, I sent in six or seven other sets of notes that became Talk pieces, among them one about the original "seat" on the New York Stock Exchange, which proved to be a real chair; the change from ivory to plastic keys on Steinway pianos, a startling event in the music world; the last day of the last livery stable in New York City; and, fifty years after the event, I interviewed the first man to use wireless to summon help for a ship in distress.

Another idea that Bill approved was about the New York City Mounted Police force, and I took so many notes on this one that I asked if I could try writing a longer piece under my own name. "The Mounted Men" was the first signed article I sold to *The New Yorker*, and I never did another set of Talk notes.

I had two reasons for choosing the subject: I love horses, and have ridden all my life (badly); and the New York City Armory where horses and riders were trained was five minutes from where I lived. With the Armory around the corner, my two boys could go there with me to watch the horse-and-rider routines while I worked.

My sons were wonderfully supportive of my writing. By the time

I was working for *The New Yorker* Richie was ten, and the minute he got home from school he would sit down on the floor beside my desk and ask me to read to him what I had written that day. I often rose at 4:00 a.m. and started writing, before I got involved in domestic routine and our seductively interesting social life. One morning Jay got up for school just after I had written the end to an air pollution article that had taken me two years, and I told him it was done. He streaked through the house waving a sign over his head on which he had written in giant letters, "HOORAY! IT'S DONE! IT'S DONE!"

We entertained and went out a lot. I was brought up — my whole generation was — to put family, home and social duties ahead of work of my own, which I squeezed into any spare moment, aside from those quiet early hours. I used to think wistfully about the English women writers whose work I admired; they all seemed to have a Mrs. Somebody lurking in the pantry to whom they could say "there'll be four for lunch," or "prepare tea for two," or "set places for six at dinner," and not have to give another thought to the marketing, preparation or serving.

My notion about the mounted police was to write about them from two aspects, which I thought of as making up a neat circle: the purchase and training of the new horse, and the training of the rookie policeman. Each had to be done separately, the new horse with experienced riders, and the rookie cop with an experienced horse. The excerpt below tells about the arrival of the horses, fresh from the Oklahoma range, and describes the first day of training for the rookie policemen, some of whom had never been on horses before!

———————— ◆ ————————

Promptly at ten o'clock Thursday—a cold day—I arrived at the Armory, where the mounted police occupy a stable area set aside for them by the National Guard. I detected a strong smell of horses and ammonia as I approached a pair of iron lattice gates covering the large, arched, medieval-looking doorway leading to the police area. While I was wondering how to get in, there was a clatter of hoofs behind me, and I turned to see a blue-overcoated officer dismounting from a bay horse. He flicked the reins over his arm and pulled the heavy gates apart. I told him I had been invited to the examination of the new horses, and he and his horse escorted me inside. "Amazing old fellow, Dr. MacLaurie," the officer said, closing the gates behind us. "Some people put his age as high as eighty-seven, but you would never guess he was much more than sixty."

We were standing now in a vast, vaulted room about fifty feet wide by a hundred and fifty feet long, its lower walls green, its upper walls and ceiling white. Two men in old nondescript clothes were standing on ladders, painting the walls. The officer greeted them, and told me they were patrolmen. "This is a state building," he said. "So the city won't authorize much in the way of repairs for it, and our appropriations aren't big enough to pay the rent and hire labor, too, so we do everything ourselves—carpentry, painting, all the rest." He tied his horse to one of a row of columns and began to remove the saddle. I noticed four large doorways opening off the room we were in and asked if they led to the stables. "Yes," he said. "Troop C horses are in the first two aisles, and Remount Training has the third and fourth. They'll have the examination down at the end of the fourth aisle there, next to the office of Lieutenant Francis Dolan, who heads Remount. Dr. MacLaurie is probably there now."

I started toward the fourth aisle, peering into the other aisles as I passed them. Down the first aisle, beyond the broad brown backs of horses in their stalls, I could see a blacksmith's shop, where an elderly man in a blue shirt and long leather apron was holding a glowing-red horseshoe in tongs over the bright coals of a forge. The second and third aisles were filled with horses and hay bales. I passed a tethered horse drinking at a long watering trough and entered the last aisle, where I was greeted by a handsome, heavyset man in khaki pants, brown riding boots, and a thick white sweatshirt. He had a round face, a ruddy complexion, and iron-gray hair. "I'm Lieutenant Dolan, in charge of Remount," he said. "Headquarters called and said you were coming. I'm afraid you're going to get a pretty poor impression of our horses at this examination. You see, when the new ones arrive from the West, at least half of them have what we call shipping sickness—a congestion of the lungs, caused by the change in climate and by germs they've picked up from one another. It's sort of distemper, rather like a cold, and we isolate them as soon as we see the signs—runny nose, red eyes, a cough, poor appetite, and a temperature of anything over a hundred degrees Fahrenheit, which is normal for a horse. If it's over a hundred and two, Dr. MacLaurie gives them penicillin and knocks out the fever in a day or so."

We walked to the end of the aisle and joined a small group of men who were standing there. I was introduced to District Inspector Omar Craig, a large, husky man in civilian tweeds; to Mr. George Patterson, a middle-aged man in a checked topcoat, from the City Controller's Office, who was wearing glasses and nervously chewing gum; to

Captain Mike Wales, a man in his late forties, stiff-backed and military, who was in charge of the squadron; to Mr. Milton Riley, a sad-faced, elderly man from the city's Department of Purchase; and to Dr. Kevin MacLaurie, a small, trim man with a neat white mustache, a full head of white hair, and horn-rimmed glasses. The Doctor was nattily dressed in a blue business suit, a blue-and-white striped shirt, and a dark-blue tie, and he looked about sixty-five. I noticed that as protection against the cold he was wearing a sweater under his vest, and shoes with heavy rubber soles—the latter to insulate him against the icy stone floor of the stables; the rest of us, in thinner soles, were already beginning to shift from foot to foot.

"What do you look for in this examination?" I asked Dr. MacLaurie.

"Oh, we look for general soundness, good conformation," he replied. "We want to be sure to spot defects that would interfere with the usefulness of the horse, such as splints—those are bony enlargements on the legs, which can interfere with the action of tendons or joints—or any malformations, ruptures, or old wounds that might be bothersome. These horses are here on a ten-day trial, which gives us a chance to get acquainted with them. We're looking for police mounts, which means that the horse must have good weight-carrying ability and a good wide chest, with enough lung space for endurance, and that he must walk and trot normally, not weave from side to side. Of course, he must have good sight and a strong tail. I would reject a horse with a broken tail as unsound, not only because it gives him a poor appearance but because he must use his tail to brush off flies. The horse should also have a full, strong mane, and I don't like feet that are too big. Clumsy-footed horses may stumble, and when a police mount stumbles, we want to know why, every time."

He broke off abruptly and hurried to look at a shaggy, rough-looking horse that had just been led in by a patrolman. I wondered how this jittery, wild-mannered animal could ever become as sleek and composed as the police horses I saw in the nearby stalls. This first candidate had a large "1" painted in white on its left side. Captain Wales put on his glasses, glanced at a paper, and announced, "Doctor, this is a dark-bay gelding, five years old. He's got a white mark on his front near coronet."

Mr. Riley, who was standing next to me, explained in a whisper that the coronet is an area just above the hoof, and that "near" means the side on which the rider mounts and dismounts—the left. Sure enough, there was a white mark low on the horse's left foreleg. Mr. Riley whispered another piece of information: "They should be as close to all brown, or bay, as possible, for the sake of uniformity. They'll be rejected if they have too much white."

The Doctor, standing on his toes, gently opened the horse's mouth and peered at its teeth. "You've aged him right," he said to the Captain. "The corner cups are there. He should have a full mouth, top and bottom, by the time he's five. He's a good size, too."

Dr. MacLaurie took a pencil flashlight out of his pocket and shone it into the horse's left eye. "See the pupil contract?" he said. He moved the light slowly around in a circle. "In a sound eye, I get a reflection in three different ways — on the cornea, on the front of the lens, and on the rear of the eye." He turned off the light and poked his finger close to the horse's eye. The horse blinked. He repeated the entire procedure on the horse's right eye, and then gently moved his hand down the length of its neck and felt carefully along its front legs and feet. Next, he held up one rough, unshod hoof, and whistled. "Look at the width of that heel!" he exclaimed.

"They've had no care," Captain Wales said, chewing on an unlighted cigar. "They've never been shod."

The Doctor was still feeling the horse's legs. "There's a scar on the left front hoof. No shoe-nail holes here at all." He moved his hands down the length of the animal's body, swung its tail back and forth, and examined the hind legs and feet and the hindquarters. Then he tool a small black notebook from his pocket and jotted something down. "That's No. 1; gelding, five years old. He's pretty clean — just that little scar. OK."

Everyone relaxed, and Captain Wales lit his cigar. The horse was led away, and I looked at my watch. The examination had taken twelve minutes.

No. 2 was brought in — an animal with a large center patch of white on its face, and two hind white socks. "I'm worried about this horse," Captain Wales said as the Doctor proceeded with his examination.

The Doctor shrugged. "He's running a temperature of a hundred and three," he said. "He's pretty droopy." He put his ear to the horse's chest and listened. "Sounds like static congestion. I think we ought to give him penicillin right away." From his black bag, on the floor nearby, he took out a large syringe, saying, "I'll give him three million units. That'll knock it out." With a powerful and sure thrust, he jabbed the needle into the horse's breast muscles, pulled it out, then rubbed the spot with a piece of alcohol-soaked cotton. The horse stood quietly throughout. "This beats the old-fashioned way," he remarked as the horse was being led away. "We used to use something we mixed ourselves and called fever medicine. We would fill capsules with it and push them down the horses' throats. This is quicker and safer. Your danger with fresh horses like these is a lung involvement.

They can sometimes get banged around in one of those cattle wagons. Why, I had one once that was scalped, when the van had to stop short and all the horses were thrown down."

The examination settled into a routine, broken only by an occasional comment on some horse's idiosyncrasies. No. 6 had large knees, and Lieutenant Dolan assured the assemblage that the animal would walk better when it was properly shod, with corrective weights on the outer edges of its shoes. No. 8 came in shaking his mane, and reared back and tried to break loose when the Doctor took hold of his mouth. Dr. MacLaurie whistled when he looked inside. "Why, he's a baby," he said. "Three and a half. Pretty well developed, too. You'll do fine with this fellow. He'll make a good street horse."

When No. 7 had first been brought in, he had refused to let the Doctor touch him, so he had to be taken out and brought back later, and even then wouldn't submit to an examination until he had been led out of the aisle, away from the group of onlookers. Standing in the outer, vaulted room, the Doctor slowly fed him a few wisps of hay and talked to him quietly, and then, before I could fully understand what he was doing, he slipped a sort of small garrote — a stick with a looped rope attached to it — over the horse's upper lip. He twisted the stick gently until the horse stood quite still, quivering. Then the Doctor opened his mouth. Mr. Riley said, "They call that thing a twitch. You might say it's a way of twisting the horse's arm. The Doctor won't keep it on any length of time, and he won't finish the examination until later, when he comes back to treat the sick horses, with nobody else around."

Dr. MacLaurie came down the aisle, frowning, as the horse was led off. "Did he act up before?" he asked Dolan.

"Not a bit," Dolan replied.

The Doctor scratched his head. "I'll be danged if I know what's bothering him, but something is. No sense examining him any further today."

Several horses were running fevers, but all except one — No. 12, an animal with a sore eye — had been given the Doctor's tentative OK, subject to further tests, when No. 15, a dark bay, fifteen hands high, was led in. "This is a thoroughbred, registered with the Jockey Club. A Jockey Club number is tattooed inside his mouth," Captain Wales said.

Dr. MacLaurie raised his eyebrows in surprise, and then turned back the animal's upper lip. A number was clearly visible on the inside, in blue letters about half an inch high. "This horse was discarded as a racer for some reason," the Doctor said. "He wasn't fast enough, or they found something wrong." He began carefully feeling the body

and legs of the horse. Suddenly he stopped. "There is some irregular-
ity, a growth of some sort, on this back leg. I'll just make a note of
that. You'll have to watch him. We've got ten days to decide."

No. 15 was led away, and No. 16 was brought in, examined, and
pronounced a "dandy little horse." The Doctor looked at his watch,
"One o'clock," he said. "We'll wind the horses next week, instead of
now. If we winded the sick ones now, we might damage their lung
tissue. Well, gentlemen"—he turned to Captain Wales, Inspector
Craig, and Mr. Patterson, who had gone into a huddle to compare
notes—"you didn't do bad picking, to my mind." They all smiled. He
picked up his bag. "I've got two horses to examine at Belmont, and
four more coming in to Idlewild from England, so I'll be going. I'll be
back to see those sick horses tomorrow, but I won't be seeing all of
you until next week." As he set off at a brisk pace down the aisle, Mr.
Riley explained to me that "winding" a horse simply meant testing his
wind.

Ten days later, at eleven in the morning, I returned for the winding
examination, and was directed up a broad ramp that opened into the
Armory's huge drill ring, which extends the full width and almost the
full length of the city block the Armory occupies, and in which, I
knew, polo matches were sometimes played during the winter. A
dozen tiers of dusty wooden folding seats ran the length of the ring
on both sides, and a cavernous balcony hung above one end, under
the steel-beamed barrel roof. A flicker of sun was trying to pierce the
sooty glass windowpanes. I could see that the walls and the waist-high
partition that separated the seats from the ring had once been painted
a soft green. I hurried across the ring, my heels sinking into the
packed-dirt flooring, and joined Dr. MacLaurie, Mr. Patterson, Mr.
Riley, Captain Wales, and Lieutenant Dolan, who were talking quietly. It was cold again, and the Doctor was wearing a checked flannel
shirt under his vest and sweater, and had an old felt hat perched on
the back of his head. At the far end of the ring, three patrolmen, who,
I had learned, were regularly assigned to Remount, sat astride three
of the new horses.

"All right, let's get started with No. 1," the Doctor called out.
"Trot him straight away down to us."

A patrolman brought the horse around the ring at a stiff trot, while
the Doctor stood slightly bent over, with his feet apart, staring with
deep concentration.

"Good trot. Has anything been done to his feet?" he asked.

"Some of the horses have been shod," Dolan replied.

"Now wind him, Bobby," the Doctor said, and the patrolman
spurred the horse directly toward the Doctor at a gallop, stopping

short just in front of him. The Doctor quickly pressed his ear against the horse's chest. "I wish my lungs and heart were as good as his," he said. "He's OK."

Captain Wales cleared his throat. "That horse is accepted," he said, in the solemn voice of a train announcer, and the onlookers, each of whom had a list of the horses to be tested, made marks on their papers.

While we were waiting for the second horse, I asked the Doctor what he was principally watching for. "How the horse travels, and whether it has respiratory problems," he said.

As the other horses trotted out, he looked sharply at each, listened to each chest, and made his decisions. When a neat brown horse whose rider had him under perfect control was identified as No. 7, I remembered that this was the animal that had balked at being examined before, and I asked Lieutenant Dolan what had happened.

"He didn't like the halter we had on him," the Lieutenant replied. "The minute we changed it, he was all right."

Horse No. 12 still had a half-closed, runny eye, and when Dr. MacLaurie examined it the horse reared. Unperturbed, the Doctor gripped the bridle and circled the eye with his flashlight. "I thought it might be a foreign body, but it's conjunctivitis," he said. "We'll give him chloromycetin ointment and ask for another ten-day extension, with final approval contingent on the condition of the eye."

When No. 15, the thoroughbred, was brought in again, the group grew tense. The Doctor frowned as he looked in the animal's mouth and felt under the chin and down the legs, and then he turned to Dolan. "Notice anything?" he asked.

"Well, he hasn't picked up any weight at all," Dolan said.

The Doctor shook his head. "Poor conformation, a bony growth; he's too small in body and bone, and he lacks weight-carrying ability. He's not the type we want. Rejected. Write Ward that at the end of the horse's probationary period he failed to meet the requirements."

The last horse was quickly approved, and the officials leafed through their notes. "That does it," the Doctor said with a sigh. "We got one reject and one extended. That eye looks good, though. He sees out of it."

I caught up with Lieutenant Dolan as we walked back down the ramp. "Too bad about that thoroughbred," I said.

He nodded. "Once in a while, we get a thoroughbred that someone donates to the Department because he can't take care of it in New York and wants to make sure it has a good home," he said. "Six or seven years ago, we were given a steeplechaser that used to be a winner at Belmont. But if someone said to me, 'I can get you a Rolls-Royce for three hundred dollars,' I'd naturally ask, 'Has it got an engine?' We used to have fine-looking horses specially bred in various eastern states for the Police Department, but, at the prices we're now allowed to pay, that's no longer possible, and the horses we get are often undersized. Also, we don't have as many lightweight men as we once did. It's a Department rule that the men dismount for ten minutes every hour, when that's possible, to give the horses a rest, but even so, you can't assign a man who weighs a hundred and seventy-five pounds to a horse that weighs anything less than twelve hundred pounds and is less than sixteen hands high. We only get what we pay for. Still, you'd be surprised how these horses will shape up with feed and handling."

◆

When word reached me from headquarters that Lieutenant Dolan was starting to train a new class of mounted policemen, I went straight to the Armory, and discovered that the course had already begun. The men — there were fifteen of them — were in their second day of training, having spent the first in familiarizing themselves with their equipment and with the grooming and walking of the horses. I climbed the ramp and settled myself in one of the seats beside the ring. The brown dust was thick on the chairs, and I could hear the blacksmith's anvil somewhere below. A black cat sat at a discreet distance on another seat, cleaning itself. Lieutenant Dolan was on his handsome dark-bay horse, Malachy, in the center of the ring, with one of his three assistants at his side. The two others were weaving skillfully in and out among the fifteen rookies, who were jouncing about on sleek, experienced-looking horses. The new men wore costumes ranging from flowered shirts and blue jeans to old cavalry outfits with wrapped leggings. None of them could ride very well, but some were worse than others. They were all concentrating intently on their riding, looking straight ahead, and one of them, bouncing along with his tongue hanging out, kept pleading to his horse, "Take it easy. Oh, take it easy, Bud. Please take it easy."

The horses clearly hadn't had such fun since the last class of rookies. They stopped and started when they pleased, went from a trot into a canter at will, and took outrageous advantage of their riders' inexperience — all with the air of authority that trained horses automatically assume with novices.

I heard Dolan call out sharply "What's going on here?" as he rode over to a husky fellow sitting on his horse at the gate to the ramp, trying to turn the animal back toward the ring.

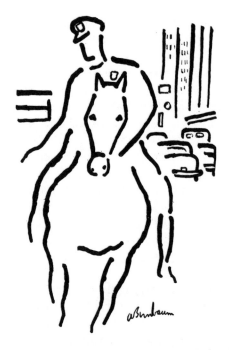

Illustration by Abe Birnbaum

"This horse gets over by the gate and it's the end," the rookie said bitterly. "This is the fourth time I've been here."

Dolan showed him what to do with the reins, and led him back to the ring.

Just then, a horse broke into a fast gallop on the other side of the ring, and his rider, gripping the beast's mane desperately, cried out in anguish, "How do you stop this horse?"

Dolan called out, with reassuring calmness, "Just lean back and pull on the reins — but not too hard."

The rider gave the reins several frantic yanks, and the horse stopped as abruptly as it had started.

An officer from Troop C came in and paged one of the new men, who was wanted downtown at the Traffic Court, where he had a case coming up. The Troop C man lingered for a moment to watch the show. "You'd think they would never get the hang of it," he said to me. "But they do, and in a surprisingly short time, too. It's very strenuous, intensive training, with a different horse every day, and even by tomorrow some of those fellows will already have caught the rhythm of the trot and canter. The first three days, they just get used to horses, because most of them have never been on one before. They learn balance and get a bit of confidence. After that, the real instruction begins."

Shortly after he left, I saw the animal that had previously broken into an unexpected gallop cutting up again. Both Dolan and an assistant shouted "Lean back!" and then Dolan turned to his aide. "Take him off that horse," he said.

The aide rode up to the runaway, grabbed the reins, and held the horse, and the embarrassed rookie dismounted. The rookie was grounded for the session, and came over and sat down beside me. "It beats walking, anyway," he said, shrugging. "The only time I've ever been on a horse until yesterday was a pony ride at Coney Island when I was a kid. I've been in the Police Department a year and a half, and this is a lot better than the precinct. I planned to volunteer for the Mounted all along, and I guess I'll get the hang of it."

Dolan ordered the men to walk their horses, and after a few flurries and several breaks toward the gate the class settled down to a sedate walk while the horses cooled off. When the men dismounted and began leading their horses down to the stables, I walked over to talk to Lieutenant Dolan.

"I always get the best and quietest horses for training, and I sometimes have to send to other stables for the ones I want," he said. "The first few days are very boring. We just walk the horses and teach the men how to turn left and right and to trot, for a whole week. The second week, we go over what they picked up the first week, and then we work on their balance and their ability to guide their horses, and we may begin backing and passing. I also make the men rise with their feet out of the stirrups. It helps them develop balance, and assume a more natural position in the saddle. We ride a military seat here, and all our men must ride in a uniform manner, with the feet not too tightly pressed into the horse and the ball of the foot on the tread of the stirrup. They must carry their hands low and keep the horses' heads up, and ride on the snaffle bit, but before they can go out on street duty they must learn to use the curb bit, which keeps the horse under better control but requires a more experienced hand. At the beginning of the third week, we take up cantering and riding in formation, and teach the men to pass left and right, and in the last week we review everything we've done, and do some jumping over low obstacles. If a man has a good seat, he learns rapidly, and if he has courage, confidence, good hands, and an interest in the public welfare, he'll be a good Mounted man."

I said he seemed to enjoy teaching, and he smiled. "I've never taught anybody but policemen," he said. "I've been with the Department twenty-five years. I spent five years on foot patrol before I came into the Mounted, but I had done a lot of riding as a boy in Brooklyn. Not everybody is interested in green horses, or green riders, and the man selected for this job has to be."

During the next few weeks, I dropped in at the Armory from time to time, and was amazed to see how rapidly the men progressed. I arrived one morning during the third week to find half the class cantering around the ring, many with the reins held casually in one hand, while the other half were practicing passing and backing, occasionally bumping into one another with shouts of laughter. Halfway through the morning, Lieutenant Dolan ordered them all to line up, had them mount and dismount, and made them ride in formations of two, four, and eight horses abreast. "Come on, stay alive down there!" he yelled to a straggler in a column of eight. "Get into line! What the hell do you think this is — a Sunday-school parade?"

One of the Remount assistants moved over near me, and I said, "They look really good now."

"They really *are* pretty good," he replied. "We don't have to worry any more. We just assign horses the way they come now. We get out in the Park once a day, and ride around the reservoir when it's nice. These men will be assigned to the Park for at least six months before they are put on street duty."

On their last day of training, the men were to be reviewed at eleven o'clock in the morning by Inspector Craig, and when I arrived, a good half hour before the appointed time, I found the class riding stiffly around the ring, eyes forward, backs ramrod straight. Lieutenant Dolan and his assistants were drawn up in the center of the ring on their horses, and as eleven o'clock came and passed they began to throw nervous glances toward the ramp. At twenty minutes past the hour, I heard the deep voice of the Inspector from below, and then he and Captain Wales appeared. Lieutenant Dolan dismounted, and the three men stood in the center of the ring and looked impassively at the riders for a few minutes. I heard the Inspector say, "I want to look them over today. I must make recommendations," and then, after a few minutes, "They look pretty impressive."

Lieutenant Dolan called out loudly, "If you men want to graduate, sit up and look good, or you'll be left back and have to stay here for another year!" Everyone laughed, and Dolan ordered the class to line up against the wall. "Forward, ho-o!" he commanded, and they all moved forward. "Halt! Back center, ho-o!"

The Inspector put on his glasses, and Dolan ordered the first man in the column to pass a horse left and then right, which the man did deftly. The second man was directed to circle his horse in one spot, which he did, and each of the other men went through some maneuver that all had learned. Then they were ordered to dismount, and the Inspector made the shortest graduation speech I have ever heard. "If you don't like the job, let me know and I'll pull you out," he said.

The men were still cooling off their horses in the ring when I left. I stopped downstairs to talk to the Troop C officer with whom I had watched the rookies training. He was wearing his uniform pants and an old quilted blue jacket, and he had a brush and a pail of water and was washing his horse. "It's my day off, and look what I'm doing," he said with a big smile. "Did anybody ever tell you how you can make a horse look fierce?" I shook my head. "Easy," he said. "By holding him fully collected — that is, pulling him up. Make him arch his neck and show his teeth and step higher — I guess you'd call it prance — and flare his nostrils, if he has that natural talent. He automatically collects himself when he's excited, anyway — by drums and bands, or by noise and excitement. Why, he can stop a fight just by looking fierce. The people become so preoccupied with getting out of his way that we simply go in and cut up the pie and let the foot men take the pieces."

I thought that one over for a moment. Then I said, "I've always wanted to ask a mounted policeman how he really feels on a horse, stalking past all the people on foot."

"I'll tell you the nicest thing ever told to me," he said. "An elderly lady came up to me in the Park one day and said, 'Officer, your horse looks majestic, and so do you.' I remember feeling as if I was on top of the world. And I guess the real word for it is the one she used. 'Majestic.'"

Excerpted from "The Mounted Men," published in *The New Yorker*, November 24, 1962.

The Biggest Foundation

———————— ◆ ————————

MY SON RICHARD says I have a "rampant" curiosity, which is probably so. One day in 1962, long before people were publicly concerned with air pollution, I stuck my head out the window and the air smelled so foul that I called Bill Shawn and said I would like to know why. He said, "Find out if anyone is taking care of us." This led to two long pieces on air pollution, published in *The New Yorker* in 1964 and 1968, respectively.

The first, entitled "Fifteen Thousand Quarts of Air," which is the amount of air a person breathes in and out in a day, changed a law in New York City. Soon after the piece was published, a young lawyer named Robert Low ran for a seat on the City Council on the promise that he would clean up New York's air. He told me he kept my piece by his bed and used it "as a bible" during his campaign. After he was elected, a law was passed by the City Council requiring that a cleaner grade of fuel oil be burned in the city's huge power stations, which were the primary air polluters. Mayor John Lindsay invited me to the ceremony when the law was signed at City Hall, a great thrill. I then wrote another article, "The Ambient Air," a study of the effects of air pollution on the human body. The United States Government reprinted and distributed fifty thousand copies of this article (with a whole column of text missing), and it appeared in a number of medical journals.

By 1968, I had found out that nobody was looking after us very much; and that the effect of normal urban air pollution, when it was combined with heavy smoking, which, as one doctor put it, "overwhelms the lungs," could be deadly. So far as I know, I was the first person to write about air pollution in a national magazine for the general public. Although I worked on other things at the same time, each article took me well over a year, and I swore I would never write another technical piece.

I forgot all about that vow one summer afternoon in New York City, when a neighbor and I took our children to the Statue of Liberty, which stands on a small island in New York Harbor. Gazing back at Manhattan, I saw that special skyline so distinctive to New York: skyscrapers, their towers shimmering like gold in the bright sun. I thought, why here? Why this special skyline on the tip of that narrow island?

The answer—Manhattan Schist, bedrock so close to the surface of Manhattan that it can sometimes be seen—came from a specialist on foundations, Robert White, who with his late brother, Edward, had worked on such historic structures as the Aswan Dam in Egypt and the White House in Washington.

In response to my query, Bill said I could go ahead on a foundation story. I accompanied Robert White when he examined I-beams damaged in a bad fire in the New York subway system, but that wasn't what I had in mind. Shortly thereafter I went with White to lower Manhattan to view the antiquated foundations of Trinity Church, which was chartered in 1697, but that wasn't what I wanted either. When he called to tell me about a one-hundred-and-ten-story skyscraper whose twin towers would be the highest buildings in the world, I knew I had found what I was looking for.

It took me seven years to complete the story, because it took seven years to build the foundation. I wrote other articles in the meantime, but every six months, Jack Kyle, Chief Engineer for the Port Authority of New York and New Jersey, who was in charge of the project, would have his chauffeur bring me down to the site, so that I could keep track of the construction. In between, there were periods when I reported intensively, when something new was happening.

Jack Kyle was a wonderful teacher. I explained at the start that I had failed a required physics course at college, and that it had taken a platoon of tutors to get me through on a second try. This was all to the good: most of my readers would probably be as scientifically simple-minded as I am. (I have often thought since how dumbfounded my professors and tutors would be to know what technical subjects I have tackled since that melancholy period.) Whenever Kyle's explanations became too complicated, I would say, "I don't understand," and he would begin all over again in simpler language. If *I* didn't understand it, I couldn't write it. It was a fascinating game, and he never once lost patience.

Seven years is a long time, and even I began to wonder when I would finish, but I did. I called Jack Kyle to tell him that the foundation piece was done, but before I could get a copy of the magazine to him, he died of a heart attack. The fact that Jack never saw my piece after putting so much of himself into it was a heart-breaker for me. Being Chief Engineer of the Port Authority of New York and New Jersey, with its heavy responsibility for human safety on bridges, in tunnels and in airports, is that kind of a taxing job. Indeed, the man who succeeded Kyle, Martin Kapp, died a year later, also from a heart attack. An official at the Port Authority wrote me afterwards, "The amazing thing about the piece is that it not only makes interesting reading, but according to our engineers, it could also serve as a textbook description of foundation construction."

◆

Soaring above the lower end of Manhattan Island is the world's largest cluster of tall buildings, whose oblongs, spires, and turrets have, since this century began, given New York the most spectacular skyline anywhere. Each one of the towers whose upper extremities pierce the clouds is rooted, below the city's surface, in a huge, unseen structure that may itself be the size of a ten-story building. The finishing touches are now being put on the biggest foundation in the world, which is below what are, as of now, the highest pair of buildings in the world. These are the twin hundred-and-ten-story towers of the World Trade Center, built for the Port Authority of New York and New Jersey. Nine or ten good-sized office or apartment buildings could have been fitted into the hole that was dug for the Trade Center, and the foundation proper is six times as large as that of the usual fifty-story skyscraper and four times as large as its closest competitor — the basement of the neighboring sixty-story Chase Manhattan Bank Building.

On a hot, dry summer day nearly seven years ago, I went down to the corner of West and Cortlandt Streets to witness the initial tests of some basic equipment for the construction of the main foundation walls of what would be the biggest building job ever attempted — in height of the structures, size of the foundation and excavation, and almost everything else. I was there to witness the test with Robert E. White, who is executive vice-president of Spencer, White & Prentis, a firm of foundation experts that is almost always called in whenever architects and builders think anything complicated or unexpected may occur below ground. Robert White and his brother Edward, president of that firm, are old friends of mine, and when I had mentioned not long before that I had always wondered what kept the tall buildings in New York anchored to the ground or whatever was underneath it, they suggested that I observe some of the steps in the construction of the foundations for the Trade Center. I knew that besides the two skyscrapers, each thirteen hundred and fifty feet high, at least three other buildings would be erected on the sixteen-acre site: an eight-story structure for the United States Customs Bureau and two nine-story ones for exhibits, meetings, and trade activities, around a five-acre plaza. To accommodate this extraordinary new assemblage within fourteen blocks of jammed lower Manhattan, the Port Authority had condemned a hundred and sixty-four buildings then standing on the site—including the big, rambling headquarters of the old Hudson and Manhattan Railroad, now the Port Authority Trans-Hudson System, known as PATH—and had closed off parts of five streets that ran through it. The city had made a neat bargain with the Port Authority. In return for municipal assistance in obtaining the huge site, the Port Authority was going to add about twenty-four acres of new real estate to New York City by dumping the dirt and rock that would be excavated—more than a million cubic yards, or enough to make a pile about a mile high and seventy-five feet square—inside a great riverside cofferdam, or bulkhead. On this man-made peninsula, with a base extending from the old Pier 7 to the old Pier 11 and the Central Railroad of New Jersey ferry slip along the Hudson, plans called for streets, parking facilities, sewers, mains for water, electricity, and steam, and, eventually, apartment houses, stores, and various other buildings—parts of a complex to be known as Battery Park City.

The backbone of Manhattan is a rock ledge, which actually can be seen in Central Park and a number of other places. Starting at Fourteenth Street, it goes gradually beneath sea level, and extends under Governor's Island, Staten Island, New Jersey, and possibly as far as Pennsylvania, where similar rock—known here has Manhattan Schist—has been found. At the World Trade Center site, the rock is seventy feet below sea level, and above it is a nightmare for all construction engineers—filled land. Two hundred years ago, New York City was a little colonial town at the tip of the island, with docks and piers reaching like fingers into the rivers on either side. As the city grew, the dirt and rock dug out for cellars and, later, for subways and other underground installations, was dumped into the rivers to create new real estate, and it is estimated that the island's shoreline was pushed out about seven hundred feet in the area around the Trade Center. When a heavy building rests on bedrock, its engineers can sleep peacefully. Once they have dug to such rock, that's as far as they have to go, which made Manhattan a superb location for many of the first skyscrapers. The bedrock is so close to the surface in midtown—

only eight feet down at Rockefeller Center—that sometimes it has to be blasted out for basements.

As Robert White and I were walking toward the test site, he said, "Some foundations, like those of the Empire State Building, are so routine they aren't interesting. A one-story service station built on a swamp could be more exciting. But on this kind of filled land there is nothing but trouble," he said, looking pleased. "For a typical downtown New York skyscraper, you normally dig down thirty or forty feet, but this foundation will have to go anywhere from sixty to a hundred feet. Around here, there's usually ten or fifteen feet of fill near the surface—rubble, old bricks, old anything. Then you have five to twenty-five feet of Hudson River silt—black, oozy mud, often covering old docks and ships. Down here we may hit parts of an old Dutch vessel called the Tijger, which burned off Manhattan in 1614. Below the silt, there's maybe a dozen feet of red sand called bull's liver, which is really quicksand—the bugbear of all excavating. The more you dig in it the more everything oozes into the hole. We expect to find it here, but we know how to deal with it. Under that is hardpan—clay that was squeezed dry by the glacier and its accompanying boulders. Finally, beneath the hardpan, there's Manhattan Schist."

As we entered the lot where the test was to take place, I noticed water running from a small pump into the gutter. White said, "People passing by complained that we were wasting water, so a city inspector came around. He laughed when he found that we were pumping out tidewater. We're working below the level of the Hudson, with the same tides as the Battery—varying from two to six feet." The lot was bare except for an enormous green crane on red wheels, a pile of bags marked "Bentonite," several oxygen tanks, a large gray hydraulic jack, and a blue box, which White said was for cutting wires. A dozen men, some in business suits and some in grimy work clothes, all wearing hardhats, stood next to a strip of concrete about twenty-five feet long and the width of a small sidewalk. White explained that the concrete strip was the top of a sample piece of foundation wall, extending about ten feet below the ground, and that what I was going to see demonstrated was part of an unusual system of foundation construction that would be used on this job. Projecting from the concrete slab, at a forty-five-degree angle, were three pipe casings, inside which, he explained, groups of rods, wires, or cables, all known as tiebacks, extended, unseen, a hundred and thirty feet down, where they were anchored to bedrock. Concrete for the permanent walls making up the foundation's perimeter, thirty-one hundred feet long and about seventy feet deep, would be poured into trenches dug to the walls' width and depth before any other excavation began. Then workmen would dig down to install tiebacks, such as those here, and they would be stretched to a tension greater than the underground pressure behind the walls, to hold them up while all the earth, rock, and other matter they enclosed was removed. Ultimately, a complex system of interior concrete partitions and floors, extending six stories below the level of the street, would take over the job of supporting the outside foundation walls. Then the fifteen hundred tiebacks would be de-stressed and cut off. The purpose of today's tests, said White, was to determine which of the three different sorts of rods, wires, and cables inside the pipe casings would make the most effective tiebacks.

The group gazing at the section of wall opened ranks for us. Several of the men proved to be Port Authority officials: John M. Kyle, the Chief Engineer, who was a short man in a white helmet inscribed "Lincoln Tunnel, Third Tube, Last Bolt, June 28, 1956"; Arne Lier, the structural-design expert; Martin S. Kapp, head of the soils division, a big friendly engineer in overalls; Harry Druding, the engineer in charge at the site; and Leon Katz, the Port Authority's information officer. The rest of the men were from West Street Associates—a group of five heavy-construction companies (of which the Whites' outfit was one) that had banded together with Slattery Associates, Inc., the lead contractor, to take on most of the technically tricky, financially risky twenty-seven-million-dollar job of underpinning the World Trade Center.

Protruding from one pipe casing were more than a dozen cables, now slack, whose far ends were cemented underground. Each of these was now to be pulled taut separately by the hydraulic jack exerting as much as twenty tons of tension to test the tieback's strength. This machine was moved into a position where its wedge-shaped jaws could grip one of the cables, and it began drawing the cable up tight. As we watched, the pressure gauge on the jack moved to two thousand pounds per square inch—which represented a quarter of the cable's theoretical breaking point—and White explained that the steel cable would be stretched about eight inches, like a rubber band. The needle crept to three thousand pounds, then four thousand. When it was at five thousand, someone said, "Get back in case the wire snaps." Everybody moved back a few feet, and White said, "I saw two steel rods break during this sort of test in West Virginia, and they shot like spears halfway across the Monongahela River." Everyone moved back a step farther. Then Kyle called out, "Sixty-seven hundred pounds per square inch! That should be enough. That's twenty tons on the cable." It was announced that the wall was taking the load well, having moved a mere seven-eighths of an inch. If it had moved substantially, that would have meant that the tieback had pulled away from its anchorage. The jack went to work on a second cable, then a third, and within an hour or so it had been ascertained that all the different tiebacks stood up well under the strain. The contractors therefore decided on the one that they believed would be the most economical—a seven-wire cable about a half inch in diameter.

After the test, I accepted Kyle's invitation to accompany him to his office at Port Authority headquarters, at Eighth Avenue and Fifteenth Street, for further enlightenment. I remember his saying, as he showed me in, "Maybe the Walls of Jericho fell down because they weren't built on good foundations."

In his outer reception room, he halted before an old topographical map of Manhattan Island—published by Egbert L. Viele in 1865 for the use of sewer engineers—which showed the island's natural springs, streams, and marshes before they were covered over by building projects. Kyle told me that this map has been a basic reference source for all underground planning and construction in New York for years. Kyle said, "Engineers make large-scale map blowups from it of the areas where they're working. Every existing stream in Manhattan shows up on the Viele map. There's the one at Forty-first Street that we hit when we were building the Port Authority Bus Terminal, and there's Minetta Creek, in Washington Square, which comes out in a hotel lobby as a fountain. And there you can see that we have a spring right under this building, whose water we use as a coolant in our air-conditioning system to save city water, and to wash down the Holland Tunnel during droughts."

Kyle told me that the World Trade Center foundation job was the most difficult and most interesting he had ever faced, and went on to explain why. Conventional deep foundations for tall buildings in New York, he said, are built by excavating the site, driving steel sheeting down to bedrock, propping it with heavy braces inside the cut, building wooden wall forms next to the sheeting and pouring concrete into them, removing the forms, installing basement floors, and, finally, removing the wall braces and the sheeting. If the ground contains excessive moisture, a mammoth, heavily reinforced slab of concrete, sometimes as thick as fifteen feet, is poured as a bottom floor, to counteract any upward pressure from the underground water. None of these orderly procedures could be applied with rea-sonable economy to the Trade Center site, he said. The original shoreline of Manhattan runs close to Greenwich Street, which bisects the site north and south, and this is a dividing line between good and bad foundation-building land. The area that had concerned the engineers from the outset was the western half, beyond the original shoreline, where borings eighty feet apart indicated that what was below was Hudson River silt loaded with underground obstructions—wharves built with wooden cribbings, foundations of stone and brick, criss-cross timbers or piles, boulders, riprap, rocks that had been used as ballast in sailing ships coming empty from Europe to take on cargo, and even some of the ships themselves. Both of the Trade Center's skyscrapers, the Customs Building, and half of the plaza would occupy this part of the site, Kyle said, and their total weight would come to a million and a quarter tons, or twelve times as much as the weight of the George Washington Bridge, including its concrete decks, its steel anchorages, and everything but vehicles.

In a foundation of orthodox design, skyscraper towers, with special concrete-and-steel footings in the rock, would have sufficient weight to stay put in ground as watery as the tidal fill around the Trade Center, but the surrounding streets might fall in and the smaller buildings might settle down, or, worse, pop up. Insufficiently anchored tunnels have risen from river bottoms to haunt engineers who miscalculated the force of underwater buoyancy, and buried gas tanks are notoriously jumpy. However, it is doubtful whether conventional foundations could have been built at the Trade Center without the contractors' going broke from cave-ins and other difficulties, such as the slow pace of excavating the entire site before starting construction, the need to pump tidal water out the whole time, the tortuous process of driving piles or steel sheeting down to bedrock through the accumulated debris, and the obstacle for other construction imposed by the huge braces needed to keep the peripheral walls from falling in until the inside floors were in place.

In addition, Kyle said, the World Trade Center had a problem that, as far as he knew, no foundation engineer had ever before faced: a railroad had to be kept running inside the foundation area while digging went on around and beneath its tracks. Actually, two railroads go through the site—the IRT local subway line to South Ferry and the PATH System, a fourteen-mile line running between Newark, Hoboken, Jersey City, and Manhattan through tunnels under the Hudson River. PATH crossed the site in two five-hundred-foot cast-iron tubes, almost three-quarters of a century old, resting on beds of mud. Some way had to be found to jack up the tubes, through which about a thousand trains rumbled back and forth daily, carrying more than eighty thousand passengers, without disturbing either the trains or the passengers. Ultimately, the tracks would be relocated under the Trade Center and the old tunnels removed.

The solution to all this was a daring one: to build one huge basement, sixty-five feet deep in some places, a hundred feet deep in others, that would take the form of a watertight box (but what a box!)

occupying eight acres on the treacherous eight-block western half of the site. What the engineers were *really* doing was building a four-sided dam around the troublesome part of the site. The bottom of the box would be bedrock, into which the walls would be tightly socketed to keep water out. During the construction of the walls, water trapped inside could be removed as the filled land was dug away and the bedrock emerged. Then the work of digging beneath PATH and constructing the basement area—containing a new PATH terminal, the underground home of the Trade Center's maintenance and air-conditioning equipment, an emergency electric generating plant, garages, and truck docks—could proceed with maximum efficiency. As it took shape, this box, the largest single basement that Kyle or any of the West Street Associates knew of, came to be called the Big Bathtub, and, finally, just the Bathtub.

While planning the Trade Center foundation, Kyle told me, he inspected subways and other underground work in Paris, Brussels, London, and, finally, Milan, where a new subway was completed in the late nineteen-sixties. In all these places, a Milanese firm named ICOS, which specializes in building walls in wet areas to keep water from flooding construction sites, had used a new process called the slurry-trench method. In Montreal, Toronto, and at a dam in Pennsylvania, an affiliate of the Italian company, the Icanda Corporation, Ltd., of Canada, was doing the same kind of work, and Icanda was eventually hired to work jointly with the West Street Associates and actually construct the Bathtub wall. To a layman, the idea of building a multimillion-dollar foundation wall anywhere from sixty-five to a hundred feet deep underground, blindly, without excavating on either side of it, is bound to seem the height of folly, and I told Kyle so that afternoon. He laughed, and said he would try to explain why it was the most practical solution. The key to the slurry-trench method is the use of a volcanic ash, or clay, called bentonite—after Fort Benton, in Wyoming, where deposits of it were first found, in the eighteen-forties. The peculiar property of bentonite, a powdery clay, is its ability to absorb enormous quantities of water in an excavation, after which it is strong enough to hold back the surrounding earth. The petroleum industry began using bentonite instead of metal casings in oil-drilling holes around 1900. When mixed with water, bentonite creates a counter-pressure to the push of surrounding earth and water, and prevents cave-ins—just how is not understood, though some experts believe that an undetectable electric charge may be involved. "If you dig a trench and put down bentonite in the right mixture, it will hold up the banks," Kyle said. "The bentonite that is attached to the earth will stay attached even when concrete goes down and displaces the water in it. The stuff acts like a membrane, and the part that sticks to the wall holds the wall up. It annoys hell out of you when you can't figure out why that is, but, basically, we aren't interested in the theory. The important thing is that it works." The Bathtub wall, he said, was to be constructed in sections. Trench segments, twenty-two feet long, three feet wide, and seventy feet deep would be dug and filled with slurry—a mixture of six per cent bentonite and ninety-four per cent water. As dirt was removed it would continuously be replaced by slurry, so that the trench would always remain full and the sides would not fall in. The digging would continue down into bedrock, with about two feet of the rock itself chipped away to give the wall a proper footing. Then a great cage of steel rods—shaped to fit into the full length of each twenty-two-foot segment of trench and holding a number of forty-five-degree-angle steel guides for the installation of tiebacks—would be dropped into the soupy mix to reinforce the concrete. Next, the concrete itself would be poured into each section. As the liquid concrete rose to the top of the trench, it would displace the slurry, which would be pumped into the next section of trench. As each section of concrete wall was completed, the workmen would excavate on the inner side of it to install tiebacks reaching diagonally down through the soil behind it. Then the earth inside that section of the Bathtub could be removed. With ten or fifteen machines moving simultaneously along the perimeter, Kyle figured, the outside foundation would take about a year to complete.

Before I left him that day, Kyle remarked that, of course, all kinds of sewer, water, and steam pipes and electric and telephone lines running through the site would have to be rearranged, adding that such work was normal in new construction, but this would be the biggest relocation job in the history of the New York Telephone Company. The company's main office was right next door to the Trade Center, at the corner of West and Vesey Streets, he reminded me, and the principal trunk lines for all phone communication between major cities in the United States and to the world outside—including the hot line to Moscow—were under what had been Greenwich Street, in the very middle of the site. Local telephone lines customarily run under public thoroughfares, too, and these would all have to be moved to the West Street boundary. As for the long-distance lines, two huge manholes, or vaults, opening into the two tunnels of PATH were to be constructed, to reconnect these lines inside the tunnels for their route across the Hudson. The vaults underneath West Street would also serve to pin the cast-iron PATH tubes to bedrock.

In order to connect the new telephone wires, one by one, to sections of cables that would be brought into the new manholes and thence dropped into the tunnels, splicers would work in shifts, sitting on benches inside the vaults and splicing each cable progressively without interfering with telephone service. Such splicing "alive" could be done so skillfully that conversations would continue, with the customers unaware of what was happening.

It took more than a year to clear the Bathtub site of condemned buildings. This had been an area of small shops, many engaged in selling hi-fi equipment, and many of the store owners left reluctantly. There were also two residential tenants in no hurry at all to depart — one of them a penthouse dweller who loved the river view from his eighty-five-dollar-a-month apartment atop a five-story office building, the other a monkey that escaped from a pet shop when it was about to be torn down, built a nest in a pile of beams, stole enough bananas daily from a nearby fruit stand to stay alive, and eluded workmen for months. In any such huge project, the pattern of logistics demands immensely precise timing and coordination. Before the demolition of the old structures was half completed, therefore, construction of the Bathtub wall had begun, excavation inside the sections of wall that were in place was under way, and the cofferdam at the river's edge was receiving excavated fill. Wherever twenty-two feet of perimeter land had been cleared, Icanda's workmen jumped ahead and built another section of wall, so that practically the entire wall could be completed before the last of the condemned structures inside the Bathtub was demolished. The steel framework for the two skyscrapers, anchored in bedrock, began to rise aboveground while workmen underground were still digging out boulders from corners and dirt from underneath the PATH tubes.

Construction engineers groan at the prospect of finding relics when they are excavating an area with a complex history, for fear their work might be delayed while archeologists poke through the rubble, but nothing worth that effort turned up. The sunken ship Tijger never appeared — at least, not in any recognizable form — perhaps because powerful shovels smashed through underground obstructions as the excavations for the wall were completed. Timber cribbings were particularly wicked to break up, because lumber underwater can be just as hard after two hundred years as it was when it was sunk, though it may disintegrate a week after it hits the air. A canister from the cornerstone of the old Washington Market turned up, full of newspapers and the cards of the produce people who had taken stalls there. A century-old bedroom slipper came to light, as did an eighteenth-century forged nail, several clay pipes, a large Portuguese fishing gaff, and a variety of antique tools and ship fittings, including rudders and several anchors of a pattern not made after 1750. An enormous iron anchor, weighing about a thousand pounds, required nineteen men to carry it up out of the site, and it now rests against a concrete wall in the Trade Center's heating-and-refrigeration plant, in the sixth-level basement—the very bottom of the Bathtub. Ancient cannonballs and bombs, the muzzle of a cannon, old bottles, bits and pieces of old china, and one small gold-rimmed cup with two hand-painted lovebirds on it turned up in the digging. Of all the china objects found, it alone was intact. A lot of coins were rumored to have been dug up, but they did not materialize in the front office.

From time to time, I dropped by the site to watch the activity in the cut far below—ants in perpetual motion to the throbbing of a chorus of heavy machines. Seventy feet above, the ground where I stood vibrated. One summer day a couple of years after my initial visit, Kyle suggested that he take me on a formal tour, since the operation had reached a point where demolition, excavation, and construction were going on simultaneously, and the Telephone Company was about to finish its splicing in the ducts inside the recently completed manholes. I stepped out of a cab on West Street in the middle of the afternoon and stopped for a moment, facing the river, struck by the beauty of what was left of an old ferry slip that was being demolished between the Trade Center and the new landfill in the river. Only the façade was intact, with high Victorian windows and a handless clockface. At the sides, the steel and wood of the old walls were falling away, dripping down like lace, and the sun was reflected hotly in a second-floor window that still had glass in it. This dreamy remnant looked ready for instant collapse. Beyond I could just see the tops of the large cylindrical caissons that made up the cofferdam bounding the huge twenty-four-acre rectangle of new Manhattan real estate in the river. The center of the rectangle was a trifle wet, but the cofferdam was well filled with excavated material from the Trade Center foundation. I turned back toward the site, and saw that the surface area of the Bathtub was now almost cleared; there remained only part of a steel building frame with an elevator shaft still clinging to it, and a large stone edifice, the Marine Midland Bank Building, which appeared to have been built to last forever—except that it was not going to; looking up, I saw the iron ball of a demolition crane pounding away at the already roofless top story. I subsequently learned that it took four months to demolish this stubborn old fortress.

Kyle was waiting for me at the corner of West and Vesey, and we walked around the outside of the Bathtub, now clearly demarcated by the sections of wall already in place. Kyle paused to show me a particularly noteworthy machine, an enormously tall blue rig on a blue A-frame that was travelling on rails along the surface, digging the trench for a section of wall. All Icanda's machines were painted blue; this one, called an Adiges, and four or five others like it, had been imported from Italy for the job. A three-ton clamshell bucket hung from the peak of the A-frame and was equipped with jagged teeth to chew away the ground. Icanda, whose contract called for cutting not only through the ground but several feet into bedrock, had discovered that boulders and ancient timber obstructions were more formidable than had been anticipated, so it had then brought in two other pieces of special equipment—a rotary drill from the oil wells of Texas, so big that it had to be disassembled and transported to the site on three trucks, and a rock slicer, which had been air-expressed from ICOS's Milan shop. This monster, which had a giant blade attached to a lofty rectangular rig, could shave off rock wedges an inch thick, like a cheese slicer, but it met its match in Manhattan Schist, which is intermixed with hard, abrasive quartzite, and quickly dulled the slicer's blade. In fact, neither machine proved useful, and Icanda eventually resorted to old-fashioned methods of drilling, crushing, and hammering rock.

Against the backdrop of exposed brown soil and gray rock, blue, yellow, and orange machines down in the excavation were spots of bright color, and moving trucks of other vivid hues made additional flecks of brightness—especially the red trucks that carried explosives. Varicolored workmen's helmets also dotted the landscape—blue for Icanda, yellow for the Port Authority, green for Slattery, white for PATH, and an occasional silver or other odd-colored hardhat that was a treasured good-luck possession of its owner. Up on the surface, the Adiges machine near me stood next to a mixer pouring wet bentonite into the open trench, whose surface was a runny beige soup. Some distance away, concrete was flowing down a pipe to make a section of wall, and, in between, recovered bentonite was running into another trench, where another Adiges rig worked. On a cleared portion of the site, ironworkers were assembling steel cages to reinforce the concrete. The cages looked like giant bedsprings, and when they were lifted vertically into the air by enormous cranes, sometimes as high as a hundred feet, and then dropped slowly—going, going, gone—into the wet slurry in the trenches, a crowd of bystanders usually formed at the fence around the site to watch.

At what had been the corner of Greenwich and Dey Streets, we came to a graded incline leading to the bottom of the excavation. We walked down, stopping often to let outsize yellow Euclid dump trucks labor uphill past us piled with loads of great boulders or rattle downhill empty after a trip across a temporary ramp under West Street to the cofferdam area. At the bottom of the incline, we crossed a plank over a lot of water and came to a large yellow drilling machine, which was slowly shattering rock. There was the smell of wet sand, and I noticed several varieties of pumps hard at work. We were seventy feet below the street, and, looking up, I saw for the first time finished sections of the new wall, excavated and exposed, with the ends of tiebacks sticking out in rows about ten feet apart. The top layer of tiebacks was in place, and workmen were drilling holes and inserting a second layer. To my surprise, the wall was not smooth and fresh-looking but, rather, full of lumps and quite scruffy, like a fairly well-preserved achievement of some much older civilization. I shouted as much to Kyle over the racketing noise of the drills. "We can chop off the lumps and put a masonry wall inside if we want to dress it up!" Kyle shouted back. "But it probably wouldn't be worthwhile for that section—it will be a garage!"

Kyle suggested that we return at midnight to visit the telephone vault, where one man from the Telephone Company would still be splicing wires in the last of the cables to be relocated. PATH traffic would be light at that hour, and when one tube was closed briefly for cleaning we could walk along the track and climb into the telephone vault from below, instead of descending through the manhole from the street. It would be somewhat wet, I was told, and to get out I would have to go up a vertical ladder connecting the vault's three floors—my least favorite form of exercise. Forewarned, I arrived clad in bluejeans and rubber boots as the clock hands reached twelve in PATH's control center, a basement room filled with dials and flashing lights to indicate the position of moving trains. I was handed a helmet, and we started out.

The trains were temporarily halted in the north tube, and we began walking down the tunnel. As I picked my way carefully through the mud and over the railroad ties, I was at the rear of a single file consisting of Kyle, Katz, and several officials from the Telephone Company and PATH. Red and white flashlights carried by the men ahead danced to the swing of their arms as we passed the arch of a spooky, abandoned side tunnel leading nowhere. I looked above me, wondering if I could see the curved top of the tube, but the darkness was a soft shroud. Although it was a hot July night, the air was cool where we were—about forty-five feet below the street, still in Man-hattan but close to the riverbank. Kyle stopped for a moment to explain to me what I was about to see. The telephone vault, or manhole—three small, high-ceilinged rectangular rooms, one above another—was a watertight concrete box, which, like the Bathtub, was fastened to bedrock and built partly around the top of the PATH tube.

When the vault was finished, a hinged segment of tube served as a trapdoor between the tunnel and the manhole.

Suddenly there was a burst of light. It came through this door, which led into a small, elevated concrete room, in which a man sat working with a large pile of multicolored wires in his lap. He was wearing a yellow helmet, a blue flannel shirt, and a phone headset, but he pushed this aside to introduce himself as Charlie McQuade and to explain that there had been thirty-three splicers working six days a week in the area for the last five months but now he was the only one left. He was about to "throw," or splice, his last cable — one that had four hundred pairs of wires, or conversations, which meant eight hundred splices for him. The wires he was working on went to Philadelphia, Washington, Miami, and Moscow, he told us, adding that he could "throw" an average of two hundred a day. I had been told that splicing was one of the most highly skilled jobs in the Telephone Company, and as he talked and worked I could see why. If the wires weren't spliced with a tight pigtail twist, conversation on the line would be very noisy, and if a short circuit occurred there would be no conversation at all. Just then, someone called out that a train was about to come by. McQuade laughed. "Don't lean back too far, or you'll get a haircut," he said. We hurriedly climbed into McQuade's concrete room, the lowest of three in the vault, and, squeezing past him, we started one by one up the vertical steel ladder. On the second level, I paused to look at the telephone cables, which hung like large black hoses from ceiling to floor. Then I leaned down to see where I had come from. I could see the outer surface of the cast-iron tunnel tube, curved and heavy, with a dull-black finish, and if I had had any doubt about what it was, that doubt would have vanished a second later, when I heard a train rumble through. I started climbing again, and the air became increasingly warm as I neared the street surface. There was a sudden draft of wind from another train passing below, and as I held tight to the ladder I felt my helmet rise about a foot above my head. I grabbed for it, but it settled miraculously back, and I climbed out onto West Street to join the others. The Trade Center site was ablaze with light, and the rock crushers and drills were steadily pounding away.

Excerpted from "The Biggest Foundation," published in *The New Yorker*, November 4, 1972.

Part Three

◆

THE NORTH

Inuit Journey

━━━━━━━━━━ ◆ ━━━━━━━━━━

I ALMOST SURELY would never have gone to the Canadian North, and might be living an entirely different life, if I had not attended the first show of Inuit stone carvings in New York City, in the parish house of a church in the spring of 1959. I was still collecting notes for *The New Yorker*'s Talk of the Town, and had never even heard of Inuit art until that day.

The first sight of the stone carvings, those figures of human, animal, bird and sea creatures that made an ordinary church room come alive with their presence, literally took my breath away. I could say now that they had some kind of a deeper meaning, because of where they led me, but all I could think of then was that I wanted to know everything I could about the people who made them.

It was not until two years later, in the fall of 1961, that I found out more, not about the artists themselves but about their general situation. At United Nations headquarters I was introduced to Donald Snowden, a young man — he was then thirty-two — from Canada's Department of Northern Affairs, as it was then called. He and I sat down in the UN lounge, and he told me that in the 1950s, Inuit were starving before the government caught up with their tragic plight. It was his job, as chief of a section euphemistically named the "Industrial Division," to find some way for the Inuit to regain their self-sufficiency, which was so profoundly undermined by the advent of the white man. The government could not have made a better choice in the person to do this than Snowden.

He told me with glowing descriptions about the Inuit in a place at Ungava Bay, in northern Quebec. They had just formed the first co-operative to deal with the production and marketing of arts and crafts, as well as future fishing and logging. After ten minutes of listening, I said, "That's the most fascinating story I ever heard."

Snowden replied, "Why don't you come with us on our spring patrol and see it all for yourself?"

I took the idea to Bill Shawn, who had just bought my first long piece for *The New Yorker*, and although neither he nor I had more than a vague notion of where Ungava Bay was, he gave me the assignment, with one simple direction: "Write about everything you see; it will all be interesting." It turned out to be one of the great experiences of my life.

The following March I went to the Canadian Arctic with Snowden's spring patrol and observed at first hand a meeting that proved to be a major turning point in Inuit history. It was the second meeting of the first Inuit co-operative in Canada, and the Inuit who met at the George River also decided then to establish homes there. For better or worse, the Inuit had begun their transition from nomadic to settlement existence.

When I came back from that first trip, I was so overwhelmed by the experience that I could not get my bearings. I arrived in New York late in the morning, dropped my duffel bag in our apartment, walked as if I were in a trance over to my younger son's school nearby, and stood outside the classroom where I knew he was. I asked a passing teacher to have him brought out to me, and when he came we just stood, both of us smiling broadly, and stared at one another. "I'm glad you're back," he said quietly.

"I needed to see you," I said. "I feel as if I'd just come back from the moon. I'll be all right now." I kissed him, went home and slept all day. After that, I was fine.

I travelled three more times to the eastern Arctic between 1961 and 1964. All four of the resulting articles appeared in *The New Yorker*, and were the basis for the book *The New People*, published in 1966. On the twentieth anniversary of the founding of the first Inuit co-operative, in 1979, the book was re-issued with additional material as *Inuit Journey*.

Years later, I asked Don Snowden how he had dared to offer me the chance to go to the Arctic ten minutes after we met, when he had never seen a line of my work.

Snowden replied, "Intuition, I guess. I wanted, more than anything, to know if I was right in what I was doing, and it was the best way to find out."

During the two years after my first trip north, the Industrial Division began carefully to extend the co-operative idea to other Inuit communities that were distressed but had economic potential. By

1969, there were eighteen Inuit and Dene co-operatives in sixteen northern settlements, all the way across the Arctic.

How right Snowden was in using the co-operative as the means for the Inuit to learn to manage their own affairs can be judged by these facts: thirty years later, there are fifty active co-operatives in the Northwest Territories and Arctic Quebec, with total sales in 1990 in the Northwest Territories alone of $47.6 million, and total assets, $38.8 million. The Eskimo Loan Fund financed by the government to provide capital for the co-ops has been largely superseded by the co-operatives' own bank, the NWT Co-operative Business Development Fund, whose first president was the brilliant and dedicated Gunther Abrahamson. The Fund is now managed very well indeed by the Inuit and Dene themselves. A sophisticated Inuk politician, Billy Lyall, is President both of the Fund and the co-op federation.

My second trip north, to observe the second step in the Inuit march to self-sufficiency, is printed here.

✦

CONCLAVE AT FROBISHER

Small Eskimo settlements are scattered across the frozen top of North America, separated from one another by hundreds, often thousands, of miles of the hauntingly bleak Arctic. About two thousand of Canada's Eskimo citizens live as far south as the fifty-fifth parallel, in the northern third of Quebec, where Ungava Bay is, but most inhabit the huge area known as the Northwest Territories, which begins about the sixtieth parallel and stretches for over a million square miles between Baffin Island, in the east, and the great Mackenzie River, in the west, beyond which are the Yukon and Alaska. Those who live on the islands of the vast Arctic archipelago see polar bears, whales, and seals, but no trees; in winter their view is glistening ice and snow and in summer it is soft gray tundra and black rock. Eskimo communities bear names ranging from stirring Anglo-Saxon ones like Resolute to native tongue twisters like Povungnituk. The settlements vary in size from Port Burwell's thirty-six people or the northern outpost of Grise Fiord, on Ellesmere Island, situated between seventy-five and eighty degrees north latitude, which has around a hundred, living in total darkness from November until the end of January, to the government administrative center at Frobisher Bay, on Baffin Island, which has more than sixteen hundred inhabitants.

◆

Early in February, 1963, Snowden wrote me that the First Conference of the Arctic co-operatives was about to be held at Frobisher Bay, and he invited me to attend. "It may well mark a turning point in the economic affairs of Canadian Eskimos," he wrote. "It is the first time that the Eskimo leaders of Eskimo co-operatives have been able to get together to find out what is being done in other parts of the Arctic. It is highly unlikely that any Eskimo has ever been at a meeting involving so many Eskimo people from so many places in the Arctic. Many of the delegates may have had even less experience at formal meetings than the George River people had had when you were there. This is to be their meeting. Our role will be purely advisory and minor. I have no idea what is likely to be said at this conference."

On a Monday afternoon, in the middle of March, I joined Snowden and his party in the terminal building of the Montreal airport for the twelve-hundred-mile flight north to Frobisher Bay. With him were Paul Godt, his assistant, kindly and worried; Jon Evans, a sandy-haired man of about thirty, whose job was to survey areas where co-operatives might be set up and determine whether there were enough resources to make the ventures economically sound; Snowden's secretary, a vivacious blond young lady named Terry Chaput, who was making her first trip to the Arctic; Dr. Alexander Laidlaw, a quiet, alert man of about fifty, who was national secretary of the co-operative Union of Canada, the co-ordinating agency for co-operatives in English-speaking Canada, and who was coming along as an observer; and a delegate to the conference from the co-operative at Whale Cove, on Hudson Bay—a handsome young Eskimo named Celestino Magpa, who had a crew cut and was nattily dressed in a tweed sports jacket, gray flannels, white shirt, and black tie. The other men, I was surprised to see, had on business suits, rather than the heavy pants and sweaters that are the customary northern attire. Everyone was carrying a parka, that traditional outer Arctic garment, but I knew that we could expect cold weather at Frobisher, and I asked Godt why he, Snowden, and the others weren't dressed in a style more suitable for the Arctic. "Well, in fact, Frobisher is no frontier outpost," he said. "You'll find hot and cold running water, oil heat, automobiles—even a cocktail bar."

As our plane, a DC-4, took off, I glanced at a timetable provided by its operators, Nordair Airlines, which showed that we were to stop at Fort Chimo and were due to arrive in Frobisher a little before midnight. Snowden sat beside me and I remarked to him that Nordair seemed to have greatly increased its scheduled flights since my previous trip. "I can't get over the speed with which things are happening in the North," he said. "We'll be having superhighways next. And when those come, I leave. But one thing we do still lack, and need badly—lateral air transportation. All our scheduled air routes in the Northwest Territories run north and south; the only east-west transportation is by expensive chartered plane. At Port Burwell, the co-operative store has to carry a year's inventory of commodities, shipped in by boat in summer, and the items that the Eskimos offer for sale—white fox, sealskins, handicrafts—cannot be moved except at great expense." He pointed to Magpa, who was sitting up ahead, and went on, "Celestino presents a perfect example of what I mean. Whale Cove, where he lives, is only eight hundred miles from Frobisher across Hudson Bay and Hudson Strait, but he must make a thirty-six-hundred-mile trip to get there. He had to go eleven hundred miles south to Winnipeg, then thirteen hundred miles east to Montreal, and now he's travelling twelve hundred miles back into the Arctic with us. Transporting the Eskimo delegates presents a real problem in logistics. If the weather is bad, the crowd from the central and western parts of the Arctic may not arrive at all."

Snowden sat back for a few minutes smoking a cigarette. Then he said, "If all goes well, we're bringing in quite a varied group. A small plane is coming from Grise Fiord, on Ellesmere Island, with an Eskimo delegate and a Royal Canadian Mounted Policeman, who was for some time the only white man there, and who has been tremendously helpful to the co-operative. He keeps the books, among other things. Another Mounted Policeman will be with the Eskimo delegate from Resolute. Two Roman Catholic priests who helped start the co-operatives in their mission areas—at Holman and at Igloolik—will accompany Eskimo delegates from those places. And you must remember George Koneak, the Eskimo interpreter at the George River. We're picking him up, along with three delegates from Ungava and two from Povungnituk and Great Whale River, when the plane puts down at Fort Chimo, which is only two and a half hours' flight from Frobisher. Our Industrial Division men in that area, Wally Hill and Don Pruden, will be with them. Pruden, who's at the George River, is about the strongest man I've ever met—heavyset, and half as wide as this airplane. Some dogs attacked his little boy this winter, and I hear that Pruden picked up one of the dogs by its hind legs and threw it so hard that it went over and over in the air.

"Do you know why I'm having this conference?" Snowden asked. "I'm trying to find out whether there is an articulate body of opinion yet among the Eskimos in the North. Their co-operative meetings are teaching them not only how to speak but how to assume responsibility and make group decisions among themselves, and I want to know if they are now capable of expressing what is happening to them as a group. If they aren't, we're doing something wrong, but if they're really enthusiastic, we've got on the right track and we should continue. I've been at conferences in Ottawa where two or three Eskimos, frightened to death, sat in an impressive room in one of the Parliament Buildings with white people from the North representing the churches, the Mounted Police, the Hudson's Bay Company, and the government. The Eskimos were anxious and depressed about the big changes among their people, but no matter how hard they tried, they were unable to talk about their own communities and their real problems. Instead, they would fall back on something like 'I have a hole in the roof of my house and it needs repairing,' or 'I need a new boat.' I'd just hate to think that this was the way the Eskimos were going to use their right to make their own decisions—especially the decision about where they fit into modern society.

"The most encouraging thing I've seen lately is that the Eskimos are showing signs of learning how to tell us when we're wrong, and I hope we get some really loaded questions about the white man's role in the North," he continued. "I don't believe that the government is infallible, and the co-ops make it possible for the Eskimos to give us hell. In this way, we are insuring that we won't have a big minority in the North that is resentful, sullen, and unheard." He turned around and called to his secretary, a few seats behind us, that he wanted to dictate a memo to her, and as he rose, he said, "This meeting is as important to me as the one we had when the people at the George River formed that first co-operative. This is a kind of act of faith with me, to show that people of different color and culture can get together. They must."

At a little after eight in the evening, we landed at Fort Chimo. I walked down the metal steps from the plane into the cool Arctic night. The sky was luminous and dark blue. The stars shone, the ground stretched far away under a white glaze, and I felt the Arctic sweep around me. I noticed that a large group of Eskimos standing on the field were staring at me—giving me an intense scrutiny of a sort I recalled from my previous trip—and I walked on over to the low, wooden airport building. Its large waiting room was jammed with people, Eskimo and white. Some of them were warming their hands at an iron stove, and others were drinking coffee that two white women served from an urn in a corner. As I blinked in the glare of the bare electric bulbs, a familiar figure stepped up to me, his hand outstretched, an enormous grin on his face. It was George Koneak. "So you come back north," he said quietly. "We glad to see you again."

Behind him I saw another man whom I remembered vaguely from the George River. I had known him there only slightly. He was Josepie Annanack, a solid, broad-faced man with a black mustache, who, I learned, would be the delegate from the George River co-operative. Behind him was kindly-looking Henry Annatuk, who still was president of the Port Burwell co-operative. A moment later, I was introduced to Don Pruden, who, though he wasn't half as wide as an airplane, was broad enough, and had a formidable jaw.

When we reboarded our plane, Pruden sat down next to me. I told him I had heard about his son's ordeal, and asked how the boy was. "The lad's all right now, thank you," he said. He had a warm smile, and spoke in a soft, deep voice with a slight burr. "He's lost some of his hair from shock, and if I speak to him harshly, he sulks for a couple of days. And of course there'll be scars. I don't mind talking about it, if you'd like to hear." I said I would, and Pruden began to tell me the story. "This Sunday, the wife and I were getting up late, and the boy, who is five, and his sister, who is three, were playing outside, flying a little toy airplane in the wind. We heard the little girl scream the word 'Dogs!' and I ran out. I couldn't see the lad, but I saw the dogs—they were Josepie Annanack's—by the corner of the sawmill, a hundred yards away, tearing at something—something blue, it was, and I knew he had on a blue parka. Then I could see blood all over, and I yelled as I ran. The snow was soft and I sank in, but when I got to the dogs I grabbed one sidewise by the leg and threw it. It began to yelp, which made the other dogs stop to yelp, too. Then I got to the lad and pulled off his little rubber boot, to use it as a club. The dogs backed off, and I managed to get him into the house. I gave him to the wife, grabbed my shotgun, ran outside, and shot one of the dogs. Josepie came running, and he took my gun and shot all the others. You can never trust a team again, you know, once they've had the smell of human blood and flesh. I went back in the house, and the boy was on the floor, in shock and bleeding badly. I made a tourniquet, gave him aspirin and some other drugs, and tried to calm him." Pruden moved his hand nervously over his hair, which was short and bristly. "When the lad came out of shock, he realized that he was hurt bad, but he took it good. I sent someone right away to report it on the radio, hoping to get word to Chimo, but there was no answer, so I got some needles ready to sew the lad up if I couldn't get him out on a plane within twenty-four hours. I planned to have one of the Eskimos do the sewing while I directed him. I wouldn't trust myself to do it. Luckily, someone at a radio up the coast had heard my message, and transmitted it to Chimo that night, so at eleven-thirty the next morning a plane came to pick us up and take us to Chimo. That night, the lad and his mother were on this very same Nordair plane, and he was in hospital at Frobisher within thirty-six hours of the attack. My wife, who is the schoolteacher at the George River, was gone five weeks, and we had to close down the schoolhouse." Pruden relaxed and lit a cigarette. "The children throw sticks at the dogs, but those animals are tough and they're not bothered at all. We'll have a compound built for all the community dogs by next spring."

"The dogs must have been very hungry," I said.

"Oh, no," he replied. "Dogs attack on a full stomach. When they are hungry, they are too tired to attack."

After that, we chatted in a desultory way, and Pruden told me he was born at Stony Point, on Lake Winnipeg. "My old grandfather, who was a fisherman and fur trapper, brought me up," he said. "I left home at fourteen and went to work in the mines, trapping on the side, at the same time. I tried business, but went broke, and next I went into the uranium mines, but I got silicosis, so I went back to school and then applied for a job with Northern Affairs. I'm thirty-one now, and I started with the department in 1959. I like the George River very much, and so does my wife. This is our first year there, and she began teaching in a tent as soon as we arrived. Now we have a schoolhouse, and everyone between the ages of six and sixteen has started school." He leaned over and peered out of the window. "Here's your first view of Frobisher," he said.

I glanced down. Frobisher from the air had a gala, Christmas appearance, with very white snow and brightly twinkling electric street lights. I looked at my watch. It was just midnight. We landed, and as I walked toward the Nordair building, my boots crunched noisily in the crisp snow. Once again, as I had been at Chimo, I was acutely conscious of the silent white world around me—above all, it was silent. I wondered if this was partly because, on Baffin Island, we were hundreds of miles above the timber line, and the land was so barren.

We claimed our luggage inside the building, and then, following the others, I went outside and climbed into a yellow bus. An affable-looking man with glasses who was standing in the front of the bus introduced himself. He was Alex Sprudzs, co-operative Officer for the Department of Northern Affairs, and he told me he was supervising arrangements for the conference. "I've kept my fingers crossed that the weather would be all right," he said. "It's eighteen below, but it's nice and clear. We're still waiting for the western crowd, though." As the bus filled up, he read off our billeting assignments. Five or six men—two or three of them Eskimos and the other whites—would share each billet, with a government official in charge of each. Paul

Godt, who sat by me on the bus, said, "We have delegates from active older co-operatives staying with delegates from new ones. We hope the men will pick up as much information at night, while they sit around and talk, as they will at the meetings."

I had been assigned to quarters in one of a number of prefabricated rectangular structures called Butler Buildings. These are large steel shells, which are easy to ship and, since they can be used alone or strung together, are capable of being transformed into almost anything—living quarters, schools, garages, laundries, workshops. The one I was in had four apartments connected by a common hall, at the far end of which was a community laundry room with an electric washing machine. My apartment contained three good-sized bedrooms and a living room, all furnished with government-issue maple furniture, including overstuffed chairs and a couch; a storage room for rations; a modern bathroom; and a kitchen with an electric refrigerator and a modern-looking stove. All the windows in the building were frozen shut, and the temperature inside was at least eighty. This tropical heat was the greatest hazard I encountered during this particular trip to the Arctic. After two sleepless nights, I discovered the community thermostat in the outside corridor, and each evening from then on I tiptoed out with a flashlight after everyone else was in bed and pushed the setting back into the sixties, which brought the heat in my apartment down to a livable seventy. Each morning, on my way out, I flicked the control back to its previous position. That first night, though, in my desperate search for air, I picked up my sleeping bag and relocated myself on the couch in the living room, where I was astonished to see a small glow at eye level, which proved to be the light on a white Princess telephone. Whom could I call? The light beckoned all that sleepless night. My sense of isolation was so complete that it never occurred to me that I could pick up that phone and call my family in New York.

At seven-thirty the following morning, the yellow bus arrived to take us to the conference buildings. I was told that the settlement of Frobisher Bay consisted of three separate communities, and that we were staying in one known as Lower Base where most of the government employees lived, and that we would have our meetings and our meals in another, called Apex Hill, which was three miles away. The third community, of small frame houses and shacks, was the original Eskimo village of Ikaluit, just around a bend in the road from Lower Base. After fifteen minutes of bumpy riding, we were deposited at the Rehabilitation Center dining hall on Apex Hill. I had learned, as we drove over, that the Rehabilitation Center had been set up by the Department of Northern Affairs eight years earlier, principally in order to provide food and shelter for Eskimos in transit to and from hospitals, but that it has gradually assumed a much wider role in Eskimo life. Physically handicapped Eskimos or those with serious emotional problems often cannot readjust to their former, primitive way of living. The Center provided a sheltered existence for some seventy-five Eskimos, who occupied themselves with such enterprises as a bakery, a coffee shop, crafts production (mainly carving and sewing), and an Eskimo-run movie theatre. Graduates of the Center who wanted to stay put could settle down with their families and buy or build houses on Apex Hill, and as our bus had climbed the hill, I had observed a general atmosphere of activity, with the stovepipes of wooden Eskimo houses smoking briskly in the early-morning air.

The conference itself took place in the Apex Hill community hall, a five-minute walk from the dining hall. A long, low building, the community hall contained a lavatory and coatroom and a large meeting area with light-blue walls and with black curtains that could be pulled across the windows to keep out the brilliant Arctic sun. As people began filing into the hall, Snowden mounted a platform at one end and sat down, facing the rest of us, at the center of a wooden table, in front of two Canadian flags and a large map of the Arctic. He was dressed in a business suit, as he had been the day before, and all the Industrial Division men were similarly dressed. The Eskimos, two of whom joined Snowden at his table and the rest of whom were taking their places at two long tables at right angles to the dais, wore suits with white shirts and ties, or plaid jackets and sweaters, but unlike the men from the South, they all had on Arctic footwear — heavy work shoes or tasselled fur boots. Jon Evans, who had walked in with me, pointed out two priests sitting with the Eskimos — Father Fournier, from Igloolik, a severe-looking man in his thirties, with bright-blue eyes, a Roman nose, and short brown hair and beard, who was wearing the standard Arctic clerical outfit of black turtleneck sweater and black trousers tucked into Eskimo boots, and Father Tardy, from Holman, who was scholarly in appearance, with graying hair and steel-rimmed glasses, and who was wearing a formal black clerical suit and collar, but also had his trousers stuffed into Eskimo boots. Evans told me that Father Tardy was the sole representative present from Holman, because his Eskimo colleague from the co-op there had missed plane connections, and had thus turned out to be the only one of the forty-five persons expected at the conference who hadn't been able to make it. Evans also pointed out the two Mounted Policemen — both of them very young — who were sitting with their Eskimo colleagues, and I was disappointed to see that they were not in uniform. One had on a business suit, and the other, a handsome, straightbacked man with a clipped mustache, was wearing a heavy brown-and-tan striped sweater, wool slacks, and fur boots.

Behind the delegates, tables had been set up facing the dais for officials from Ottawa and for observers, and at each place was a neat brown envelope. One of the envelopes bore my name, and inside it were a lined pad; a pen and a pencil; several printed pamphlets about co-operatives; the latest issue of the Northern Affairs Department magazine *north*; a list of the Eskimo co-operatives, in the order of their incorporation, with the names of the delegates they were sending to the conference; the agenda for the five days of the conference; and a program, which had a green cover ornamented by an impressionistic black stencil of two Eskimos shaking hands. The program was printed both in English and in syllabics.

Sealskin stencil print by Sheouak

ᕇᕗᑕᐸᒥ

ᒪ ᑲᓕᒪᕿᑲᓂᐅᕗ ᐃᓄᐃᑦ ᓄᓇᖃ

ᑯ ᐅᐊᑦ ᐱᕿᓂᕈᒍ

FIRST

CONFERENCE OF THE ARCTIC

CO-OPERATIVES

Leafing through it, I found greetings from the Minister of Northern Affairs; a message from the Commissioner of the Northwest Territories; a statement by Snowden of the meeting's purpose ("What you decide here will be of great importance to Eskimo people far into the future. . ."); a suggestion by Godt that the Eskimos "look ahead to the day when the co-operatives in the North form their own big co-operative to undertake. . .things which individual co-operatives cannot do"; a message of welcome from R.J. Orange, the Regional Administrator at Frobisher; and a description of the co-operatives by Alex Sprudzs. I read that the membership of the co-operatives now totalled five hundred (representing with their families, more than twenty-five hundred Eskimos), and that their products were currently selling at an annual rate of about half a million dollars.

While we waited for the scheduled nine a.m. opening of the conference, I first chatted with my right-hand neighbor, Dr. Laidlaw. Then a slight, wiry fellow with a lean face and a wry expression slipped into the seat on my left and introduced himself as Jack Veitch, Co-operative Development Officer for the western Arctic. He told me that he and his colleagues in the western group had not arrived at Frobisher until three-thirty that morning.

At this point, Snowden began to speak over the public-address system. "It is ten minutes to nine, and I would like to start, even though we are ahead of time," he said, by way of opening the meeting. First, he introduced the Eskimos at the table with him—a tall, distinguished-looking, immaculately dressed man of about thirty, known simply as Simonie, who was the head of the Frobisher Bay housing co-operative and a leader in the community, and the interpreter, a local resident. The latter began translating Snowden's remarks into Eskimo very haltingly, and seemed to be having a great deal of difficulty. I looked around for George Koneak. He was sitting on the edge of his seat at the side of the room, his mouth open and his hands tightly clasped, listening intently. Simonie made a one-minute welcoming speech first in Eskimo, then in English, which was followed by a few words from the eastern Arctic Co-operative Development Officer, Richard Nellis. The interpreter was now in deep trouble, scratching his head and pausing for long intervals while he gazed helplessly at the ceiling. Snowden leaned over and spoke softly to him for several minutes, and then said to the assemblage, "This conference brings to Frobisher Bay many people like me, who don't speak Eskimo. This is a new experiment for all of us, and we must have patience with one another. We have talked it over and decided that it is better to start with an interpreter I am used to." He called to Koneak, who quickly came forward, stepped onto the platform, and stood beside the table. Koneak said a few words in Eskimo and smiled, and everyone seemed to relax.

Snowden went on, "Four years ago almost to this very day, the first co-operative was started in the Arctic. None of us thought at that time that we would be sitting down with so many people from co-operatives right across the Arctic. . . If we tried to write down what co-operatives are, we would have as many different answers as there are people in this room, and it's because we have different ideas that we are here today. For the first part of our meeting, delegates will talk about what they are doing. We are going to hear a lot of things that will get our thinking straight on what co-operatives are and what they can do for us. So far, most of us think in terms of the money that co-operatives can make for the members, and there's nothing wrong with that. Co-ops are the best way I know to make money in the Arctic." He was speaking rapidly, and Koneak was interpreting tensely, in short sentences.

Suddenly Koneak stopped talking in Eskimo. "Excuse my language," he said to us in English, "but I use as much power as I have to bring it out in one piece."

Snowden said, "At the start of this week, it may be for you — as it is for me — something that makes me very nervous, because I have never done this before. But it will get easier as we get to know one another better." He introduced the delegates, who stood up self-consciously as their names were called. There was one woman delegate, a dour-looking Eskimo named Mrs. Bessie Irish, who was wearing a red cotton dress and blue sweater, and had straight black hair hanging to her waist.

"She's from my territory — from Aklavik," Veitch whispered. "Bessie is unique. Hers is the only co-operative composed solely of women. They make and sell fur garments." He shook his head sadly. "Bessie won't be able to talk," he said. "She'll clam up when her turn comes."

As an alert, high-spirited Eskimo from Fort Chimo, Noah Angnutok, was introduced, I noticed that Wally Hill, the Industrial Division's man at Chimo, was sitting next to him with a small child on his lap. Behind me, I was aware that Don Pruden, who had risen from his place was pacing nervously to and fro, and I asked him in a whisper who the child was. He explained that Hill's wife was in the hospital having a baby, so Hill had had to bring their smallest child with him.

"What's wrong with you?" I asked Pruden. "You seem nervous!"

He looked anguished. "I *am* nervous," he said. "Josepie Annanack is going to speak first, because the George River was the first co-operative, and Josepie is just about the shyest man in the world. He'll never be able to do it!"

Snowden was winding up his introductions with the two Mounted Policemen. "If I may make a personal remark, I want to say how delighted we are to have the co-operation of the RCMP," he said. "Thanks for being here." He then mentioned the half-dozen others present, among whom, in addition to Dr. Laidlaw and myself, was an anthropologist, Dr. Frank Vallee, from the government's Northern Research Center. Finally, he outlined the rules of procedure: "Simonie and I will be co-chairmen of the meetings. Anyone who wants to talk must stand up, and the chairman will ask him to talk. If lots stand, the others must sit down. Now we'll have our first report."

Snowden called the name of Josepie Annanack. Annanack came up onto the platform, and Snowden made room for him to sit next to Koneak, who was now seated at the end of the table, the original interpreter having withdrawn to the audience. Annanack lit a cigarette, and his hands were shaking so violently that he quickly thrust them under the table. Snowden moved his chair nearer to Annanack, to bring himself, Annanack, and Koneak into a little half circle, and said, very gently, "I would prefer to make this first report a discussion among three people, just the way we talked at the George River." He was speaking carefully, and there wasn't another sound in the room as Koneak translated. Hill's little boy had fallen asleep in his father's arms. Almost all the Eskimos had begun taking notes in syllabics, and I was struck by the seriousness and dignity of the proceedings. Snowden went on, speaking to Koneak, "Say to Josepie that you and he and I have talked many times. I want him to tell me about the co-op at the George River and forget about the other people here." Snowden was now leaning over so that his large frame practically blocked Annanack's view of the assemblage. Koneak interpreted, and everyone waited breathlessly for Annanack to speak. Pruden, back in his seat, put his head in his hands. Annanack slowly brought his arms up onto the table, crossed them, and leaned on them. Then he took a deep breath, and began to speak. His voice had an unusual mellowness, which I recalled from my previous trip as being characteristic of the George River men. As soon as he started talking, Snowden sat back. After every few sentences, Annanack would stop and nod to Koneak, who would translate into English.

Annanack said, "When the people of the government came to the George River with this new idea, we could hardly understand, and didn't realize how good it was. Before, we were mostly short of food. There was not enough game and we hardly got anything. We had to go ninety miles by dog team to Fort Chimo for government relief. We thought we should go to another place so we could live better. When the white people brought in this new idea, we decided to wait and try. Now we make money at home and feel much better." He halted, looked around, and said, "I'm not the best man for speaking. It doesn't come into my head all at once, and I have to stop for thinking."

Snowden nodded. "I wonder if Josepie would tell us what his co-op does," he said. "The others don't know and would be interested."

Annanack explained that in the winter the members cut logs and in the summer they fished, and he told about a new chemical called Biostat, which they used to keep the fish from getting soft while they lay on ice in the boats bringing them to the freezer that the co-op had set up. He said that the co-op was also making small boats, and had sold some to the Port Burwell co-operative. Snowden remarked, "This is one thing we'll see more and more — the co-ops will be selling to one another."

Henry Annatuk, president of the Port Burwell co-op, stood up. Snowden recognized him, and Annatuk said, "We have no wood at Burwell, so we would like more boats and also a price that is a little bit less."

Several other Eskimos rose, to ask Annanack about Biostat and about the boats. Then there were queries about pricing and marketing, which Josepie could not answer. Snowden answered for him, and then said to Koneak, "It is important that we should all understand what happens in a co-op. I'm not sure whether the Eskimos do things because the white man thinks they should be done, or because they want them themselves. I myself want to know this."

There ensued a long conversation in Eskimo between Koneak and Annanack. The latter moved restlessly in his chair, and asked Koneak several questions. Koneak suddenly began to talk in Eskimo with considerable emotion, clenching his fists. I knew that until Eskimos completely trust a white man, they usually tell him what they think he wants to hear, and I wondered whether the small drama we were witnessing represented Annanack's struggle between his desire to answer Snowden truthfully and his natural distrust of a roomful of strangers, half of them white. Finally, Annanack began to talk in a low voice, holding his hands tightly gripped before him. He said, "The co-operative idea came from the white people. We could take the idea, and it works well. We never tried to produce before, because we had nothing to produce with, so we would not refuse to do this, as long as we thought we could do it. Now we have a chance to build with something, among our own people."

Annanack looked uncertainly at Snowden, who said, "That was a difficult question, and Josepie has answered well. The whole idea for a co-op did come from the South, but it is now something that belongs to the George River. Do they feel that it is something they *must* do or something they *want* to do?"

When Koneak translated this, the Eskimos laughed, and Simonie said a few words that made them laugh again. Annanack, relaxed and calm, lit another cigarette, and said, "As we were working along at the beginning, we never thought of this, but everyone realizes now that the people can do something, and that's why every year it's getting better. We do not always make a good job, we are a little bit short of equipment or it breaks down, but we like very much to proceed as much as possible."

Snowden announced that it was time for lunch, and, with a nod toward Annanack, said, "As the first delegate to report, he has had the most difficult job that anyone will have this week, and he has done it so well. It will be easier for everyone else, now that we have seen how it can be done."

Everyone applauded loudly.

Walking over to the dining hall, I asked Snowden if I had only imagined that there had been a struggle between Koneak and Annanack over the answer to his question. "I'm not sure, but I think George was trying hard to explain my question to Josepie," Snowden said. "I asked that question because the Eskimos have never been at a formal meeting before, and right from the start I wanted no confusion in anybody's mind about the purpose of this one. I wanted everybody in the room, Eskimo and non-Eskimo, to understand that I wished the Eskimos to say what they really wanted to say, and not be dominated by us. Since Josepie was the delegate I knew best, and the first speaker, I wanted this idea established, through him, for the entire meeting. As for my asking whether the co-operative idea was something they wanted or something they felt they must do, if the Eskimos had felt they were not making their own decisions, I would have considered our whole technique wrong, and would have changed it."

At lunch, it was agreed that the conference was off to a fine start. On one side of me sat a young Eskimo who spoke perfect English. He told me he was Paul Oolateetak, and that he was from Resolute, where he had learned his English working at the Royal Canadian Air Force base. I asked what his co-operative did. "We sell polar-bear skins," he said. "We had twenty this year, but I only shot one bear myself."

◆

When the afternoon session began, Henry Annatuk, from Burwell, was seated on the platform ready to start talking, but before he could begin, Snowden announced, "I want to do as little work as I can. I wonder if Simonie would take over as chairman?" He said this so casually that it wasn't until Simonie had started to conduct the meeting in Eskimo that it became clear what had happened. The conference had become an Eskimo affair. Now it was the white people who had to wait for the interpreter to tell them what was going on.

Brushing the hair back from his eyes, Annatuk spoke in a low tone, and with a quizzical, half-amused expression on his face. Burwell's story was similar to the George River's, he said. The Eskimos had been destitute and about to leave when "the people from Ottawa" came along with the co-operative idea and showed them how to harvest their rich resources. He told how in four years, the Eskimos had built up a flourishing fishing, handicrafts, and fur business, and, because they were a hundred and twenty miles from the nearest Hudson's Bay outpost, how they had established the first Eskimo-run co-operative retail store in the Arctic. Seals were very abundant in their area, and they had such a plentiful supply of seal meat, for feeding both human beings and their dogs (reputed to be the fattest in the North), that he said the Industrial Division had sent a food expert into Burwell with a portable cannery to experiment with the canning of the meat for sale to other settlements.

Of all the delegates to the conference, the next speaker was the one I was most eager to hear. His name was Oshaweetuk, and he was a noted carver from Cape Dorset, the west Baffin Island community where the magnificent walrus-ivory carvings and prints made from stone blocks or sealskin stencils, already well known in the American and European art world, originated. In 1959, Oshaweetuk had walked into the office of James Houston, the government administrator at Dorset, and himself an artist, and, noticing a package of Player's cigarettes on the table, had remarked, of the familiar picture of the bearded sailor on the wrapper, "It must be terrible to have to paint this little sailor on every package every time." Houston had replied, "But that isn't the way it's done," and the next moment he had introduced Oshaweetuk to the art of printing. Taking from his desk a walrus tusk on which Oshaweetuk had incised likenesses of familiar Arctic figures, and some ink and tissue paper, Houston had, by good luck, succeeded in printing a fine impression of the various objects—caribou, a man in a kayak, a goose, a walrus— that were cut into the tusk. Upon seeing the print, Oshaweetuk had said, "But we could do that!" He and his companions did, making printing blocks and stencils from more easily worked materials, and the Dorset community went into the Eskimo-art business. Soon afterward, they formed the third, and the most prosperous, of the Arctic co-operatives.

Oshaweetuk, a slight, neat, highly intelligent-looking man, walked to the platform, took his seat with dignity, and began to talk. "Before the co-operative started, the people suffered," he said. "They didn't have much ammunition and they didn't have lumber for kayaks. Now they have lumber, but they also have money to buy outboard motors, so they don't use kayaks much." Describing how Houston had provided the Eskimos with the technical knowledge that enabled them to produce the prints, he said, "A lot of people didn't know how to carve and were learning from each other — both the ladies and men, even myself. At first the price was not very high, but as we get better the price is going higher. We also learn which carvings make the better price, but now the prints are higher priced than the carvings. We can afford canoes to travel on the sea, and, working for the co-op, we can buy ammunition. That way, we get a better life." He lit a cigarette, and said, "In the beginning, we tried to make the prints fancy, but they were not as good as the prints made from an idea. Now the prints are not even pretty to look at, but they are higher-priced than the pretty prints. The way to make prints, you draw an idea on paper and carve a copy of it on soft stone and use it like a stamp. If the stone is nice and smooth, and the carving is well done, you can make lots and lots of prints. But the ladies' prints are always higher-priced than the men's prints." Everybody laughed, and someone asked him why. He smiled. "Because the ladies are not thinking only about animals, like the men always think, but of something of their own ideas." He paused, then said quietly, "The help we got from Jim Houston we still have, and it is still growing. Before he came along, we could hardly go hunting and could not afford even a half gallon of coal oil. Now everybody can get more of anything, because Jim Houston helped us. We are still thankful to that man, and can never forget him."

Simonie asked if there were any questions, and Father Tardy rose. Speaking with a heavy French accent, he asked, "What kind of 'elp Mr. 'ouston give to you? Did he teach you 'ow to draw?"

"At the beginning, people didn't know how to start," Oshaweetuk said. "Houston showed them how."

A small man named Pauloosie Seuak, from Povungnituk, who was sitting up front, near the platform, bobbed up and asked, in a staccato tone of voice, "Who is the boss at Cape Dorset — the white man or the Eskimo?"

Instantly, Oshaweetuk said, "The white man."

Snowden quickly turned to Simonie. "Could I clarify that?" he asked Simonie. "Would it be all right?"

Simonie nodded, and Snowden said, "At Cape Dorset, the leader is a white man, in the sense that two white people from the South work for the co-operative, one as manager of the co-operative and one as manager of the retail store, but the co-op, not the government, pays their salaries. If I am Prime Minister of Canada, and I don't like one of these two men, I cannot have him fired. Only the members of the Dorset co-op can fire him. People really control their own affairs when they can hire and fire their people, so although the two men seem to be leaders in some ways, they are actually the paid employees at Cape Dorset."

Pauloosie Seuak's turn as speaker came next, and he described the stone-carving industry at Povungnituk, a settlement that has become almost as famous for its art as Cape Dorset. "The carvings have to be a certain size to sell, not larger than is measured by the hand, from the middle finger to the middle of the thumb, standing on a base," he said, holding up his hand and demonstrating. "The small sell easier than the big."

In a few minutes, there was a coffee break, during which Seuak took Snowden aside and, with snapping eyes and in rapid-fire Eskimo, hastily translated by Koneak, described the events surrounding his presence at the conference.

"Did you know that I was chosen by the people, by the Eskimos, but the white men had chosen someone else?" he asked.

Snowden scowled and said, "No, no, we wanted the Eskimos to choose the man they wanted to come."

Seuak rushed on to tell how he and the mission priest at Povungnituk, who had helped found the co-operative, had taken a trip to Quebec City to promote the Povungnituk carvings. There the priest had been injured in an automobile accident. "So I returned home alone, and when I get back, I learn that the priest and the government man picked someone to come here already before, without asking the people." he said. "But I was told by the people, 'We want you to go along instead of the other fellow to represent Povungnituk.'"

Snowden told Seuak that this had been the right procedure, and that he was glad things had turned out that way.

That evening, I accompanied several Frobisher residents to the town's only night club. Often known as Gallagher's, from the name of its proprietor, it was a series of shacks pushed together and covered with red shingles. Its official name was the East Coast Lodge and Tavern, and it was divided into two sections known as the Rustic Room Grill and the Captain's Corner, but the most popular name for the whole place was the one the Eskimos used — the Easty-Coasty. The interior, which had low ceilings, shaded lights, and bamboolike tropical decorations, looked more like a stage setting for "Rain" than a cocktail lounge on a snow-covered, treeless island. A glass of beer cost fifty cents, and a steak cost six dollars. Several quietly drunk Eskimos were sitting at a table on one side of us, and several quietly drunk white people were sitting at a table on the other side, and nobody got out of hand. "They run a pretty fair show here," a man who worked in Frobisher said to me. "We hear that whiskey is ruining the Eskimos here, and I wouldn't deny that some have been affected, but a three-week waiting period has been imposed on orders at the government liquor store, and that has checked a lot of impulse buying."

I asked if the Eskimo and the white populations mixed much.

"The schools are integrated—they're three-quarters Eskimo and one-quarter white—and there is some mingling on that account, but generally the whites just do not mix with the Eskimos," he said. "They aren't interested. We have some basic prejudices to break through here, especially among people who only come north to make money. Not all our government agencies have helped, either. In 1959, for instance, when a man from another department went into the office of the Northern Canada Power Commission to suggest that the Commission should hire Eskimos, he was summarily told to leave. But last fall the Commission finally took on four Eskimo lads, to train them as power-plant operators. We are working all the time to break down barriers. The Department of Transport, for example, still operates a bar that doesn't welcome Eskimos. But give us time. All that will change."

◆

During the next three days' meetings, Snowden sat at the back of the room listening to the individual reports, while Simonie served as chairman. The spokesman for the co-operatives described a wide assortment of their activities: fishing for trout, cod, and Arctic char, which was being sold as a luxury item by now not only in southern Canada but in the United States, France, and England; arts and handicrafts production; fur trapping; boatbuilding; and the operation of tourist camps. Four co-operatives now ran retail stores, and two had credit unions—called in Eskimo *qikartissivik*, which means "the place where the money is stopped."

When Paul Oolateetak, of Resolute, spoke, he said that his co-operative had appointed Constable Bell, the Mounted Policeman, to be its treasurer. "He was to look after the money, because no one else was too good at adding," he explained.

A man from Chimo stood up. "Is the co-op paying the treasurer?" he asked.

Oolateetak said, "No. He is paid by the Mounted Police and it is part of his duties."

Constable Bell promptly popped up and said, "But it's a good idea!" This brought a roar of laughter.

Then the young policeman told how, at the Canadian Air Force base in Resolute, he had set up a table in the mess hall to sell the Eskimos' carvings to the servicemen. "A group of carvings is gone in half an hour," he said. "Almost every Eskimo family has at least one member working at the airbase, so the income from carvings is extra spending money, and the Eskimos use it wisely—on stoves, beds, and other furniture. Everybody is now one hundred per cent behind our co-operative, although at first there were several who sold their carvings under the counter. That pulled prices down, so we had a meeting and explained this, and since then the Eskimos have found that prices have been twenty to thirty per cent better."

Akpalleeapik, the delegate from Grise Fiord, on Ellesmere Island, which is about seven hundred miles north of the Arctic Circle and about a thousand miles south of the Pole, was introduced as representing the northernmost co-operative in the world. (I later learned that he had never seen a tree.) Akpalleeapik, who was a famous hunter, had a small mustache and a round haircut, and he was nervously chewing gum as he sat down on the platform to talk. He said he had formerly lived on north Baffin Island, and explained, "The reason I ended up at Grise Fiord, the government was moving people from the east coast of Hudson Bay to Grise Fiord, because they did not have too good a life in their old place. I was asked to teach them how to live in darkness, which I already knew from north Baffin. Where we live, darkness comes from November through January, and then it gets brighter and brighter and will eventually be brighter than where other places are." The Grise Fiord co-operative's activities were similar to those at Resolute, which is two hundred and fifty miles away to the southwest and is the nearest settlement. He went on, "Since very few people knew bookkeeping, we had to turn to someone who did know—Constable Currie—and since we have turned to the RCMP for help, we feel we have done well."

Henry Annatuk asked if there were fish at Grise Fiord, and Akpalleeapik replied, "If you want to live there by fishing, you might as well give up the idea of living, because you are going to starve pretty fast. Sealskins are our main source of income, and we also hunt polar bears and trap white fox, and are getting quite a lot from carvings."

During the coffee break that day, Dr. Vallee, the anthropologist, remarked to Snowden that the tensions were breaking down and people were beginning to make jokes. Snowden was pleased. "There was an undercurrent of suspicion among the Eskimos that the whole show at Resolute and Grise Fiord was being run by the Mounted Police, but it's obvious to everybody now that the Eskimos understand just what they are doing," he said.

As we returned to our seats, I noticed that Akpalleeapik was nowhere to be seen. Koneak reported that Akpalleeapik was ill, and had waited only to give his report before being taken to the hospital. "Probably the flu," Paul Godt said to me. "That's what usually happens when someone from an isolated community comes into contact with a lot of other people."

It was the turn of Noah Angnutok, from Chimo, to talk, and there was one message that he was determined to deliver. He said, "The members of my co-op want me to say, if there are men from Ottawa at the conference at Frobisher, that the people of Chimo wish to have a store. If I can't get an answer right away, I would like an answer sooner or later for my people back home. We have a Hudson's Bay store in Chimo, but everyone looks for something that costs less than in the Hudson's Bay store. My people are happy, never sad, but they will be very happy to get this."

Angnutok then spoke of the current activities of the Chimo co-operative, but before he sat down, he looked straight at Snowden, in the back of the room, and said, "Chimo would like to know. We haven't got an answer on a store. Will we get an answer here?"

Snowden got up—reluctantly, it appeared. "I was rather hoping you would forget, but not really," he said. "We will discuss this later in the week."

I asked someone afterward why Snowden had been so uncharacteristically evasive. "This is the gray area that government people must stay away from, and they do," my informant said. "It is a hellish problem, because the fact is that where there is already a Hudson's Bay Company store, as there is at Chimo, the government officials are not allowed to help set up retail stores in competition." I assumed that he meant they were prevented from doing so for political reasons. "Dr. Laidlaw is here as a private citizen, representing a powerful union of southern co-operatives, and he looks interested," he said. "Perhaps he'll come up with something."

When the report from the co-operative at Holman was called for, it was the scholarly-looking Father Tardy who rose to give it, since his Eskimo colleague had missed his plane. He was extremely nervous, and obviously something was bothering him. Speaking in halting English, he began by telling us that in 1960 there had been five cases of tuberculosis among the Eskimos in Holman, and that he was certain that a prime factor in this had been the inadequacy of the living quarters—unsanitary shacks built of old boxes, canvas, and paper. "Something had to be done to alleviate, so I thought of developing local industry," he said. He started the Eskimos making tapestries of sealskin, with appliqué designs in different shades of fur, and then decided that a second industry was needed. In 1962, he saw his first Cape Dorset print. Since the artistic talent of the Holman Eskimos had already been demonstrated in the tapestries, he decided that they should try making prints, and he found an article in *Beaver*, the Hudson's Bay Company's magazine, that described the Cape Dorset process of making stencils and printing. "We try to make, using poor paper and ink, but the first time, not good," he said. "At last, we find a nice paper that worked, so we make our first print collection. We hanged the prints, everybody came and looked, and we arrived at conclusion we liked and they are really our own. The Eskimos choose the fifteen best and we sent to Canadian Eskimo Art Committee in South. None are accepted, and letter comes back that says prints are not really Eskimo and that somebody tell Eskimo 'ow they should do it." In an agitated voice, he said, "I wish to defend our prints against this comment and get your impression of them."

Slides of the prints were shown. They depicted Eskimo figures and polar bears against a background of mountains in perspective. Puzzled by the rejection, I later sought an explanation from some of the government men. I was told that the Canadian Eskimo Art Committee—a group of five experts, one of them James Houston, and the rest from Canadian museums and art publications, who met at irregular intervals to give the Eskimos guidance on such matters as the quality, printing, and pricing of their art works—had said that the prints from Holman showed real promise, and were not bad for a first attempt. But because no other Eskimo drawing had ever had background or perspective, the committee felt that the prints revealed a degree of white influence not evident in the work from Dorset and Povungnituk. The committee had urged the Holman Eskimos to try again.

I subsequently saw photographs of some of the sealskin tapestries made under Father Tardy's supervision. Intricately worked into the fur design were figures depicting the Last Supper and the fourteen Stations of the Cross; the figures wore Grecian-style robes, and grapes and tropical leaves had been painstakingly appliquéd around the borders. It was obvious that Father Tardy had become confused about the delicate line separating the imposition of ideas from the teaching of techniques. This distinction, however, seemed to be quite clear to the Eskimos, who, during a coffee break after Father Tardy had spoken, spiritedly discussed the matter, through Koneak, with the government officials. I heard one of the officials say, "I remember Jim Houston telling me that he would never think of telling an Eskimo what to draw, any more than he, as an artist, would ever think of drawing the way the Eskimos do. He also believed that the Eskimo *should* reject anything imposed on him, because his thinking is so different from ours. The whole philosophy of art is involved here." He added, "But it would be wrong for any white man to speak of this to Father Tardy. It will have to come from an Eskimo."

When we returned to the hall, Simonie reopened the discussion of the Holman prints, and sought Oshaweetuk's opinion.

The Dorset artist rose slowly and faced Father Tardy. "First off, I would like to ask how did the people start to develop the prints?" he said. "When I have heard that, I will talk about them for a little while."

"They have never been teachered, just by themselves," Father Tardy said. "They tell each other what to do—it is purely Eskimo. Our first appreciation was by the Eskimos themselves. Everybody said, 'This is our country, something belonging to us.'" He raised his voice. "The Dorset man said before, 'The best art is what comes from a man's mind.' Each Eskimo community has its own way of expressing itself. I could do it the way the committee wants and our prints would be sold, but they would not be pure Eskimo!"

"Thank you for all the information," Oshaweetuk said, in a soft voice. "These prints, we like them very much, but we don't know how much money you would get if you sent them south to the same place we send our prints. Even those that come entirely from the Eskimo, we don't know how much."

"If you like them, we don't see why they shouldn't sell at a good price," Father Tardy said eagerly. "I want you to see that there is no white influence in these prints." There was an electric quality in the quiet room. "I would refute all the arguments," he continued. "They have been judged already by the Eskimos."

Oshaweetuk said, "We never had a chance to meet before, but I hope you can understand what I try to say. People at Dorset did not get information on what to draw from elsewhere. But are those drawings from Holman not followed from pictures that came from other parts of our country? Those drawings, they must be by people who have seen Cape Dorset prints before. Or was this information passed in a letter?"

"Maybe one of them saw a print made by Cape Dorset from the

magazine, but he didn't know what it was, because he didn't know 'ow to read," Father Tardy replied.

Oshaweetuk asked, "Do you supervise for the co-operative at Holman?"

Father Tardy said, "Yes, I 'elp the people with paperwork and bookkeeping. I find I 'ave to give a model for 'andiwork, but no one does for prints. In our co-op, I'm just the secretary, and in the rugs I 'elp the women with the drawing. But in the prints the drawing are supervised by the man who did not get here."

At this point, Simonie gently suggested that perhaps it was time to move on to the problems of another delegate, and he proposed that Father Tardy and Oshaweetuk continue their discussion in private.

There was something very touching about Father Tardy's appeal, and I sought him out at lunch a day or so later. While we ate, he told me that he belonged to the Oblate Order of Mary Immaculate, that he had come from a little town on the French Riviera, and that during the Second World War he had been in the French ski corps. "There, I saw so much death it was a relief when I received my call and went into the Church," he said. "Five days after I was assigned to my present post, I was in the Arctic. Believe me, it was a tremendous shock to go so suddenly from the Riviera to the Arctic."

I asked him how he liked the Arctic, and he smiled.

"The Eskimos are a primitive but interesting people," he said. "I like living at 'olman. I use my big room as a chapel, and besides I have a bedroom and small kitchen, but I am too lazy to cook. In the middle of the day, I 'ave a small lunch of fish; in evening, caribou. I don't take time — mostly eat meat and fish." He laughed, and touched his receding hairline. "Maybe diet makes me lose 'air. There are about one 'undred and ten Eskimos at 'olman, and twenty-four are Catholics, but the main thing is not straight missionary work. We look to improve whole community by charity and advice and by the medical, which is always the same. I get instructions by radio from doctor or nurse, and slowly get knowledge. If serious, I ask for plane."

We ate in silence for a time, and then he said, "The thing I enjoy most in Arctic is we 'ave time to think. My faith goes deeper and deeper. If I 'ad any doubts, I could not stay, not one day more."

The delegate from Great Whale River, on the east coast of Hudson Bay, was a tough little dark-skinned Eskimo with very fine features, named Pauloosie Napartuk. Looking at the wall and smoking furiously as he talked, he said, "This winter, when we learned that delegates from all over are meeting in one place, we are very glad. I want to say thank you very much. I did not pay my fare, not even one penny, and I don't know much about co-operatives." I looked on one of the information sheets that we had been given and saw that Napartuk's co-operative, although it had been incorporated two years before, listed only one activity — carving.

Napartuk said, "I make notes here. Each delegate as he reports, I have down on my sheet of paper, but I won't blame my people if they can hardly understand, because they are hardly organized. No one has come to tell us more about the co-operative since two winters and one summer, and we are tired of waiting. Someone should have come sooner, and specially. The people haven't done much carving this year. We have people who can carve, and people who can make things, and fishermen, and also we can build canoes. We don't understand what we should proceed on, but no doubt we are going to be feeling like really getting started after we have been talked to."

Snowden asked to speak. "We know that we can't start a co-operative on a sound basis just by sending one of our men into a community for two weeks, no matter how good he is," he said, "but we now have only two co-operative officers for the whole North — Dick Nellis for the east and Jack Veitch for the west. It is too big a country for two men to handle. We also have only two officers in Ottawa, Paul Godt and Alex Sprudzs, and as there are more and more co-ops, more and more work keeps them away from the Arctic. We know the problem Pauloosie has. Others have the same problem, and we are very, very sorry. We don't know how long it will be, but we will send someone as soon as we can."

Simonie's deep voice interrupted. "Are there any whales at Great Whale River?" he asked.

Napartuk replied, "The whales are getting scarce, because more ships come in and make more noise and the whales don't come back as often as before, but our place is still called Great Whale River, just as in the old stories." He turned back to Snowden. "So no one has come to us since the first time, and this program was catching us before we fell down," he said. "Before the co-op, it was just as if we were sleeping. The people from Ottawa came and woke us up. After I get back, I will tell my people we must try and do something for ourselves."

When it came time for Mrs. Bessie Irish, from Aklavik, to give her report, Veitch's worries about her not being able to talk proved unjustified. She sat down at the table on the dais, lit a cigarette, and began to speak, in a low, pleasant voice, and Veitch whispered to me, "Good — she's relaxed. She's under control." A few minutes later, Veitch said in an awed voice, "My goodness, if she tries to tell her whole story, they'll have to shut her off. She'll never stop!" She described how she had trained twenty women to make fur mittens, slippers, parkas, and other articles. The parkas made of muskrat sold for a hundred and seventy dollars, those made of sealskin for approximately two hundred. Despite Veitch's fears, Bessie eventually did stop talking, closing on a splendid note. She suddenly tossed her head, waved an arm in the air, exclaimed "Old Aklavik will never die!," and was silent.

Noah Angnutok stood up. "Are only ladies working, or are there men, too?" he asked.

Bessie puffed on her cigarette, and smiled. "Well, you know as well as I do that among our people the men catch the animals, the women sew the fur, and the men never go near it again," she said.

Everyone laughed except Angnutok. "Is there no man who helps the ladies in the co-op?" he asked.

Bessie gave him a contemptuous look. "There is no man who helps in the co-op, and no men who are interested in sewing," she answered.

"In Aklavik, do you have a co-op store?" Angnutok asked.

"Not yet," she said.

"Do you have trees?" he asked.

"More trees than *you* could shake a stick at," she answered, and picked up her papers and cigarettes and left the platform.

◆

After the rigorous daytime schedule, the delegates and government men usually spent the evening sitting in their quarters and talking, or else visiting around, but occasionally some went to the Easty-Coasty. On a couple of evenings, there were square dances at the community hall, in which the Eskimos participated enthusiastically. Snowden's superior, R.A.J. Phillips, the Associate Director of the Department of Northern Affairs, looked in on the conference on his way back to Ottawa from a trip to the western Arctic, and while he was there he took me to my first curling match. We arrived on foot at a long, narrow building in the Lower Base area, in front of which half a dozen cars were parked, all with their motors running to keep them from freezing in the twenty-below-zero cold. Inside the building was the curling rink, with two ice-covered alleys, each eighteen feet wide and a hundred and twenty feet long. On each team were four players, who, by turns, sent the curling stones—smooth, rounded stones that had curved metal handles—gliding down the ice to a circular target area, while two teammates, brandishing oddly elongated brooms, tried to control the stones' movement by brushing the ice before or behind them. There are times when almost everything that goes on in the

Arctic seems dreamlike and unreal, and you wonder what you are doing so far from home. I felt this way at the curling rink, and also later when I visited a house that belonged to the owner of Frobisher's only three taxicabs. The house, built on an A-frame, had a two-story living room that overlooked the enormous expanse of Frobisher Bay, and the view from its picture window at night was wonderfully clear. I could see the peaks of the frozen whitecaps in that immense body of water, which was solid ice now for fifty or sixty miles. Inside the house, we sat back in deep chairs and listened to an electric phonograph, which shifted from Bach to jazz. Occasionally, I got up to take a better look at the incredible view.

The next morning, I was taken to see the new Eskimo Housing Co-operative of Frobisher, whose president was Simonie, and whose members — many of them government employees — using capital borrowed from the Eskimo Loan Fund and their own labor, were building themselves modern residences. When Simonie had given his report, he had mentioned the difficulties in building the houses, which were near Apex Hill. The prefabricated parts had come by ship, and there were many missing. Blueprints and parts hadn't always matched, and the electric wiring had just arrived by plane, with us. Despite these handicaps, fourteen houses had been constructed, each consisting of three bedrooms, a bathroom with a chemical toilet, a combined kitchen and living room with an oil heater, a storage room, and a porch, and each costing its Eskimo owner thirty-five hundred dollars. Simonie's house, though not quite finished, was on display. The interior was cheerfully painted and papered, and had a pine-panelled divider between the living room and the kitchen, and spotlights in each room. The oil heater had not yet been turned on, and even so the house, with its flowered wallpaper and soft colors, had an atmosphere of warmth and cosiness.

Later, Mr. Orange, the regional administrator, took me on a tour of Frobisher. It had originally been a small Eskimo settlement, and its modern history had begun during the Second World War, when the United States Air Force established a base there. In 1955, the Department of Northern Affairs started developing the present community as an administrative center for the entire eastern Arctic. Orange, a lean, blond man in his late thirties, was responsible for overseeing five hundred thousand square miles; he had a staff of a hundred and twenty-five people at Frobisher, and fifty more in twelve outlying settlements on Baffin Island, on the nearby Melville Peninsula, and in the high Arctic, and he spent half his time travelling by single-engine Otter plane through his outsize district.

As we started off on our tour, in a government station wagon,

Orange told me he had lived in town for two years, with his wife and their three children. "I am enthralled with the Arctic," he said. "It's bleak, it's barren, harsh, and cold, but, boy, it's beautiful!" We stopped first at the various units of the Rehabilitation Center, on Apex Hill: the sewing cottage, where parkas and fur boots were being made; the crafts storeroom, in which row upon row of Eskimo stone carvings stood awaiting shipment to the South; the carving workshop, where a sad-faced, almost toothless Eskimo was polishing a black soapstone bird he had just made. This man, Orange said, had once been the best lumberman in his community, and one of its leaders, but after a series of illnesses he was unable to readjust to his old life.

Leaving Apex Hill, we drove past the Hudson's Bay store and toward the Lower Base. The road climbed and we passed a steel skeleton, which Orange told me was the beginning of a new, twenty-eight-bed hospital, to replace the present thirteen-bed one. "We're on Astro Hill now," he went on. "If we go ahead with our present plans, we'll be building a six-or seven-story town building here pretty soon. The Lower Base is really a temporary town, and we expect the permanent town to be here." He turned down a curving road that took us to the Eskimo village of Ikaluit. I noticed some wood-and-tarpaper shacks, but there were also many solid frame houses. "This is the traditional camping ground for more than nine hundred Eskimos, and many still move out of their houses into tents here in summer," Orange said. We passed a stray dog—the only Eskimo dog I saw in Frobisher—and a man on foot dragging a dog harness, and then I caught sight of two vehicles, driven by Eskimos, that were entirely new to me. They had skis on the front end and tractor treads at the rear. One, a bright-yellow machine with an exposed leather seat behind a plastic windshield, was about the size of a motor bike. "That's a Skidoo," Orange said. "It costs about six hundred dollars, has a gasoline motor, and is used by some Eskimos instead of a dog sled, although the Skidoos are not quite as reliable." The other machine, which was bright red, looked more like a small tractor. Orange said that this was an Autoboggan, which cost somewhat more and could pull heavier loads.

Going on to the Lower Base, we passed a large quonset hut that contained a branch of the Bank of Montreal, and then more prefabricated buildings, housing a barbershop, the Frobisher laundry, a second Hudson's Bay Company store, a crafts shop, and the post office, and then we zoomed down the open road, past the civilian air terminal and the adjoining airfield, to the former United States base, which had been part of the US Strategic Air Command until only a few months before. Orange stopped outside a huge, square building. "One hundred and thirty-five Americans, whom we almost never saw, worked, played, and lived here," he said. "This building has the only gymnasium within five hundred miles — a beauty, too — and the best bar in Frobisher. It cost six and a half million dollars and its various interior levels have a total floor space of one square mile." He drove around to the airfield. "A row of airplanes was always poised on this strip, ready to go up on five minutes' notice, if it had ever been the real thing," he went on. The production of large new aerial tankers that could refuel bombers in midair had made the SAC setup obsolete, he said, and the entire twenty-million-dollar installation had reverted to the Canadian government, which planned to use part of it for government offices, and as a school and residence for pupils from all over Baffin Island. Just before he turned the car to take me back to the meeting on Apex Hill, he gazed for a moment at two big black birds sitting on a post. "Ravens," he said. "We love them, because they are the only living things in the sky at this time of year."

When Orange brought me back to the community hall, the last of the eighteen co-op delegates had finished delivering his report, and Jon Evans was describing the efforts of the Industrial Division to find additional sources of income for the Eskimos. They listened closely and took notes as he outlined a new government plan that would allow them to borrow from the Eskimo Loan Fund to buy boats, and then told them about a fish that scientists had found in Ungava Bay — a "big fish, very flat, called halibut, which lives at the bottom of the sea." He added that shrimp were also believed to exist in Ungava and Hudson Bays. Finally, he told of the canning experiments being made with seal and whale meat, and announced that canned seal meat from Burwell would be served that night at supper. (The Eskimos complained that the canned meat, which I found smoky and oily, had too much seasoning, and ate very little of it — but the competition was stiff; the menu also included roast beef, a luxury item for any Eskimo.)

Snowden was now back on the platform, sitting beside Simonie, and at the close of Evans' speech he opened the meeting to general questions.

Celestino Magpa rose, and, speaking in English, said, "When summer comes, Skidoos could be shipped to us by boat. How much could be taken off our taxes for the purchase of Skidoos? Would we get a tax concession, like the farmers do on their machinery in the South?"

Snowden looked amazed at this sophisticated question, and I glanced over at Paul Godt to see his reaction. He, too, looked amazed, and I heard him mutter, "Say! Isn't that fascinating!"

Snowden looked hard at his hands for a moment, and then said,

"Celestino is raising a whole new idea, and one that is very, very interesting. In the South, the government gives lower taxes to special kinds of business. The farmers get a tax rebate for a farm machine because it is a harvesting agent, and Magpa considers the Skidoo a harvesting agent. He is suggesting that Eskimos, who fish in the sea and hunt on the land, are doing a certain kind of farming in the North, so they want a certain kind of lowered tax, like the farmers in the South. Have I interpreted you correctly?"

"Correct," said Magpa.

"It's a wonderful question," Snowden said. "Canadians in the South have been trying to settle that kind of question for a hundred years, and we could spend a year discussing it. As a beginning, this is what we will do. The Industrial Division will undertake a study of the types of equipment and vehicles used in hunting and trapping, and see if any tax aid can be given. I think none can be."

◆

By Saturday morning, it was evident that the conference couldn't possibly end that day, as it was scheduled to do, but must continue on Monday. Then it would have to end, because almost everyone was scheduled to leave on the Tuesday-morning plane for Montreal, even though a number of the delegates were suffering from flu. Coughing and sneezing could be heard throughout the hall. There were several empty seats on Saturday, and, for the first time, Hill's little boy, who had a bad cold, was not with him.

The meeting was thrown open to general discussion, and Noah Angnutok repeated his demand for a co-operative store in Chimo. This time, Dr. Laidlaw rose to reply. "I hope that during the summer we will be able to send a man from the Co-operative Union of Canada to help you organize your stores where you wish to have them," he said. "This man will be an experienced person, but he will have to have an interpreter. We must convince the people that they can run their own business."

Napartuk rose and said excitedly, "Now I have information to take back, and I am proud! Dr. Laidlaw says the big co-ops want to help the small co-ops in the Arctic. Perhaps we can't go fast enough at Great Whale River, but we don't want to stop. We need help! Somebody put it down on a piece of paper, so nobody forgets us!"

Both the Eskimo delegates and the government representatives at the conference had repeatedly mentioned the need for a central marketing outlet in the Canadian South for Eskimo carvings, prints, and handicrafts. The Department of Northern Affairs was handling the marketing of Arctic handicrafts, but other art works, except for the much sought-after prints, which were selected, priced, and distributed through the Eskimo Art Committee, were marketed individually. A committee of four Eskimos—Oshaweetuk, of Dorset; Angnutok, of Chimo; and the delegates from Povungnituk and Coppermine—met with Godt and Dr. Laidlaw on Sunday afternoon to discuss the formation of a marketing agency that would be financed by the Eskimo co-operatives, and the first business on Monday morning was a report on their meeting. They not only recommended that such an agency be established, but felt that it should have eastern and western warehouses and sales offices, and that shipping costs should be pooled, so that Grise Fiord Eskimos would pay no more to export their goods than Eskimos closer to the South.

Snowden suggested a vote on the project, saying, "Now the delegates must decide, as a group, whether to recommend to their co-ops that the central agency is a good idea and should be established. Everyone knows that the delegates here cannot make a final decision for their co-operatives. If the delegates recommend an agency, then my people will prepare a paper in Ottawa telling every co-operative how such an agency can be set up and what it will cost. After all the co-operatives have had a chance to study this paper, then *they* must take a vote."

Napartuk stood up, and said, "Before we go home to a lot of questions, we want to know: Is this going to be a better life?"

"My answer is yes, but that is only *my* answer," Snowden replied. "I say yes because more and more is being produced by the co-operatives all the time, and they will be able to pay for a central agency. I also believe that responsibility should be taken out of the government's hands and put in those of the co-ops, where it belongs. This doesn't mean that the government is losing interest, though. We are always available for advice." He said to Koneak, "Do they understand what they are voting for? They must vote for what they believe, not what we think."

Angnutok said, "Suppose when I get back to Chimo, my people don't like that vote I made here at all. What should I do? Let them crawl all over me?"

"You are not making a final vote here," Snowden explained. "When your people have studied our paper, they will decide yes, we like the central agency, or no, we don't."

"So we could raise our hands here, even though we don't know what our people are going to do," Angnutok said. "They decide later at home."

Snowden said, "I will ask who says yes and who says no, and you can't vote both ways." Turning to Father Fournier, from Igloolik, he added, "Father, I am going to take one vote from each co-operative, so I will take the vote of the Eskimo, Kolaut, from Igloolik."

The vote recommending that a central marketing agency be established was unanimous.

The meeting recessed for lunch, and I walked up to Snowden, who was smiling. "We had two major objectives here," he said. "The first was education in the broadest sense. I knew that if the people in Grise Fiord became aware that the people in Chimo were thinking the same way about pricing, or about hiring white men to work for their co-ops, or about establishing retail stores, they would get a sense of unity and, all together, would have a voice. The second objective was to determine whether it would be possible for the Eskimos eventually to have a marketing agency of their own. We thought it would seem like a farfetched idea to them, and the most we hoped to do was to familiarize them with the thought." He pulled his parka over his head, and as we started toward the dining hall, he said, "Of course, we had a third objective—to find out how effective our own work had been. When we got on the plane at Montreal, we were terribly afraid that the conference could be a farce. A lot might be said, but if the Eskimos weren't discussing, arguing, and constantly questioning what was being said, it would be a failure. I began to feel that it would be a success when our plane stopped at Fort Chimo on the way up. A number of the delegates had had to wait there for about a week before flying up here, and our men at Chimo told us they did nothing but sit and talk among themselves about their co-ops—about what they were doing and how they were doing it."

When we returned to the hall from lunch that last day, all the delegates and all the government representatives—except for Jon Evans, who was in bed with a high fever—were present, though many of them were still half sick and coughing. Even Wally Hill's child was back, looking pale and sleeping heavily in his father's arms. Snowden opened the session by asking the delegates to help compile a list of the things that white men were doing for the co-operatives and that the Eskimos, with proper training, could do for themselves. The government planned to provide such training, Snowden said, but first it had to know what was needed. It was finally decided that priorities should be given to courses in bookkeeping, motors and motorized equipment, electricity, English, and store management.

During the coffee break, I encountered George Koneak, who had been so busy that we had scarcely exchanged a word in days. I asked how he liked Frobisher Bay.

"I find it very interesting, because I have never been here for longer than an hour before, but I wouldn't want to live here," he said.

"Why not?" I asked.

He shook his head. "Too many people," he said. "It costs too much to live here. There are too many little places to go in the evening to spend money, and I am the type of man who would spend it."

Koneak was suddenly called to the back of the room to interpret, for Orange and Snowden were conferring there with Henry Annatuk, of Port Burwell. Orange was telling Snowden that an unknown disease, believed to be hepatitis, had killed most of the dogs at Cumberland Sound, on Baffin Island, about two hundred miles north of Frobisher. Only two hundred dogs had survived out of a dog population of a thousand, and there were five hundred Eskimos in that area, in desperate need of replacements. "The Eskimos' camps are anywhere from twenty to a hundred miles from the settlement of Pangnirtung," Orange said. "We had to set up an airlift to bring people from the camps to the settlement to get their supplies." Snowden thought that the Burwell Eskimos might want to sell some of their fat dogs to the government, which could fly them into Pangnirtung within a few days. Annatuk agreed to this proposal, and the deal was closed. Burwell would sell forty dogs, at ten dollars each, and Orange hurried off to arrange for their transportation.

When the session resumed after the coffee break, Henry Annatuk had an unexpected question: What kind of opposition could the co-operatives expect from the Hudson's Bay Company in the near future? Snowden fielded this one deftly to Dr. Laidlaw, who rose and said, "You should not spend time finding fault with the Hudson's Bay Company. Work hard instead to build your own business. You can expect prices in the Hudson's Bay stores to come down when you establish your co-operative stores. But one thing to remember is that, unlike the Hudson's Bay Company retail store, each co-operative store must stand on its own feet. It cannot depend on other co-operatives to maintain it. The Hudson's Bay Company can operate one store without a profit when it is competing with a co-op, and make it up someplace else, because the Hudson's Bay Company is very big. Last year, its operating profit was ten million dollars."

"Was that money from Eskimo land?" Napartuk wanted to know. "The Hudson's Bay Company is surely a strong and powerful mountain!"

"If it is a mountain, it was people who built the mountain," Dr. Laidlaw replied. "If the co-operatives are going to have strength, they must join with bigger co-operatives in Canada." He had a suggestion. He invited the Eskimos to send one of their number to a conference of his organization, the Co-operative Union of Canada, which was meeting in the South the next month.

There was a buzz of excitement when George Koneak translated the invitation, but no action could be taken immediately, for it was now dinnertime. However, we hurried through our meal and reassembled in the hall, though almost everyone still had his packing to do. Snowden opened the final session by announcing, "In exactly thirty minutes, this conference is going to end." He went on to say that the delegates must now pick the man who was to go to the meeting in the South, and that this man should be able to speak English, so the choice should be limited to the six Eskimo delegates who were bilingual. A written vote was quickly taken among the Eskimos, and Simonie was chosen.

When Simonie heard the news, he stood up, looking very proud. "So you're the people to choose me," he said. "I can go. Probably I will feel shaky, but I will try and do the best I can for you." He went on, "My head was half asleep at our first meeting, so I didn't say much. I don't want to hold you longer, but I'm very glad we had a chance to get together, and everybody is satisfied about this conference. Wherever you people are going, and many go a long distance, God bless you all!" There was huge applause as he sat down.

Donald Snowden looked at his watch, and I looked at mine. It was eight o'clock. We had been meeting continuously from eight-thirty in the morning until six-thirty at night, except for mealtimes and on Sunday, for seven days, and I was tired. Snowden looked exhausted. He said slowly to the group, "This conference has done many things for all of us. It has made friends of people who didn't know one another before. But the most important thing I've seen this week has been that the people of the North are beginning to control their own affairs. There's a long way to go, but I can't think how a better start could have been made, and the co-ops were represented by as good men as there are in the North, or anywhere."

The Eskimos had stopped taking notes and were looking at Snowden. Suddenly embarrassed, he picked up a pencil and began making scratch marks on a sheet of paper before him. "We have seen what a week's meeting in the North, the first of its kind ever held, can do," he said. "In my work, I attend many meetings in many places, but I can't think of any as satisfying as this has been. I have never been at a meeting where people worked so hard. Thank you all for coming, and I hope we meet again soon."

Then Snowden stood up abruptly and said, "The First Conference of the Arctic Co-operatives is adjourned," George Koneak repeated his words in the Eskimo language, and the Eskimos quietly began gathering up their papers.

> First published as "Conclave at
> Frobisher," one of a series of articles in
> *The New Yorker*, November 23, 1963.
> Published in different form in *The New
> People*, 1966; updated and reissued in
> *Inuit Journey*, 1979.

I used to hear about other writers who found themselves weeping in the process of writing, but I never believed it until it happened to me.

When I was writing up the Frobisher conference, I came to the point where Snowden turned the meeting over to an Inuk chairman, Simonie. It was the real climax of that historic occasion, and it happened so easily that it seemed routine, except that this was the first meeting that any of the co-op representatives had ever attended outside their own settlements. They had had just that morning to meet each other, and to learn how a formal conference was held. Snowden was convinced that the only way the Inuit could acquire a firm grip on their own destiny was to start doing it from the very beginning.

I was trying to keep the incident as simple and beautiful as Snowden had made it, and I could hardly see the paper in my typewriter through my tears. If there was one true symbolic moment that gave the Inuit control of their own fate it was this instant: when they took over the management of their own affairs at that first meeting, with a quiet switch in chairmen.

I have received a lot of wonderful mail from readers over the years, but a letter that was sent to *The New Yorker* the day after the article "Conclave at Frobisher" was published is my all-time favorite. It was written on a piece of white loose-leaf paper with blue lines, by a gentleman at the Bell Telephone Laboratories in New York. It said,

Dear Sirs:

Thank you for the beautiful and profound story on the Eskimos in your issue of Nov. 22. It reminded me of the great virtues of civilization, before what ever goes wrong goes wrong.

Sincerely,
Peter Linhart

Baker Lake Art

✦

I MADE A THIRD TRIP to the North, to the central Arctic, in the spring of 1964: this time to the Hudson Bay area and the Keewatin, with Don Snowden and Gordon Gibson, Jr., assistant to the Minister of Northern Affairs. Our purpose was to observe the results of one of Snowden's ideas: to can Inuit food. Don had found a German chef, Erich Hofmann, who had trained in the French Foreign Legion and enjoyed cooking any time, any place, especially at sixty below zero in a tent, with a gale blowing off Hudson Bay.

Hofmann produced a prodigious collection of canned seal and whale meat; also whale flippers, and various innards; smoked, pickled, baked and boiled; as goulash, in Spanish sauce, sweet-and-sour, in vinaigrette, and as a paste. One delicacy he canned that was especially delicious to Inuit palates was *muktuk*, the outer layer of whale skin.

We went to five settlements in the Central Arctic, where the Inuit had been given sample cans ahead of time to open and taste, so that Snowden could call a meeting and ask the people directly what they thought of the food. The Inuit were mildly enthusiastic, and some went so far as to buy it in their co-op store. Subsequently, the program was dropped because of the high mercury content discovered in the food item most frequently used for canning, the meat of the beluga whale.

Our first stop was at Baker Lake, the home of the inland Inuit, known then as the Caribou Eskimos. I had been given strict instructions by Bill Shawn at *The New Yorker* to avoid the subject of Inuit art, because he felt that enough had been written about it already. Nevertheless, Snowden thought I should see the wonderful art work that was beginning to show up in this strange sad community, home to many families who had suffered from starvation on the neighboring Barren Lands in the 1950s, when the caribou mysteriously disappeared.

"I am going to have the first show ever of Baker Lake art at the art gallery in the Winnipeg airport," Snowden said. "No one down south has even seen or heard of Baker Lake art. You would be the first to write about it." So I took a lot of notes on the artists and their work, just in case.

After the whole trip was over, we stopped in Churchill, Manitoba on the way home, and Snowden called *Maclean's* magazine. He offered them the story of Baker Lake art and they accepted his suggestion. Peter Gzowski was my editor at *Maclean's*, which published the following story in 1964.

◆

In a faraway region of the Northwest Territories, in an area unique even in the Canadian Arctic for its lack of resources to sustain life, some remarkable stone sculpture is being created by carvers who belong to one of the strangest groups of people on earth. They are the Caribou Eskimos and they live in and around a place called Baker Lake, the only inland settlement in the great, bare district of the Keewatin. Keewatin is 228,000 square miles of land which lies north of Manitoba, bordered on the west by the Mackenzie District and stretching in the east along the coast and out to the islands of Hudson Bay.

The history of the Caribou Eskimos is an interlacing of tragedy and taboos, of death and indomitability. The responsibility for their welfare lies with the federal government's Department of Northern Affairs and National Resources, and that agency's Industrial Division is engaged in a desperate battle to bring these impoverished people, decimated by disease and starvation, back to a full life. Only in their astonishing sculpture, which is just beginning to trickle south, has there been any indication from these weary people of some mysterious inner flame—a talent that may prove to be richer than any other known natural resource in the wasteland surrounding Baker Lake.

"Keewatin" is an Indian word meaning "the north wind." Survival in the primitive camps of the Keewatin requires a strength that borders on madness; or so it would seem to a non-Eskimo. Two hundred miles inland from Hudson Bay is the heart of the Barren Grounds, a rolling, treeless, deserted plain. It is covered for almost ten months of the year by a light snow that drifts in the crazy, wild, winter winds above a jagged debris of glacial rocks and grey tundras. An unfriendly place, with an unfriendly climate: thirty below zero is the midwinter temperature average, and it can drop as far as seventy below. Yet roughly five hundred persons live in the Baker Lake area, even though one of the Industrial Division's own area economic surveys has pronounced it fit to support only a possible fifty. Efforts to entice a substantial part of the Baker Lake population to more comfortable country on the coast of Hudson Bay or farther east have failed. Forced resettlement is not tolerated in a democracy, so the relief bills at Baker Lake have soared while Northern Affairs men looked for some way to keep the people from becoming forever dependent on handouts.

The inland Caribou Eskimos lived in small family groups of ten or twenty along the rivers, principally the Kazan, the Back, the Thelon, the Prince; and beside the lakes, chiefly the Ennadai, the Yathkyed, the Maguse, and the larger Garry and Baker lakes, each over nine hundred square miles in size. Their normal history, even into this century, was one of feasting in the fall, when the great migrations of caribou swept across their land, and hunger in the late winter and early spring, when their caches of meat were exhausted and no plentiful new supply had yet appeared. But in the 1950s almost total disaster struck, and it was three-pronged; first, in 1956, there was sickness, in the form of a measles epidemic, followed by respiratory ailments to which Eskimos are peculiarly susceptible; and then, in 1957 and 1958, there was poor fox hunting and a drastic reduction in the caribou herds.

The caribou, traditionally a primary source of the Caribou Eskimos' food, clothing, and even shelter, has a special significance for them. Without caribou, they seem to feel that all life stops. Although fish and game were reported to be abundant in 1958, the Caribou Eskimos scarcely attempted to hunt or fish. They waited instead for the source of all life to reappear, the *tuktuk*, the caribou. Almost no caribou came. At Garry Lake, a building with emergency food supplies burned down, killing the occupants, and other Eskimos in the area then starved to death. The total death toll was seventeen.

Fear among the white officials, as well as the Eskimos, set an insidious routine in motion. Worried government men, severely criticized because people had starved, knew that the Eskimo, more often than not, waits too long before seeking help. He stays in his snow house until, desperate for food, he makes a feeble attempt to fish and then, too late, he strikes out for help. So the local administrators encouraged the people in camps to move into Baker Lake in the two following winters, where officials could be sure that in the bitter cold months the Eskimos would at least stay alive. In their turn, the

Eskimos, haunted by terrible memories of starvation, became thoroughly frightened when reminded of how they might starve again in their camps. They settled down, too hopeless even to hunt, to a passive pattern of receiving welfare. This year, encouraged by the present capable administrator, Barry Gunn, and assured that there will be regular inspection tours, some of the Eskimos are moving out to their camps again but their background of suffering has left many scars. A missionary at Baker Lake said recently, "The people here are half dead."

If the people are half dead, their sculpture is not. It indicates a tremendous latent energy and will to create, and what makes its flowering so dramatic is the last-ditch nature of the government crafts program from which the carvings have sprung.

The beginning for Baker Lake art occurred in 1960, when Mrs. Edith Dodds, wife of a Northern Service officer at the lake, started handicrafts there among the women. Later that same year at an Arctic air field, she happened to meet James Houston, administrator at Cape Dorset on Baffin Island, who was then promoting the growth of the subsequently famous Dorset graphics industry. Houston is an artist himself and in 1948, when he was traveling on the east coast of Hudson Bay, he saw some stone carvings the Eskimos had made, bought them, brought them south, and sparked the development of Eskimo art as a means of livelihood. Now, he asked Mrs. Dodds if she had seen anything at Baker Lake that might be included in Dorset's second graphic art collection which he was rounding up, following the international success of the first series in 1959. The result of this query was two prints, *Tattooed Faces* and the startling surrealist *Inland Eskimo Woman*, both by a widow, Una, from the Kazan River. She was, and still is, the only Eskimo outside Dorset to have her work included in the Dorset collection.

The following year, 1961, the Dodds were stationed in Ungava Bay in the eastern Arctic, where Bill Larmour, crafts development officer from Ottawa, was working with the Eskimos at Port Burwell. Mrs. Dodds urged Larmour to add Baker Lake to his visiting list, and in 1962 he went there for the winter. The first thing he saw, on the desk of the area administrator, was what he later called "a quite extraordinarily small carving of a caribou of red sandstone, about four inches long, two high, and *one eighth of an inch thick*, in a curious angular style." It was the work of an elderly Eskimo, Angosaglo, head of one of the camps on Back River. "It was pretty exciting," Larmour recalls, "for *there* was the evidence that the potential for the arts must surely exist among these people."

Larmour moved into a small, central house and raised a sign that read in English and Eskimo, "Baker Lake Eskimo Craft Centre." He wanted the Eskimos to feel welcome at all hours. "That was a bit rash on my part, but it paid off," he says. "Small boys would come in the middle of the night. 'Wake up! Wake up!' they would cry. 'Come and see what Kingalik has made now!' and so I would stagger out to find one of his birds sitting on the table surrounded by admiring Eskimo children who'd been unable to wait till morning to find out what my reaction would be."

The children came first to the crafts centre, in pairs. Gradually they began to bring in things made by their parents, to see what Larmour would say. Then came the very old ladies to get crafts materials, but still no men. Many Eskimo communities have an Eskimo council, made up of Eskimo men, and Larmour addressed the one at Baker Lake. Here he had good luck. A respected member of the council was an Eskimo named Moses, who had been at Port Burwell with his family in 1961 when Larmour was there, and had seen how well Larmour was received by the Burwell Eskimos. At the council meeting, Larmour says, "Moses spoke longer than I did about my work."

"Those people had no confidence whatsoever when I went in there," he says. "To a man, they said they could not carve and never had. My stock answer was, 'Well, you won't ever know if you don't try,' to which they would always reply, 'Ima' — 'Perhaps' — and march off with a piece of rock under their arm."

Larmour had a second piece of luck with the return to Baker Lake after seven years in hospital of a nineteen-year-old Eskimo named Willie. Willie was a member of Angosaglo's family, and was so badly crippled by polio that he was scarcely able to walk. His family couldn't care for him. He came to live with Larmour. "He was a very popular Eskimo," Larmour explains, "and I attribute a great deal of the success of the project to the gratitude of the Eskimos for keeping Willie in their midst as long as possible. Their desire to please by making good carvings existed anyway but it was reinforced by Willie's presence in my house." One morning old Angosaglo, who represented a large clan, had a long talk with Larmour and decided "that it would be desirable to teach the young people the old ways of making things, so that they should be remembered," thus paving the way for the reproduction of Eskimo artifacts, an art in which Angosaglo himself excels.

Bill Larmour clearly remembers the moment when the first really important carving was brought to him at Baker Lake. "I paid thirty-five dollars for it," he says, "and the result was sensation in capital letters. Certain hunters, who had looked disdainfully on carving as an unsuitable occupation for a man, began to have second thoughts. Pricing was a hectic business at first and the Eskimos used to crowd the little room, breathless and silent. But there was almost always approval, and even hugging among them."

Larmour left after six months but the following year, in April, he returned to install a regular crafts officer, Gabriel Gély. An artist trained as a lithographer, who has spent eleven years in the Arctic, Gély is a lean Frenchman with a bushy red beard and an eager, kindly manner. He lives with his attractive wife and two small children in a home close to the two-room crafts centre. I visited Baker Lake on a sunny, snowy day this spring, while the temperature was still thirty below zero, and accompanied by Gély I climbed the wooden steps of the cottage and entered a warm room with an oil stove and a large work table. Encircling the table were four or five Eskimos in drab parkas, who kept their heads bent at their work as they covertly glanced at me. Besides encouraging the Eskimos to carve, Gély is developing handicrafts, especially the production of jewelry from walrus teeth and from caribou hooves that have been boiled, flattened and polished until they have a translucent, soft brown sheen.

One Eskimo was filing a piece of walrus ivory and polishing it to make a needle case; another was cutting a bird in flight from a flattened caribou hoof; and the others were chiseling at small pieces of stone for an elaborate decorative carving of dogs pulling a *komatik*, or sled. The stone sculpture is regarded by its Eskimo creators as much too personal to be worked on in public, and is always done at home. Its production is totally their own.

Gély explained that two hundred and ten men and women are involved in the crafts program, with seventy coming to the cottage each month by rotation and earning anywhere from thirty to seventy dollars a month from the government. Eventually, when the products have steady markets in the south, the program will be financed by the Eskimos themselves and the profits will go directly to them. At first, the Eskimos from different parts of the region refused to work under the same roof, but they are now collaborating quite happily on the special project.

"Perhaps two hundred and five of the two hundred and ten Eskimos in the crafts program are very very skilled," Gély said to me, with great enthusiasm. "This community is unique, yes, incredible! To have such a large number of artists living in the same area! Many of our best carvers used to be the nightmare of the administration. They were the nonconformists, thought by both Eskimos and whites to be the unemployables. They didn't like steady jobs. Now a good carver earns from one hundred to one hundred and fifty dollars a month, and we've established a new class that sets its own pace. The Kazan River people, for example, are great carvers, purist and resourceful, yet they were called The Bone-eaters before, because they were so poor they ate nothing but bones."

He nodded toward a wild-looking man with a mop of black hair hanging over his forehead. The man was wearing an old, half-buttoned checkered shirt and he was sitting alone against the wall, polishing a stone, his eyes downcast. He looked up, revealing an aged, heavily seamed face. "That man is Magpa, one of our finest carvers," Gély said. "He does not mix with the others, he's—what do you call it?—a loner. He refuses to do any other work, only carving. The other day he came in and pulled seventy-six dollars from a fishing tackle box under his parka. He really surprised me. He had saved that money, and he asked me if he could start buying a house."

I asked Gély how he worked with the Eskimos. "They listen to my hands and they understand," he said. "I paint, or carve, or sketch. They do not copy what I do, but if I do it they think they can, too, without being a subject of scorn or public laughter. Their profession is now as dignified as hunting and our best carvers are among the best hunters. I can only guide them. At first, I explained that they were using too many foreign materials, that string should be replaced by caribou sinew, wood by bone, and that shoe polish, with which they used to shine up their carvings, should be eliminated. Also glue. If the legs of an animal broke, they would glue them back on, and nobody wants a flaw in contemporary art. Magpa once brought in a life-sized carving of a seal's head with whiskers suggested by two long pieces of Fiberglas insulation that had been glued to the head. You have to be careful. 'Terrific,' I said, 'but it would be even better if you got some bone for the whiskers,' which he did within an hour. He was very pleased with the results."

Gély said something softly in Eskimo to the men around the table. They looked up curiously at me and stopped their work. They did not have the ruddy glow of most Eskimos; their faces were dark and full of sadness. They had fine features, with long cheekbones that heightened their grim expressions. One of them, John Narkjanik, who had spent six years with TB in outside hospitals, acted as interpreter. I spoke first with Kingalik, a good-looking man of twenty-five, whose birds, several of which were on an overhead shelf, have a lovely, lyric quality. Kingalik said, "I make a bird now, an owl, at home, in the day and evening. Before I was carving, I was carrying the garbage and water." He paused and stared down at his hands. "I like much better carving," he added. "In winter is too cold for outside working. But in summer I like hunting in canoe and fishing. Only the old men carve in summer."

A very small man, scarcely five feet tall, who appeared to be in his middle thirties, spoke up. He was Tungwack, renowned equally for his carving and hunting. "Bill Larmour started me, but I don't know whether I like carving yet," he said in a reedy voice. "After working here, I can try everything myself, making animals or men. Sometimes I break a stone, and that makes me change my mind. I like to carve what is in my mind, what I remember. Before, I was always fishing and hunting fox, also caribou." He smiled suddenly. "In three days I'll go for the caribou. With dogs." Then he added, with obvious pride, "I have three dogs now."

Magpa, sitting with his chair tipped back and his head down while he polished and polished his stone, abruptly exclaimed, "When I go hunting, I use no dogs, no canoe. I use a *komatik*," He sprang to his feet and dramatically acted out the part of a man pulling a sled, making the motions of putting the reins over his forehead and shoulders, and pulling against a great imaginary weight with his whole body. "Do you like to carve?" I asked. His dark face lit up. "Yes! I like!" he said, and nodded vigorously.

Gély took me into the next room, which serves as a shop. The impact of the stone sculpture reposing on shelves and tables was stunning. Group and individual figures, parka hoods only suggested, arms foreshortened so that the hands were taken for granted, yet with a form complete and satisfying; birds with small angular indents barely suggesting their features and intriguing, even humorous expressions; a walrus, a bear, a caribou, carved with direct, sure lines, lines that could only be cut by people who know these creatures intimately. The room had once been a kitchen and still retained the cupboards and counters, along with a large cookstove, on which a pot of caribou hooves was stewing. The counters held various handicrafts; embroidered, bright red, duffle mitts; functional objects such as needle cases, snow goggles, and *ulus* (the Eskimo knife), children's parkas, miniature *kamiks* (boots); and dolls costumed in caribou clothing with long sinew fringes of a style unknown elsewhere. Gély had also persuaded the Eskimos to draw pictures and many of the faces in the drawings bore the tattooed lines that were customary in the past and may be seen occasionally even now on some of the older Caribou Eskimo women. There were hunting and fishing scenes and drawings of igloo interiors that frequently showed whole families on their knees in prayer. With these as a beginning, Gély hopes to start a graphics industry.

The program has an immediate purpose—to bring in more of the people in the community who need part-time work. But beyond that is a bigger goal—to have the Eskimos form their own co-operative, as has been done successfully in seventeen other settlements in the Canadian Arctic. Working for themselves, with the initial income from carvings, handicrafts, graphics, trapping and a tourist industry, they might eventually invest in a bakery, or a barber shop, or a retail store, or other enterprises that would make Baker Lake a more healthy and diversified community.

A year ago, former governor general Vincent Massey presented a ptarmigan by Kingalik as a wedding present to Princess Alexandra, daughter of the Duchess of Kent. Last October, at the National Gallery Association auction in Ottawa, two of Magpa's sculptures, a kneeling young man and a mother and child, sold for ninety-four dollars and three hundred dollars, respectively. It was the first time an Eskimo's carvings had been sold at an auction on equal terms with other Canadian sculpture. Dr. Ferdinand Eckhardt, Director of the Winnipeg Art Gallery, has scheduled an exhibition of the stone sculpture of Baker Lake for September at the Winnipeg airport. It will be the first time a major exhibition of Baker Lake carvings will have been shown in southern Canada. The exhibition will include about seventy-five pieces from a score of the best sculptors.

Although it is too soon to predict with certainty, the Caribou Eskimos seem, even now, to be carving a more secure world for themselves; a life on the land, camping beside the lakes and rivers in their own wild country, supplied by their own creative efforts with the material things of the world outside, without which even they can no longer survive in the north.

Published in *Maclean's*, July 4, 1964.

Almost thirty years later, Gabriel Gély still is involved with the art of Baker Lake, although he no longer lives there full time. Baker Lake carvings and the magnificent tapestries made by the women have gone all over the world as ambassadors for Canada, to queens, chancellors, sheiks, shahs—even the Pope. A government official said to me: "Inuit art has become Canada's image abroad." Then he added, "An Inuk woman once said to me, 'Who has benefited the most from our art?' and she answered her own question, 'Canada, more than the Inuit'."

The Beautiful Day

◆

I WAS THIRTEEN when a school librarian introduced me to the great Russian novels with Tolstoy's *Anna Karenina*, and I started reading Dickens, too. From then on I wanted to be a fiction writer. I keep right on thinking that's what I will be some day, but when I sit down to write, I find the real world infinitely amazing, beyond imagination and irresistible. Who could invent the political upheavals, the scandals and intrigues, or the bizarre behavior of public figures in the last twenty-five years?

Most fiction is based on real people and happenings anyway. They are often recognizable, as I discovered when I studied Tolstoy's diaries after reading *War and Peace*. Almost all his characters were inspired by some one person or a combination of people in his family: the people he knew best. That's where I lose my nerve. The people I know best are my nearest and dearest, and I treasure those relationships too much to endanger them.

"The Beautiful Day" is the only published piece of fiction I have ever written, and it is a true story. It is my memory of the last day I spent with my father, a month before he died. That day became a song running through my head, with its own rhythm. Early one morning, I sat down at my typewriter to write it, and by evening I had finished the whole story, in the first person.

William Maxwell, who edited fiction at *The New Yorker* and is the other great editor I have been privileged to work with, had been encouraging me, so I sent it to him. He suggested I rewrite it in the third person as fiction, which I did, and then he bought it.

After this story was published, many people wrote in to tell me that it expressed their own feelings when a beloved parent had died. I suppose because it came from the heart, it hit some kind of a universal chord. There was the same reaction to my last book, *Fishing with John*, only even more so. Both times, I really was surprised.

I have placed this story here, between articles on Canada's North, because that's where it belongs chronologically. My father died in January 1963, between two Arctic assignments, and his death became a dividing point in my life. I felt as if the big roomy protective umbrella that had been over my head and spirit all my life had been snatched away. I was on my own, and having adopted my father's philosophy of never looking back, I had no choice but to go straight ahead.

My father was very proud of the first piece I wrote about the North, "Mr. Snowden Among the People." He even carried it around in his pocket to show people. So when I told him I was planning to go north again, he said, "Oh, take me with you."

We both laughed, and I said, "I wish I could." He died a week later, and then Don Snowden called to give me the final arrangements for the Frobisher Bay Conference, to be held in March.

"I can't possibly go," I said. "My father just died."

"All the more reason to come," he said. And he was absolutely right.

◆

It was a beautiful day. The snow was so deep on the road into the valley that they decided to leave the car at the farmhouse and walk over the last hill to the cabin. Amelia Medford's father sat in the front seat beside her husband, barking out unheeded directions to turn here, and look out for that rut there. Amelia had placed herself between her sons, Pete and Sam, to deter the usual back-seat riots. The boys were growing up in New York City, but every summer of their lives they had been coming to stay with their grandparents in Ohio. Sometimes they got off the train with their mother and went straight to the cabin in the woods—they loved it so—without bothering to go to the big house in town. But they had never seen the valley in winter and now they were excited by each familiar form—a tree, a house—in this new setting. For Amelia, it was a turning to before the boys were born, when she was her father's child and not somebody's mother. It had been that long since she had been to Ohio in the winter.

The sun shone on the packed snow and made it glisten. Bill Medford stopped the car at the white frame house, and John Barnes, the farmer who was their nearest neighbor, could be seen briefly at the window, where he must have been standing, waiting for their car. Amelia had come home for her father's eightieth birthday, with her family, and when it was over, the next morning, she had this craving to see the country in winter, after so many years of being there only in the lush green season. She called John Barnes to tell him they were coming, and when she hung up, because of the heavy snowfall and the threat of more she was assailed with doubts about the wisdom of the venture, so she called back to say she had changed her mind. "Too much snow," she said. "Too cold. Too slippery. Too dangerous. Too everything." He listened politely on the other end of the phone, which snapped and wavered because it was a party line, and when she was all done he simply said, "Well, in the old days you would have come."

So here they were. Everyone got out of the car, and John Barnes joined them, slowly buttoning his jacket over his blue overalls as he walked. He stopped suddenly. "What a beautiful day!" he exclaimed. "Wait a minute, while I go back and get my camera." He returned, carrying an old-fashioned Brownie box camera, and they started off down the road, the boys slipping and sliding and tumbling over one another. Amelia's father walked lightly, with the spring of a man twenty years his junior, but for all that the thought whisked through her mind that he was moving with more care than usual. "It's because of his birthday yesterday," she said to herself, hastily hiding the thought under an excuse, but she moved ahead and casually took his arm as they started down the hill. Her father stopped and made a snowball, and threw it at her older boy, hitting him between his shoulder blades. "Who did that?" Pete shouted fiercely, waving his arms and roaring with pleasure. He scooped up some snow and pelted his father and younger brother, but not his grandfather, and she thought, Pete is remembering how old he is, too.

They were at the gate now, and John Barnes said, "The snow got ahead of me before I could plow out the road. I've never seen snow like it is this year, day after day, so there's no keeping up with it. It's banked up so high we won't be able to open the gate. We'll have to climb it." Amelia's father bent over and went through the fence below the top bar, and the farmer snapped a picture of him halfway through, one leg across, his face upturned, smiling forever on that very last day Amelia had with him.

It was a joyous day that stayed joyous forever, like the photograph of Amelia's father smiling. The others followed him through the fence and up the road. He led them, as he always had, making tracks they could step in with his stub-toed, high-laced rubber boots, right up to the screen door. The snow was so deep that they could walk onto the porch of the cabin without climbing the steps, which had disappeared under a snowy cover. Amelia's father pulled out his big pocketknife and carefully picked the ice from the lock. Then he put the key in and opened the door. They went in, stamping the snow off their feet and peering into empty rooms, at the bedding piled on the stripped beds and at the drained plumbing fixtures. The rooms were musty from being closed up, and cold, and Amelia wanted to build a fire in the fireplace, the way they always had when she was a child, but her father was in a hurry to feed his birds. He unlocked the back door and darted across the big dining porch and out to a small shed in the yard, where he kept his tools and birdseed. He had put a combination padlock on the door of the shed, and it was a family joke that he had done this so nobody could use his things, since nobody else could ever remember the combination. He moved the wheel back and forth until the lock fell open, and then he went into the shed and came out carrying a coffee tin full of birdseed. He had placed the feeders in such a way that he could watch the birds while he ate on the porch. He smiled happily as he moved from feeder to feeder, and when he came to the suet holder he unbuttoned his jacket, pulled out a brown paper bag, and removed a large piece of white suet. John Barnes reached up and unlatched the top for him. Amelia noticed that the farmer was smiling, too. He had taken off his cap, and the wind blew through his thin hair and gave him a boyish look. He was ten years younger than Amelia's father. He must have been just a few years older than my boys, she thought, when my father first came out here.

The sun had a dazzling brightness, and the little clearing was warm. Amelia's father took off his hat, which had fleece-lined earmuffs, and rubbed the perspiring top of his bald head. "Tell the boys how you first came out here," Amelia said. "I don't believe they've ever heard it."

Her father put his hat back on, pulling the flaps down over his ears. The boys had been lying in the snow, making angel wings with their arms, and now they scrambled to their feet and came over by their grandfather.

"I was not more than twenty, and I came out the first time in a horse and buggy," her father said. "I came with Amos Finch, from my office. He knew a lot about birds and wildflowers and loved the woods. It was all new to me, and I wanted to learn."

"Amos kept his camping equipment in a wooden box he built and nailed to a sycamore tree in front of where this cabin stands now," John Barnes said. "He had a cup and saucer, frying pan, and binoculars for bird watching. And a hatchet. I don't remember what else."

"Yes," said her father. "At first when we came, we just spent the day hiking and listening to the birds. Amos could identify most of the birdcalls. Then he built a one-room shack right here—"

"In the middle of my pasture," John Barnes said.

"I used to wake up in the morning," Amelia said, "and the first thing I'd see would be cows' faces pressed against the porch screen. When we went to the stream to brush our teeth, the cows would run away and then stand and stare at us. I've never really liked cows since."

"You were *very* little, Amelia," her father said. "That was after Amos sold me his cabin. Then I bought the land underneath it from John, and—"

"And we lived happily ever after," John Barnes finished, smiling.

Everyone was silent, watching the birds as they swooped down from the bare tree branches and snatched the seed. John Barnes backed away from the group and snapped another picture. Then Amelia's father locked the shed, and they walked back to the cabin.

"I'd hate to have these birds go hungry. They depend on me to keep them alive over the winter," Amelia's father said. "I've hardly missed a week."

"Sundays are certainly dull when I don't see your car coming down the road," John Barnes replied. "But when you can't get out, I come down and feed the birds anyway."

"I know that," Amelia's father said.

He stopped at the door of the cabin and removed his glasses; some snow had fallen on them from an overhanging branch. The boys pulled icicles from the eaves of the porch and sucked them as they went inside. They sat and talked a few minutes, and Bill Medford and the boys drew pictures of snowmen on a blackboard by the door. Amelia's father talked to John Barnes about planting new trees in the spring. Suddenly her father pressed his cigarette out in an ashtray and announced that he was hungry. "It's after two," he said. "I hate to leave, but we'd better get going."

So they left. Locking up carefully, retracing their steps across the snow, with a brief side trip to the stream, to peer down at the blue-black pools of water that seemed so still beneath the crust of snow. Amelia had a sudden longing to see the river in spring, when it would be rushing past the cabin, the tiny brook transformed by the thaw into a roaring turbulence, with great blocks of broken ice pounding their way down into the main stream that began beyond the gate and the bridge.

"Maybe I'll come back in the early spring for a few days," she said to her father.

"I wish you would," he said. "Try to do that."

That last day spent with her father remained suspended in Amelia's mind, away from other days, vivid and clear, a fragment of beauty to which she could turn whenever she wanted. Her father died

a month later—suddenly, unknowing, after a splendidly active day.
And so she came back before spring, before the breakup, when the
snow was still falling as if it would never stop, making the drifts deeper
and deeper. Her younger son came with her. While she was still
wondering how she would ever be able to go to the cabin again, he
said, in the most natural way, "When are we going to the country?"

He said that on a Sunday, the first Sunday, a beautiful, glistening,
unbearable Sunday, and while she was figuring out how to tell him
she never intended to go there again she was called to the telephone.
It was her friend Mary Knowles, who spent the summers in an old
house on the road into the valley.

"We're going to the country today, and you and Sam must go with
us," Mary said. "It's no good waiting, and, of course, you know you'll
have to go sometime. So it had better be now. Such a beautiful day,
too!"

"I really can't," Amelia replied stiffly. Even to herself, her voice
had a starchy sound. "Not yet. Maybe never."

"We'll be by in an hour," Mary said.

They went, bundled in heavy clothes and ski pants. Mary's
husband drove, and the two women sat behind him chatting busily
about schools and work. Sam and Priscilla, Mary's daughter, invented
riddles that made them fall over laughing at their own wit in the back
of the station wagon. Amelia had a long medical discussion with
Mary's husband, Ted, who was a doctor, and found his back strangely
reassuring; in fact, she felt quite relaxed, and was wondering why she
had so dreaded coming on such a beautiful sunny day when they went
around a curve and were at the edge of her father's property. Amelia
looked out into the woods, seeing through the leafless trees the piles
of brush her father had left everywhere as winter shelter for the
animals. She had such a sharp physical pain that she bent forward
and gasped, quickly turning her face away, toward the car window.

Ted Knowles drove on past the cabin, turned the corner at John
Barnes' farmhouse, and continued up the hill to his own place. They
ate their lunch in the cold kitchen of the Knowles' cottage. They had
brought sandwiches and cake, and thermoses of coffee and cocoa.
After they had eaten, they took a long hike; it was a favorite trip,
through a deep gulch. When they got back to the cottage, Sam and
Priscilla started building a snowman. Amelia and Mary stopped to
watch them. Amelia said, "I think I'll go down to the cabin. I ought
to see if everything is all right." Then, turning to Sam: "Do you want
to go with me?"

He shook his head, too absorbed to answer, so she started off
alone. As she passed John Barnes' house, she went in and found him

alone. "Hello," he said, getting up from the rocker where he had been reading the Sunday paper. "I was wondering if you would come today. I'm glad you did."

Amelia sat down on a kitchen chair and opened her coat. She began biting her nails, something she hadn't done in years. He took off his glasses, put them in an old-fashioned metal case, and carefully placed them in the chest pocket of his overalls. Amelia blurted out a message from her mother: "Could you use any of my father's clothes? He would have liked you to have anything you might want."

"Your father and I were a different size," he said. "I'd like to wear them, but they'd never fit. Maybe a jacket or sweater might do. Something of that sort."

That was over. Amelia sighed with relief and stood up. John went to a hook by the door and took down his heavy coat and cap, and they left the house and walked down the road. The same kind of day, she thought, and for a wonder she felt comfortable and quiet. When they came to her father's gate, they climbed through the fence, laughing, both of them remembering her father and the picture John had taken. They talked about what had to be done in the spring — new screening for the porch, a survey of the west line of the property, tree pruning; she wanted her boys to try to prune the way their grandfather had taught them. "I hope Pete is strong enough to run the hand tractor," Amelia said. "There's such a lot of underbrush to be cleared away."

"He can do it," John replied. "He has a real feeling for the place."

They were at the door of the cabin, and Amelia took her father's keys out of her purse and handed them to him. He opened the door with them, although he had his own key, and they walked in, stamping their feet to shake off the snow. There on the blackboard were the drawings that her husband and the boys had made of the snowmen. Amelia noticed that the ashtray still contained the stub of her father's cigarette. "Everything looks just the same," she said. "I really don't know what I expected."

John Barnes made no reply, but opened the back door and went out into the yard and over to the shed, putting on his glasses while he walked. He turned the combination padlock to right and left until it opened, and then he went in and filled the empty coffee can with birdseed. With Amelia trailing after him like a small girl, he went from feeding station to feeding station, scattering the seed. When they reached the suet holder, Amelia took from her pocket a brown bag that her mother had given her and handed him a piece of suet, which he put in the feeder. "Your father thought a lot of those birds," he said. "So I thought I'd keep on feeding them."

Amelia said, "I didn't think I could ever come out here again."

"Your father would not have liked that. Not at all. He wasn't that sort."

"I'm not sure I know what you mean," Amelia said, looking puzzled.

"He just wasn't the sort of man who dwelt on things, that's all. He liked to get going on something new all the time."

John Barnes got a hammer and nails, and repaired a bird feeder that had started to come apart. Amelia looked at her watch and saw that it was getting late. "I'll go in and close up the cabin," she said. "They'll be coming by to pick me up any minute."

He nodded, with his mouth full of nails. Amelia went into the cabin and sat down in the wing chair by the cold fireplace. A conversation she had had with her father was ticking through her head.

"How does it feel to be eighty?" she had asked her father on his birthday. "What do you *really* think about?"

"Not about dying, if that's what you mean," he had answered. "I've got an awful lot of things to do." He gave her his working schedule for the next day and, warming up to his subject, went on to outline enough plans for his future to keep him busy for the next ten years. He looked at Amelia almost sternly and said, "You can't do anything about the past, so never look back. At least I never do. Just ahead. If you want my secret, that's it."

Amelia heard the car honking, and the children shouting for her to come. She shivered and rubbed her arms as she got up from the chair. It really was cold in the cabin. She pulled back the fire screen, emptied the ashtray with its lone cigarette butt into the fireplace, and carefully replaced the screen. Then she went over to the blackboard and erased the drawings of the snowmen. She locked the front door and went outside to wait for John Barnes, who came around the corner of the cabin and joined her. They walked down to the car, and although she had always turned around before for a farewell look at the cabin and the tall swaying sycamore trees when she was going away, this time she did not look back.

Published in *The New Yorker*, March 19, 1966.

Denison's Ice Road

◆

In the summer of 1964 I went to the eastern Arctic for the fourth time, to observe an area survey being made on a lake north of Frobisher Bay on Baffin Island. It was August, and my sons were at a summer camp in Vermont. It was vital to me that I be back in New York to welcome them at the train when they came home, but I had to wait in Frobisher for the lake ice to melt so our float plane could land on open water.

When I had only three days left, I felt I couldn't wait any longer, so I called Bill Shawn at *The New Yorker*. With his permission I hired a small plane, which I thought very daring, and went by myself to the George River, where I had gone with Snowden four years earlier.

Then, the George River had consisted of the one small log community hall where we stayed, with the Inuit camped around it in tents; now it was a thriving settlement with streets lights, several rows of houses, a dock and a schoolhouse.

I had only two and a half days left. Don Pruden, whom I knew from the Frobisher Bay meeting, was still the projects officer at the George River, but when I arrived he was at the coast, twelve miles away. I had never met his wife, Gwen, but she came out to the plane in a canoe and put a message in a tin can that my pilot dropped where Don was working. He sped back in his large outboard canoe, and I got the story I wanted, thanks to the Prudens' hospitality and Don's ability to act as an Inuit interpreter. I was at the train station to welcome my boys when they arrived home, and the trip became the final chapter of my book *The New People*.

All the time I was in the eastern and central Arctic, I kept hearing how different the west was. Everyone seemed to be talking about

Yellowknife, and I became more and more curious to see what it was like.

I went finally to the western Arctic in 1968, with an assignment to write about Yellowknife. I travelled through Ottawa on my way from New York and spent a night with the Prudens, who were stationed there at the time. The friendships I formed with the men and women who worked in the North in those early days were forever; it's as if we are members of a family, and although we don't see one another often, we know we are there, and those of us who are still living keep in touch.

In Ottawa, the Prudens had arranged a reunion of all our northern friends, but I felt so ill I had to lie down. Gwen sat on the bed and said, "You know, I have a feeling you aren't sick, you are just scared, and you'll be fine as soon as you get on the plane." That is exactly what happened.

I felt lost in Yellowknife, though, because I didn't know a soul. The first night, I sat in the bathtub washing my hair under the faucet and cried. I had just gotten a divorce, and I don't think I have ever felt so lonely. Where I came from, women didn't go to the kind of places I was going, especially alone.

The next morning, I took the list of people to call in Yellowknife I had been given by my friends in Ottawa and telephoned the first name, Rae Parker. "Come right over," she said, and I went to her office. Rae was a young social worker, very attractive, with long dark hair and a terrific smile; she became a friend forever, like the others. She took me off to dinner with her and later introduced me to everyone I needed to know.

The following night Rae invited me to her home, and that's where I met John Denison. I had promised Bill that I would stay in Yellowknife and not get sidetracked, so when Denison offered to take me on the ice road, I said I'd think about it. The next evening I had dinner at the home of the Commissioner of the Northwest Territories, Stuart Hodgson, and casually mentioned Denison's invitation. Hodgson, who is a big man with a walrus mustache, got very excited. "You've *got* to go," he shouted at me, pacing up and down. "John never takes anybody on that road! *I've* never even been on it! Think of it! You, a woman! A pioneering endeavor! A chance to write a great northern story! I want to see the mystery taken out of the North!"

I went back to the hotel, called Denison and told him I would go. "Just to see what it's like," I said. "I can't write a story, because I'm not supposed to report about *anything* but Yellowknife."

"Be ready at eight tomorrow morning," he replied.

Back in Yellowknife after that first trip up the ice road, I called

Bill Shawn and told him what a great piece it would make. He agreed that I should go back the following year to do it. The next winter, right after the New Year, I went with Denison and his crew when they were building the ice road for that season. The following are excerpts from the article that resulted.

✦

A road hundreds of miles long is made out of snow and ice every winter in a beautiful part of Canada so strange, so far north that hardly anybody lives there. The road makes travel possible for three months of winter across the frozen lakes that lace the Northwest Territories between Great Slave Lake, near the Territories' southern border with the province of Alberta, and Great Bear Lake, on the Arctic Circle—two of the world's largest inland seas. The length of the road changes each year, in accordance with difficulties encountered during its construction, but it usually runs for about three hundred and twenty-five miles, some of them a little rugged. For ten years, the creator of this road of snow and ice was a lanky, laconic Canadian in his fifties named John Denison, whose eccentric specialty was building winter roads where nobody else dared to and hauling over them any freight that could be fastened on the back of a lowboy trailer truck. Denison, who was a partner in a trucking firm, has retired, but the road is still built each winter by his former associates, whom he serves as a consultant. By braving savage cold, blinding snow, wild winds, and perilous terrain to build the Ice Road, Denison doubled the time available each year for shipping freight cheaply in and out of a silver mine at a tiny point of human habitation called Port Radium, on Great Bear Lake. Only a handful of communities on the entire thousand-mile shoreline of the lake are inhabited throughout the year, and one of them is Port Radium, whose hundred or so residents dwell in frail wooden houses clinging to the sides of a steep hill on a small inlet, Echo Bay. These people stay at the outpost not because they like the beautiful scenery but in order to dig minerals from the surrounding ground. Uranium gave Port Radium its name, and the famous Eldorado Mine, opened at Echo Bay in the nineteen-thirties, provided the raw material for the first atomic bombs. Eldorado closed in 1960, but four years later another company, Echo Bay Mines, Ltd., began extracting exceptionally high-grade silver ore from the same site, using the old mine buildings and adding a couple of its own.

The birth, life, and death of a Northern mine, no matter how great its mineral wealth, are governed by the cost of reaching it to bring in supplies and heavy equipment and to carry out the tons of ore, which must compete with the products of more accessible mines to the south. During the brief, ice-free summers, which begin in July and end in early September, freight barges call at Port Radium, and all year long costly small shipments come and go by air. Besides adding three winter months for freighting, the Ice Road provides door-to-door delivery of cumbersome objects. An entire prefabricated building incorporating a cookhouse, a dining room, a recreation hall, and several bathrooms came by road on trailer trucks one February, and was delivered directly to its permanent site at the top of the hill. The unit, from Edmonton, in Alberta Province, arrived in four sections, and the four huge vehicles that brought it rumbled for almost a thousand miles over the Mackenzie Highway and its extension into the Territories.

That haul from Edmonton to Port Radium is routine to a point on the Mackenzie Highway seventy miles short of Yellowknife, the capital of the Northwest Territories, on Great Slave Lake. Here, where the highway swings east toward Yellowknife, is the beginning of the Ice Road, which runs north to Port Radium. At the turn off the highway onto the Ice Road, John Denison put up a garage several years ago and, just for fun, named it Fort Byers, in honor of Byers Transport Ltd., the freight company of which he was part owner. Fort Byers has not survived Denison's retirement, but it was an important part of his operation. He outfitted it with fuel-storage tanks and a trailer containing bunks, a kitchen, and a radiotelephone that occasionally worked. The garage replaced one in Yellowknife that had burned down, and the new site saved truckers a trip into the capital and out again. Denison's drivers—en route from Edmonton or from the Byers warehouse at Hay River, a community on Great Slave Lake—paused at Fort Byers for repairs, food, sleep, and the latest news on drivers ahead of them. Then they climbed back into their trucks, turned north off the highway, and plunged into the scrub bush and onto the Ice Road, known locally as the Echo Bay Road, the Denison Trail, or sometimes simply Denison's Road.

The men who drive the Ice Road come back year after year to make the dangerous run that Denison carved out for them. Their huge trailer trucks carry in everything from tractors to peanuts—refrigerators, cribbage boards, small pickup trucks, groceries, lumber, gasoline drums—and carry out millions of dollars' worth of silver ore so high-grade that it is shipped uncrushed in a sealed van. The trip is lonely and hazardous, even in convoy. A driver who misjudges a curve in the road or fails to notice a snowbank can overturn; on a lake that a truck ahead of him just crossed safely he may plunge to the bottom. On the Ice Road, especially during a lake crossing, a driver is apt to keep one hand on the steering wheel and the other on the handle of the door beside him, which he may have left ajar. When a driver and his truck run out of ice, it's time to jump, and every second counts.

◆

Soon after we arrived at Fort Byers, I put my parka on and went out to the garage. The temperature was thirty below and there was still a sharp wind, so I put my head down and ran the few hundred feet to a small door in one side of the shed. Inside the shed, where the air was saturated with gasoline and oil fumes, I gazed through a forest of trucks, tires, automotive parts, welding machines, and heaters. I recognized the rectangular-box form of a Herman Nelson heater — a machine with a powerful gasoline motor, used for warming up frozen machinery outdoors in the North. The black arms of an overhead crane loomed under the slanting metal roof. Then I saw the cab end of a trailer truck over a repair pit and, across the cab's open radiator hood, the green visor of Denison's cap and the graying top of Henry Ford's head.

I walked around the truck and looked up at the two men, who were perched on a fender several feet above me, peering down into the motor — two physicians in consultation over a sick patient. Trucks have a sameness only until you know them. I would now recognize this colossus, this gigantic red truck, anyplace, even without the numerals 36 painted in gold on its door. It was the largest truck I had ever seen. The trucks used in building the Ice Road were customarily referred to by their identifying numbers in the company's books, but someone had named Truck No. 36 the African Queen, and the name suited her. Her size was queenly, and she moved with heavy, majestic dignity. When I rode in the African Queen later, sitting beside the driver on the wooden box that held the batteries, it was not comfortable, but the view from her great height, at least eight feet above the snow and ice, was superb. She was an old-fashioned, unstreamlined shape thirteen feet high and eight feet wide, and she had six-wheel drive (dual wheels in the rear and singles in the front). From the front of her stubby fire-engine-red radiator — to which Denison had attached a two-ton snowplow of his own design, with wings like an angel — to the back end of her flat trailer, she was thirty-four feet long. She could easily carry on her back a huge tractor or a serpentine road grader, a two-ton pickup truck or a house. Travelling empty, she weighed just thirty-nine thousand pounds, or about twenty tons, but when she was fully loaded she could weigh as much as a hundred thousand pounds, or fifty tons — a sizable matriarch, and overweight for anyplace but a private road or pretty thick ice. She had started life as a Mack truck, and had been rebuilt by the Canadian Army for use on the Alaska Highway. Denison had bought her for six thousand dollars. A new truck anything like her would have cost at least fifty thousand dollars, and, anyway, Denison would not have been satisfied with a new one until he had reconstructed it, as he did most of his trucks, to meet the peculiar needs of his road. The only parts of 36 that were still Mack were the transmission and the differential.

A driver is assigned for the whole winter to one vehicle, and he becomes deeply attached to it. The man and his machine form a close partnership of mutual dependency, which evokes strong emotions: grief when the truck breaks down; jealousy when another driver takes the wheel; pride when the truck performs well and brings them both smoothly through a bad trip. The driver knows his truck inside out. He must be able to repair breakdowns, even welding parts together, in wind, snow, darkness, and sixty-below cold. All radios in the North have an unhappy habit of conking out when they are most needed, but even when they work, help or spare parts arrive after a long wait, on another truck or by chartered plane. The alternative to self-help is to sit down in an ailing truck with the motor running (if it still can run), or to light a propane heater (if there's one along), and hope someone will come past in another truck to attach a towline before the fuel supply runs out.

At the far end of the garage, I found the camper, a red pickup truck, which had been driven inside so I could sleep in a warm place. My sleeping bag and overnight case were on a long bench at one side of the door, and across a narrow, carpeted aisle was a square table mounted on a metal pole with a bench on three sides. A sliding door opened into a small kitchen furnished with a wall refrigerator, cupboards, a four-burner yellow enamel stove with an oven underneath, a miniature steel double sink, and a little counter. In the overhang beyond, at the level of my chin when I stood in the kitchen, was a large bunk, piled now with sleeping bags. I hung my parka in a closet beside the refrigerator, sat down, and pulled off my boots, delighted with my comfortable surroundings. Denison and Jimmy Watson removed the table pole and dropped the tabletop to the level of the bench to form a neat, square bunk for me, with the seat cushions laid flat as a mattress. When they left, they snapped off the garage lights and slammed the outer door shut. I was alone with the big truck shadows, the reaching arms of the black crane, the wind beating against the tin garage walls. I pulled off a sweater and one pair of socks, unrolled my sleeping bag on the new bunk, turned off the camper lights, and went to bed. In the darkness, I inhaled gasoline and oil fumes, and tried to imagine what the Ice Road would look like.

◆

We left the next morning at eleven o'clock — an hour after dawn. It was a gray, windless day, and exhaust smoke from idling truck motors hung in the dry, cold air at Fort Byers as if it had been pinned there. We crossed the highway onto a rough road just wide enough for two trucks to pass. Denison told me that the road was an old one that ran for sixty-five miles north through the wilderness to Rayrock, a uranium mine that had been closed for nine years, and that he had brought his tractor in by barge this past summer to fix the road up. As we bounced along, I braced myself to keep from hitting the windshield, the ceiling, and Denison's two-thousand-dollar two-way radio, which was mounted on the dashboard, and I wondered what the road had been like before it was fixed up. After two miles, we arrived at Marian Lake, the first of the chain of lakes serving as a base for the Ice Road. The air was so gray that I didn't see the lake until we dropped from the road onto its flatness. The other end was somewhere twenty-five miles distant, and the shoreline on both sides was marked by willow bushes and low spruce trees. We were driving at forty miles an hour down the middle of the lake on a smooth white road bordered by two-foot-high snowdrifts. Denison inserted a Guy Lombardo dance recording, "Golden Medleys," in the stereo tape player that was mounted under the dashboard, and the music blended with the cozy hum of the tires on the ice. "Want to dance?" Denison said suddenly. We both laughed.

"Do you ever think about falling through the ice?" I asked. I was looking straight ahead, but I couldn't see the end of the lake. The wind suddenly came up with a fury that made the camper shudder.

"Funny you should mention that," Denison said. "I was talking with an old friend, Del Curry, about ice just two days ago. Del has a construction business in Yellowknife, but when he came north, in '43, he freighted with Cat trains on Great Slave Lake. Cat trains are sleighs hooked together and hauled by tractors, and their top speed is four miles an hour. We call all tractors Cats, although in the beginning they were just the ones made by the Caterpillar Tractor Company. Del said he knew he had to get out of the business of hauling winter freight across lake ice when he found he was afraid to send one of his men in a lead Cat and drove it himself instead. One particular trip, he was doing the same thing he had been doing for maybe ten, twelve winters, and he realized he had lost the confidence to make that snap decision to tell his men, 'That ice is safe. Go across.' He says the only fellow who knows ennathing about ice is in his first or second year working on it, because he still has some confidence left. The longer you stay with it, the less you know."

I was shivering. The wind roared through an open space that had been cut in the floor to make room for the winch lever. In this kind of rough, off-road travel, a winch is an essential piece of equipment, and most of the vehicles that were used to build the Ice Road had one. Ours was mounted on the front, but on the big trucks it was behind the cab. Truckers like to say that a winch triples the power of their engines, because it supplies them with leverage to pull themselves up out of a hole without using their wheels. A button on the dashboard put the winch into gear; letting the clutch out wound up the cable. Looking down past the winch lever, I could see the white road beneath. A thin layer of snow had blown in and was building up around the base of the gearshift and around my feet. Denison turned the heater up a little, and said, "Wind is our worst enemy. It's always colder on the lakes—especially a big, open one like this—because of the wind. More snow. More plowing to keep the road from blowing in. That's about a twenty-five-mile-an-hour wind blowing now. Over thirty, we've about had it—and it can get up to a hundred. It'll get warmer in among the trees.

"I'll probably pull out, like Del Curry did," Denison went on. "Maybe in a couple of years. Ennathing can happen on ice, ennathing. No two years are the same, and your ice conditions change hourly. You can have six inches of ice and get across, and have thirty-six inches, which is what we think we need to cross in the loaded trailer trucks, and fall through. As a rule, it's the first man over who cracks the ice and the second guy who goes through. It all depends on how the cracks are formed and where they are. It's smart to go slow when you're not sure—about six miles an hour—so as not to bend the ice. Because if you make a wave, it has no place to go, and will snap back and break the ice when you're coming near the shore. The heavier the load, the more ice you need, so I don't take contracts after April 15th. It's pretty mushy after that. I usually go on, but I'm not happy about it, even though mostly just a wheel or two goes through." He shrugged. "Almost everyone who works with ice has had a pretty narrow escape. Del Curry was telling me that Hughie Arden, one of the most experienced men around here on ice, rode his Cat down because his overshoe got caught in a gear. He had to tear his shoe off under thirty-five foot of water in Yellowknife Bay to save himself."

"Did you ever go through?" I asked.

Denison laughed. "Couple of years ago, I was driving a Bug of mine across Prosperous Lake, twelve miles from Yellowknife, and I didn't see the ice crack. The stupid thing went in, but it floated six or eight minutes, so I climbed out of my seat and jumped out the other door. A Bug has a hull like a boat, full of holes, but a Cat—now, that's something else again. It's solid iron and drops through water like a rock."

I asked what had happened to the Bombardier that sank in Prosperous Lake.

"Oh, I left it there and went home," Denison said. "I sent a man out to find out how deep the water was, and he probed two hundred and fifty feet and couldn't touch bottom. I said, 'I've got to have it—it's the only thing I have to make a road with. Probe to five hundred.' You see, we had to know how deep the water was, so that we'd know how long a line we needed to sound for the Bug. We finally hit the bottom at three hundred and fifty feet. Then we found a spot where gasoline from the Bug had discolored the ice; that told us roughly where it was. We drilled about fifty or sixty holes in that area, and then we put a small iron bar on a string and dropped it through each of the holes, sounding for the Bug. When we found it, we hooked it with a big heavy grappling hook and started winching it up. The hook came off seven times and caught on the eighth. We lifted the Bug with the winch, which was on an A-frame, through a little hole we cut in the ice with a chain saw, and set the Bug over on a pad. The gas tanks had collapsed, but we had brought extra ones along, which we installed, and then we dried the Bug out with a Herman Nelson heater and drove it home. The same Bug is now at the bottom of Hardisty Lake, almost a hundred miles father north on this road, and I haven't had time to go and get the stupid thing, so it's still there. I don't think of it as really lost—just in cold storage. A machine doesn't deteriorate under water—only when the air hits it. Not much damage is done if the engine is turned off before the machine hits the water. I've dropped five machines in the lakes around here in seven years, but that's the only one I've lost. I'm more likely to put a piece through than any of my men are now, because I'll go where they won't dare. The men have spent their life on ice and dropped more Cats through than I have, so they're more scared than I am. Maybe I'll get time to go back and pull up that Bombardier this year." He opened the window to look back at the Bug we were hauling, then rolled the window up again. "I don't mind ennathing else, but I do mind the cold," he said. "When the temperature hits forty below zero—about what it is now—nothing but trouble! Air lines freeze, and you just don't have any brakes."

The portage road at the end of Marian Lake was the longest on the Ice Road—forty miles. It was terribly rough, and as we were

crawling at four miles an hour around a very narrow curve, Denison said, "It was right here that one of my drivers, Shannon O'Reilly, rolled his truck last season." I must have looked puzzled, because the language was new to me. "Rolling a truck is laying it on its side," Denison explained, "And when a driver says he has rhubarbed, that means he went off the road in a ditch but stayed on his tires. Last year was the first year since I've been making my road when nothing got wet, but we had one truck that turned completely over, got a short, and burned up the whole cargo. I turned my camper on its side once, too. All the food went out, and the ketchup went splat all over the inside walls. What a mess!"

A few minutes later, we came up behind another great snowplow truck, like 36, standing on the near bank of the Emile River. Denison walked over to the truck, which had a gold 34 painted on the door, climbed into its cab, and emerged shortly with two men I had met when I worked in Yellowknife the previous year—Al Frost, a young Indian driver, and Tom Berry, a driver and a master mechanic. After we had exchanged greetings, Berry returned to his truck, Frost unhooked the Bombardier—John called it the Bug—that we had been hauling, with its motor on, from the camper and got into it, and our vehicles crossed the river one at a time, over a narrow, rickety metal bridge that creaked and complained. We climbed the opposite bank on a half-cleared, deeply rutted road, and at the top we found a large red TD-14 International tractor slowly advancing toward us, crushing trees and bushes in its path to clear the overgrown portage road. A man's head with black hair and a black beard stuck out grotesquely above a canvas sheet that was stretched high across the open front of the Cat for a windbreaker. We stopped, and Denison got out again, this time to climb up on the tread of the tractor and shout over the clattering noise of its motor to the driver, Gilles Chartrand, who nodded vigorously. When Denison returned and we drove on past the tractor, he said crossly, "I've been seeing piles of snow in the woods all the way from Rayrock. I told that fool to stop wasting valuable snow—to put it back on the road, where it belongs, and pack it down. When you're making an ice road, you take snow off the lakes but not off the portages. On the portages, you use it, because it's like cement and you've got to mix it as if that was what it is. You've got to beat the goddam air out of it right away, so it will freeze solid. Take the two feet of snow that we have around here now. Well, we'll keep dragging it, take all the air out, until we have only two inches of snow left, and when the weather gets cold again like this, it'll turn to ice right away. Making ice roads is a science. I wish I had my books with me to show you how the Russians and Swedes have been studying it." He grimaced. "But everything those guys write, even translated into English, is in technical terms I don't understand. So I make my roads my own way."

"What way is that?" I asked.

"First, I go by plane over the area where I'm planning to make my road, to see if it's possible," Denison said. "Then I scout the ground between the lakes—the portages—to find the best route through, and sometimes there isn't any. I use the Bug we brought with us for scouting and marking out the route; it's the fastest, lightest vehicle over ice, when it runs. Then our twelve-ton Cat clears trees and stumps and rocks away so we can get the rest of the equipment through, and the third step is to knock the snow down from two feet to two or three inches with special steel drags I've designed, which we hook on behind the Cat and, later, behind the trucks. Then we pack the snow down some more—with heavy trucks like 36 and Tom Berry's 34, and the Cat, and a couple of trucks you haven't met up with yet that go back and forth over it at least a half-dozen times to level it down. We try to camp ahead of where the crew will be working so that I can go forward and scout the next morning, while the crew goes back to pack down the portage we've just cleared. The portage roads and the lake roads are two different kinds, of course. On the lakes, which make up ninety per cent of the Ice Road, we just go through with a snowplow truck and open a road. After we get the road in, the plow keeps going back and forth, clearing off excess snow that blows in, and we send along the freight trucks. Without snow as a blanket insulating the ice, the frost keeps going down through to make the ice thicker and thicker. We go on plowing all season."

Denison's eyes were fastened on the road. It was less a road than a half-broken trail, so rough I had to grip the seat and the door to avoid bouncing into the radio; we were rocking from side to side over ruts a foot deep. Suddenly, we slapped down onto a small lake. "When we come down on ice like that, how do you know we won't go through?" I asked.

"We've got to go over the lake ennaway, so what's the difference?" Denison replied.

We reached Hislop Lake at four o'clock, when it was completely dark. We made our own road for a few feet through crusty snow on the lake, which had not yet been plowed, and then stopped. "We'll spend the night here," Denison said. "The others'll be along any minute."

✦

After lunch the next day, Denison, his nephew, Jimmy Watson, and I set off in the Bug to scout the next lake, Tuche, and the portage between it and Rae Lake, where we had spent the night. I sat on a plank on the floor in the back, below an escape hatch in the ceiling which had formerly had a door but was now covered by a flimsy rag of a coat. There was an ominous clink in the engine. "I don't trust this old pile of junk, but there's no point spending ten or twelve thousand for a new one when I use it only this once a year," said Denison. The Bug was having transmission trouble, and to keep the transmission from jumping out of position into neutral Watson had to hold his foot pressed against the gearshift. During the return from our expedition, the Bug developed more trouble, and stopped. "The temperature and oil are both down," Denison said. "We must have burned a bearing."

Both men got out and tinkered with the motor. I was so accustomed by then to miracles that I was not surprised when the engine started chugging again and we were able to move on. At the south end of Tuche, at the beginning of the woods between Tuche and Rae, we came to a halt. Denison said that the route we had taken through the woods earlier was too long for the Bug in its crippled condition and that the route now ahead of us, which was more direct, was too rough. Our crew was only about a hundred yards away, on Rae Lake; we could see the smoke of our trucks through thick undergrowth and hear the sound of voices. But between us and the men was a deep, densely wooded ravine. Denison sent Watson on foot to tell the men where we were. The sun was going down, and Denison grew impatient. Why didn't Watson return? I asked why we didn't follow him in the Bug. "The way this old Bug is now, she'd never make it," Denison said. "We'd have to go right through the trees." He looked at his watch, swore, got out of the Bug, and disappeared into the ravine.

In the crippled Bug, with its engine still running, I had for company Jimmy Watson's tool kit, an oil drum, a gasoline drum, an ice auger, a shovel, an axe, and two propane heaters, one of which Denison had lit before he left. I was quite warm, and since it was dark out I curled up on the floor with a sleeping bag as a pillow, and took a nap. When I woke, it was after five. I stepped out of the Bug, wondering if I should follow Denison but remembering how often I had read about novices in the North who had frozen to death a few yards from shelter. I was turning to get back in the Bug when I saw an electric lantern swinging toward me, and a moment later Denison emerged from the darkness. He climbed into the driver's seat looking grim. "The Cat's in the water," he said. "It's down four feet, about thirty from shore, turned over on its right side. If we had a winch on a truck, we could pull it out in a few minutes, but the winch on 36 has a burned-out bearing, and the only other winch that's strong enough is on the Cat itself. The radios are dead, so I'll have to go back to the garage for help. But the first thing I have to do is get this Bug back to the other vehicles while it's still running. Keep your foot against the gearshift, and let's go!"

I sat where Watson had sat, my left foot pressed against the gearshift, my left hand pressed on my knee to keep my foot steady, my right arm bracing me on the seat. The Bug went forward with a horrid lurch. I looked up into the stream of brightness made by our headlights, and gasped. We were driving directly into a very large white tree, its thick trunk coming up to meet us out of the dark. Brush crackled under our treads as the tree trunk came closer and closer. I looked at Denison; he looked straight at the tree trunk, making no effort to swerve. Swerve where? We were surrounded by trees. "Keep your foot on that gearshift!" Denison snapped without turning his head. So I held on to the shift and the seat, and the tree came up to our windshield, separated from my face by the short, curved front of the Bug.

Crack!

The tree snapped off. Unbelievably, it fell over, laden with snow, as neatly as if it had been cut with scissors.

Crack! Crack! Crack! The trees fell before us as we crashed through that woods. The old Bug rattled and shook with each blow.

Crack! Crack! Crack! Finally, I didn't even close my eyes when we hit. I noticed that it took a birch longer to break than a spruce.

A yellow patch of light appeared in the black sky above the trees ahead. Suddenly we leaped onto the ice, into a circle of headlights. The Cat, a great wounded animal, was lying on its side, its right track under water, with broken ice floating around it. The other vehicles were standing at a respectful distance, shedding light—comforting companions and mourners. Denison shouted "Lift your foot!" and as I did the transmission slipped into neutral and we came to a halt, the motor idling. My toes were stiff from the cold air that had been blowing on them through the hole at the base of the gearshift. I felt as though we had come miles, but it had only been about a hundred yards.

Denison got out and walked around the Cat. The men clustered silently near him, waiting for an instant remedy. There was none. Everyone drove back to the camper, on Rae Lake, and Denison tried the radio. He wanted to call to have parts brought by plane to repair the winch. There was no response—only static. That settled it. Someone had to go back for help. Tom Berry started at once for Fort Byers, to return with another tractor and its owner to drive it— Hughie Arden, an old-time Northerner, who was an expert on Cat salvage. The power steering on 34 had broken, so Berry needed to go back anyway.

The radio was silent all the next day and the day after. Denison was really ill, and stopped eating. He lay on the back bunk as still as death, his eyes shut. He opened them and turned his head only when one or another of the men came to report on his work. Without a Cat to clear away trees and rocks, no portage road could be broken open. The shack on the truck the men called Fud had fallen off, and had been fastened in position again and her water lines hooked up, so Mukluk and Jimmy Watson had returned to dragging and packing down the portages behind us and plowing out the road on the lakes to keep it clear of drifts. Bob Burns, grieving for his crippled Cat, spent the days in the camper, his head down, a paperback mystery open and unread in his hand, smoking cigarette after cigarette and drinking coffee. It was fifty below outside. I drove up with Watson in 36 to see the Cat. It was well frozen into its icy prison and coated with tons of ice at the waterline.

On the second night, I asked Watson how sick he thought Denison was.

"Pretty bad, but not so that we have to get a plane to fly him out, like some of the other times," Watson whispered. "Last year, he was flown out three times. He'd be out for a day, and then he'd be OK and he'd come back. John'll pick up when things get better. He shouldn't be doing this kind of work, but you can't stop him."

I dreamed that night that all the lights were on and someone was standing in front of me shouting. I woke to find Tom Berry standing in the door, back from Fort Byers, with a flashlight in his hand. It was the first time I had ever seen him agitated. "It's through!" he shouted. "I just went through the ice in 34!"

Denison had pulled on his boots and struggled into his parka before Barry stopped shouting. "I heard you drive in, Tom." he said. "I *knew* you were through the ice. I could *feel* it, and I heard a crunch. I thought, By Jesus, I'm not going to worry, and then I heard some more crunch, crunch, crunch, and you yelled." Denison followed Berry outside.

I put some water on the stove for coffee and then joined the group outside around the endangered truck. Both ends of 34 were standing on the ice, but it sagged in the middle, where the back wheels of the cab and the front wheels of the trailer were partly under water. The rescue squad to retrieve Denison's Cat from its water hole had arrived with Berry—Hughie Arden and Davy Lorenzen, a man in his thirties, who worked winters for Denison and had his own sand-and-gravel business in the summers. Arden and Lorenzen had come in Lorenzen's tow truck, a modest ten-ton Diamond T model, which was standing at a discreet distance on the ice behind the accident; on its trailer hitch was a giraffelike machine, a cherry picker, which had a long neck with a lot of pulleys and cables for lifting heavy objects. Two additional pieces of equipment had been brought out on the lowboy of 34— Arden's silver caboose, and his yellow Cat. Burns prepared to drive Arden's Cat off the back of 34's trailer. The other men started up a Herman Nelson heater, to thaw the back wheels of 34's cab and prevent the water from freezing around them. After serving coffee to the men, I started packing up for travelling, without being told. The radio was still out, more parts were needed to get 34 running, and there was no way to get them except by driving back to Fort Byers and on to Yellowknife. Around three in the morning, Denison, Watson, and I set off in the camper. Denison had become withdrawn again—so formidable in this silence that I could not imagine talking to him.

◆

On the morning of the twenty-third, we were at the north end of Yen

Lake, facing our last land barrier to Great Bear Lake. On the other side of this final portage was Gunbarrel Inlet, a narrow entrance channel four miles long and only a mile wide, leading onto the big lake. On this morning, Denison shaved. The thinness of the face that emerged from behind his grizzled beard was shocking. As he watched the Cat mount what appeared to be an almost perpendicular hill and disappear abruptly over the top, he restlessly drummed his fingers on the camper's steering wheel. "Two days late," he muttered. "I said I'd be in Port Radium two days ago."

"This looks like a steep portage," I said.

"It used to be a complete bottleneck a few years ago," Denison said. "We had to winch every truck up it and down again, which meant keeping a Cat here most of the time. The snow is unusually deep in this portage — about three feet — and last year we blasted a great big pile of rock out."

The Cat passed back and forth over the top of the hill two or three times, clearing away the rocks. The Beaver followed and disappeared over the top — a signal for Lewis Mackenzie to start up in the African Queen. The huge truck dipped and twisted, seemed to fall back, then rose in a surge of strength over the top. Denison, suddenly impatient, shifted gears and drove up the perpendicular embankment. Halfway, we became caught in deep snow. The Beaver came back over the hill and tried, unsuccessfully, to give us a push. The others tried to go by us and got stuck — Lorenzen in the Diamond T, Mukluk and Lowen in 37. Burns, waiting on the side of the hill in the Cat, pulled us out. When we were free and had been detached from his winch, Burns moved slowly to each of the other trucks and gave them a shove that got them going. Meanwhile, we had got stuck again.

When I glanced into the camper's rear-view mirror, I saw smoke pouring from the space behind the cab. Denison saw it at the same time; he jumped out, picked up an armful of snow, and threw it into the smoke. As he climbed back into the camper, he was laughing. "No wonder I've been having so much trouble making it over this hill," he said, looking sheepish. "I had my brake on. It was my goddam brake that caught fire!"

At the top of the hill, two red-and-white gasoline drums marked the road. When we reached them, we peered over the crest at the sheerest drop I have ever seen on anything that could be called a road. We teetered on the top of the portage for a second. I gripped the seat with both hands, held my breath, and shut my eyes as we tumbled down the hill toward the glassy surface of the inlet. We glided out onto the ice and waited for the others to come down.

After lunch, Spotlight George, Bob Burns, Lewis Mackenzie, and Davy Lorenzen said goodbye to me. Only Herb Lowen and Mukluk — in the new truck, 37 — were going with us to plow the Ice Road the last forty miles to Port Radium, from which I would be flying to Yellowknife. The others were turning back to put the finishing touches on the road we had left behind — cementing the snow into ice on the portages, and plowing the lakes to keep them free of snow. Barring any more accidents, Denison would be calling Fort Byers from Port Radium by the end of the day, and the trucks from Yellowknife, from Hay River, from Edmonton would be on their way.

As we came out on Great Bear Lake, Denison pointed out a pressure ridge — a wide bank of broken ice, several feet high, that was light blue against the flat, snowy ice surrounding it. It ran for miles in a curving line, vanishing somewhere in the middle of the lake. Of all the disturbances created by Northern weather, the pressure ridge is the one feared most by the men who constantly deal with ice; it is treacherous, dangerous, and frequently impassable. We followed the curve of this raised band of ice for several miles, until it blocked the way ahead so directly that we could not avoid crossing it. Denison got out and walked over to it, digging into its craggy ice chips with his feet. He waved Lowen ahead and got back into the camper, and we drove over a low spot, lurching across the bumpy ice. "This is a very small pressure ridge, and it's dead — it's quit moving and the cracks are all froze up," Denison said.

"How blue it is!" I exclaimed.

"That's because fresh water is directly underneath," Denison told me. "Ice is a solid, same as metal. It shrinks when the weather is cold, expands when it's warm. Temperature variations change the texture of your ice. On a cold night, on these really big lakes you'll get cracks opening as wide as four feet. On a warm day, you can actually see the expanding ice moving back together again, and if it expands beyond its original size, it overlaps and breaks, and leaves real fresh water underneath that spot. Sometimes, when the ice overlaps, it piles up twenty feet, even higher. The trouble with pressure ridges is that they are such a terrible temptation to cross when they're low. I have a real bad habit of finding the lowest place, breaking it down with a needle bar, throwing some planks down, and going through. It looks so easy, but since the cracks may not have froze over, the ice can separate again and tip you down into open water."

At four o'clock, the sun had almost set. An orange-red sphere, it was slipping down into an orange strip at the horizon; the blue sky was slowly turning a soft gray, with little streaks of salmon pink. The lakes' surface—which the wind had swept clean, except for some tufts of snow scattered about like powder puffs—was a glassy blue green. "God, but it's beautiful up here!" Denison exclaimed.

At five o'clock, we could see the lights from Echo Bay Mine twinkling at us in the darkening sky. We soon came to a second pressure ridge, higher than the first one by a foot or so, and curving far out into the lake. We back-tracked several miles, until we found a hole through the pressure ridge—a reasonably smooth patch of ice. We were farther out now on Great Bear Lake, travelling to the left of a little island, doubling on our own tracks, making a second, parallel white road on the other side of the pressure ridge, but we were heading straight for the mine again. As we came closer, I could see Port Radium's old-fashioned white frame buildings scattered along the narrow shore of Echo Bay.

"Today is the twenty-third of January," Denison said. "Last year, I was here by the twenty-first. Two days late. But that's all behind us now."

"I wonder why you do this kind of work when it makes you so sick," I said.

"Oh, I don't know," Denison said. "It's just something about the North. You're on your own. You feel more as if you are your own person, somehow."

The darkness had settled in around us, and the twinkling lights of the mine were moving closer, getting brighter. It was a lovely moonlit night. "We could have come in without lights," Denison said. "Neither truck really needs lights tonight, but I turned mine on so we can be seen at the mine."

We crossed from the bay ice to the shore and climbed a little incline. "This was a real good trip," Denison said as he stopped the camper on the dock, where in a day or two his trucks would be unloading freight, "Except for dropping the truck and the accidents—all that falling through the ice—opening my road to Echo Bay this year went better than ever before."

Excerpted from "The Ice Road," published in *The New Yorker*, December 30, 1974.

One evening right after my article on the ice road had been published, I was entertaining my friends Bill and Emmy Maxwell with some of my experiences on the ice road that I had *not* put into the piece, partly due to lack of space, and partly out of embarrassment. "For example, you may notice that I said very little about cooking for the crew," I said. "I did a lot of that, and it caused me a lot of grief."

I explained that since I was a woman and was travelling in the camper, which was the crew's cookhouse as well, they assumed that I was the cook, which was a total surprise to me. They had been told I was there to write about the ice road, but the way they saw it, that was a useless thing to be doing. I was a reluctant unpaid second cook to Denison until he became so ill that I had no choice. I did all the cooking from then on, to a chorus of complaints. Then when the men went off on the road and I was left alone, there were always the dishes to wash for six men and myself, in one to two inches of water.

"Oh dear," Emmy said, laughing. "What did you cook?"

"There was the matter of breakfast," I said. "First of all, I was too slow. Denison said he could get an hour's work out of the men in the time it took me to cook their breakfast. Then there was the morning I burned the bacon and fried nine eggs, turning them to order, and broke seven, while they all watched me in total silence. Denison was sick in the back bunk, leaning on his elbow, observing. 'You lose your nerve at the last minute, every time,' he said."

Emmy and Bill were both laughing. "You have to write this," Bill said. "What else?"

"Well, there was the time I made macaroni and cheese, which they wanted, and I had never made it in my life. I was so agitated I couldn't read the directions, so I put the macaroni from the box into the baking dish, without boiling it first." We all laughed at that. "I did remember to put the cheese on, but the damage was irreversible."

"Yes, it would be," Bill said. "You have to write this."

"I had two friends in Yellowknife who found these details amusing too," I went on. "Rae Parker and Kay Vaydik used to rush over to the Yellowknife Inn as soon as I came in from a trip, and I would pour out my sorrows. They would start laughing the minute they saw me, I was such a wreck, and the worse my stories were, the more they laughed. We made so much noise laughing that everyone in the coffee shop would be staring at us."

"You *must* write all this down," Bill and Emmy kept saying, and kept asking for more. So I told them one of my favorite stories, about Denison and his nephew, Jimmy Watson, who were sharing a bed in the overhang of the camper; they had this incredible conversation about Denison going to sleep with his hat on.

Bill asked, "Do you have enough material for a book?"

I thought I did, so he told me to try it. I took all the notes I had about Yellowknife and the ice road, started working with them all over again, wrote forty pages, and showed them to Bill Maxwell. He read them, handed them back to me, and said, "Start all over again, and tell it the way you did to us." I went home and felt like shooting myself, but I knew he was right. So I started all over again, and this time it became my book, *Denison's Ice Road*.

Here is the story of Denison, Jimmy, and the hat:

———————— ◆ ————————

When Jimmy went to bed, although I wasn't sleepy I went to bed also; it was just too much trouble reading by candlelight. Before the fire we had in the camper, when my sleeping bag fell into a heater while we were travelling, and we still had electric lights, all of us read after dinner or in bed. I lay there listening to Denison breathing steadily in the back bunk, and Jimmy moving around restlessly beside him. Suddenly a flashlight went on and I heard Jimmy say in a loud whisper, "John?" Then louder, "John!"

There was a stirring and John said, "Yup?"

"John," he said. "You've gone to bed with your hat on."

I pulled myself up on one elbow and looked out from my bunk. It was true. Denison was wearing the green cap he had worn all day, lying on his back with the visor over his forehead, covering his eyes.

"John," Jimmy went on, in a normal speaking voice. "*Nobody* goes to bed with their hat on."

"I do," said John.

There was a silence. Jimmy continued to stare at him, holding the flashlight with its beam turned on the green hat. Denison hadn't moved and the visor still shaded his eyes. "But *why*?" Jimmy finally said.

"Dunno. Had it on, I guess. Never took it off."

"Well, why don't you take it off now that I've called your attention to it?"

"Don't want to. I've got it on now."

There was a long silence. Jimmy turned off the flashlight and lay down. The light suddenly went on again. Jimmy was sitting bolt upright, staring at John. There was something very surrealist about this. A small surrealist drama.

"John," he said.

Silence.

Jimmy drew a long sighing breath. "John, I've *never* slept in a bed with *anyone* who was wearing a hat," he said. Another sigh. "I don't know whether I *can*."

"Sorry about that," John replied. Silence. Nobody moved.

It seemed like a long time before Jimmy turned off the flashlight and lay down.

Published in different form in *Denison's
Ice Road*, 1975; 1982; 1991.

Writing sometimes brings unique rewards. John Denison's mother, Ethel Denison, was in her eighties when *Denison's Ice Road* was published. She always referred to it as The Book, and after it came out she invited me to celebrate with her in Vernon, British Columbia, where she lived.

I had met her once before, when I went to Vernon to get more information on Denison's background. She was a tall, slim, very dignified woman, with white hair, glasses and fine features. She dressed simply but had an air of elegance; I was not surprised to find out that when she and her late husband were running a lodge at a lake near Vernon, no matter how hard she had worked during the day she always stopped at four o'clock, changed her clothes and served tea.

John was the oldest of eight children, and when he was a boy, they lived on a farm. He told me that his mother used to come out and help him clean the barn, after everyone else had gone to bed. By the time I met Mrs. Denison, she was not very well, but was living alone, fiercely independent still, in a cozy basement apartment. She and I instantly liked one another, and I spent a memorable afternoon talking to her.

The celebration I returned for was an elegant tea given in my honor, but really in hers too, in the exquisite garden of her eldest daughter, Dorothy. Mrs. Denison sat in a chair at the center of the party as if she were on a throne, surrounded by friends and relatives, radiating pride. It was a great day for her; for me too.

Don Snowden, 1929–1984

◆

WHEN DON SNOWDEN DIED suddenly in 1984, I was in New York, about to return to Canada. Gunther Abrahamson, then Chief of Social and Cultural Development for Northern Affairs, met me in Toronto and asked me to write Don's obituary for the government's magazine, *Inuktitut*. It would be distributed all over the North.

Writing Don's obituary seemed unimaginable. He was an extremely complex man, and was already a legend larger than life. Besides, he was much too young to die. He had recently made an extremely happy marriage with a fine young woman, Mary McGugan, who was just right for him, and he had all kinds of fascinating work lined up for the future.

It was hard to accept that I would never see him again doing the thing he liked to do best: drawing people out to express their deepest thoughts and wishes. Listening to a meeting he directed with the Inuit always made me think of the music achieved in concert by a great orchestra conductor; it had the same clear, pure tones. A man who appeared to have supreme confidence when he was working, he hid his personal shyness under bravado that was misleading. He would have liked, for example, to know Bill Shawn, who in the course of publishing my articles in *The New Yorker* had expressed a keen interest in meeting him. When I suggested such a meeting, Don refused, saying, "I admire him so much, I haven't the courage; I wouldn't know what to say."

It was a sad privilege that Gunther handed me, and I sat down at my typewriter and did the best I could. How could I say what Snowden meant to me, or to any of the people, whether he knew them personally or not, to whom he gave himself with all his heart?

───────────── ◆ ─────────────

For those who knew Donald Snowden, it is hard to accept that a man so vibrantly alive can have died, as he did suddenly on April 4, 1984, across the seas and far from home in Hyderabad, in south central India. The end came a month before his fifty-sixth birthday, with the characteristic swiftness and intensity with which he had lived. It was a hot day and after an early morning swim in a hotel pool he went into the dressing room and had a heart attack. It was all over in half a minute.

Many who live in the Canadian North have never heard his name. But those who are old enough to remember how life was for the Inuit thirty years ago when they were caught by changing times in a spiral of unemployment, poverty and slow starvation, will remember the big, laughing young man from the government who radiated joy and optimism and introduced them to the idea of co-operatives. And whether they remember him or not, every Inuit man, woman or child who lives in the Northwest Territories, Labrador or Arctic Quebec today leads a better life because of Don Snowden's vision and singular determination. "We are religious people," he once said to a friend, and his religion was the dignity and beauty of the human spirit.

Snowden came to the North first in 1954 as an information officer for the Canadian Government's then Department of Northern Affairs. One summer he went on a patrol voyage of the icebreaker C.D. Howe and what he saw then made a deep impression; he was caught up in the tragic situation of the Inuit, and the magic beauty of their surroundings. Two years later, in 1956, as Chief of the Industrial Division in the Department of Northern Affairs, he was given the job of tackling the twin problems of poverty and unemployment in the North by providing some kind of an economic system that would help to make the Eskimos self-sufficient. He could have brought in businessmen from outside to run things, or imposed some other solution on the Inuit without consulting their wishes. Instead he and his superiors chose the more daring route of assisting the Inuit to make their own decisions. He had a vision for the future of the North, of an independent native population of Canadian citizens governing themselves. It was his firm belief that if people are given the right tools and shown how to use them they can help themselves better than anyone else can, will make wiser decisions for themselves than others can make for them, and will make important contributions to society in doing so.

The tool that Snowden and his hard-working staff put in Inuit hands was the co-operative, because it seemed to fit into the Inuit way of living and sharing together. He also saw the co-operatives as a training ground where Eskimos would learn to speak up and assume responsibility. He used to say, "I don't believe the government is infallible. The co-ops make it possible for the Eskimos to give us hell."

The Industrial Division's first move was to have studies made of renewable resources in the Arctic, and on the basis of what was learned, Snowden went on to organize fisheries (he sold the first arctic char himself, taking it from restaurant to restaurant in Montreal), the production and marketing of Eskimo art and the Northwest Territories Tourist Office. Twenty-five years later he could look back on a proliferation of forty-three co-operatives involved in a wide variety of business operations across the North, and his vision was a reality. Almost all who are leaders in the powerful Inuit organizations today received early training and confidence in running their own affairs in their local co-operatives; and Inuit now participate at the highest levels of municipal, territorial and federal governments.

Don Snowden was the first to say that these astounding results in just twenty-five years were achieved not by any one person but by the dedicated efforts of many people: by those higher up in government who supported his unorthodox methods of swift action, cutting through red tape, apathy and outright resistance; by his own staff, whom he chose, not for their ability to get high scores in civil service examinations, but for their strong characters, quick intelligence, practical skills on land and sea and their respect for the Inuit; but most of all by the Inuit themselves, whom he admired and loved. Whether people liked Don Snowden personally or not — and he was not afraid to make enemies — there is general agreement that without his driving energy and single-minded approach that went right to the heart of any matter, it would have taken decades longer, if it had happened at all.

Shortly after he left the federal government, after ten years with Northern Affairs, Snowden wrote: "In humanity there is so much that is latent, so little ability to loosen the fear of ourselves, and so much vitality and sunshine when we do. It may be that some men in some places may find they walk with more certainty because we have met, and they have exposed me to their dignity and their unspoken longings which are the same as mine."

Don Snowden was born in Winnipeg on May 9, 1929, and after getting a degree in journalism from Carleton University in Ottawa, he worked as a newspaperman briefly on the *Winnipeg Free Press*. He left to become Director of Tourism for four years in Saskatchewan, and then joined Northern Affairs. When a competition opened for the job of economic development in the Canadian Arctic he applied, winning over three hundred other applicants. The North was his personal proving ground, when he learned what he could do and could exercise his particular genius for taking a mix of familiar ideas and weaving them into a new pattern. He also had an extraordinary gift for persuading people to speak their thoughts, and was a good and thoughtful listener.

When he left Northern Affairs in 1964, he explained, "I love to be in on the beginning of things. Now that I know our program works, I have to go on to other places. I am a sort of a learner and some sort of a teacher, and desperately inside me, there is the need to keep both these things flowing all the time without interruption."

He went then to Newfoundland, where he made his home until his death, finding new frontiers as Director of Extension and Adviser to the President of Memorial University. He is credited with doing much to transform the lives of the rural population of Newfoundland, bringing the University's education programs to all the outports and Labrador for the first time, giving the population outside the capital of St. John's a visual arts program that included the operation of provincial art galleries, and creating a fisheries co-operative program that attracted students from twenty-five countries.

The connecting thread through all of Snowden's work was his passionate belief that when people can communicate their thoughts to one another, the possibilities for a better world are virtually unlimited. It was the lesson he learned when he and the Inuit twenty-five years ago finally understood and trusted one another and he never forgot it.

In Newfoundland, he devised in association with the National Film Board, a new, unique method of communication called the Fogo Film Method, so named because it was first used in the Newfoundland community of Fogo Island. The provincial government was determined to move the islanders to the mainland where their needs could be more easily serviced, but the Fogo Island residents liked where they were. Snowden, and his Film Board colleagues, went among the Islanders with portable videotape equipment, that recorded them talking among themselves about the threatened relocation. They expressed their true feelings about why they did not want to move, when they met together in their own familiar surroundings, in an open way they could not have done in a formal conference room away from home. The tapes were then played for the government authorities who had proposed the move, and they replied on tape as well, thus setting up a dialogue that led to greater understanding between the two formerly opposed groups. The Fogo Islanders were able to stay where they were, and formed fishing and boat building co-operatives that gave them a fresh economic base. Snowden's film crew had also trained local personnel to run the videotape machines and by exchanging tapes among themselves the Islanders came to know one another better too.

For the past ten years Snowden has taken the Fogo Method to distant parts of the world including the Caribbean, the United States (especially Alaska), Africa and India, training government and rural people in its use wherever he went. One of the projects that pleased him most was a recent one that involved the Kaminuriak caribou herd in the Keewatin.

He was asked by the Department of Indian Affairs and Northern Development to bring together government biologists, Inuit and Indians, all of whom were concerned about the welfare of the herd but did not agree on methods of management. "A part of myself has been restored by the chance to work in the North again," Snowden announced. Thirty-three tapes later, natives, government biologists, and game management personnel were sitting down together and discussing the best future use and management of the caribou herd. The Keewatin tapes, as well as a thirty-minute film about India, *Eyes See, Ears Hear*, won awards of merit at the Atlantic Film Festival in 1983.

When he died, Snowden was working with the National Dairy Institute of India, training local people to make tapes for education and village development in the little town of Taprana, and he was about to go to Bangladesh. A favourite story that he delighted to tell was how the Fogo Method had helped the Taprana drivers of rickshaws — small, two-wheeled carriages pulled by one or two men that are used as taxis in India — who wanted to buy their own vehicles. The tape made of the meeting where the drivers discussed this among themselves was taken to a bank in a neighboring town and shown to the manager, who replied on videotape that he would make such a loan. The drivers formed a co-operative, purchased the rickshaws, and the film itself became so real to them that they were certain they had actually seen the bank manager in Taprana, although he had never been there.

Snowden served on many official bodies, including the Canadian Eskimo Arts Council, the National Film Board and as Chairman of the Royal Commission on Labrador. Recently he was invited to serve on the advisory board of the Dag Hammarskjöld Institute in Sweden, and participate in a world study of communication in development of Third World countries. He was to have gone to the first meeting in Sweden in May, and was to have held one himself in Labrador in September. The meeting is expected to take place as planned, which is what Snowden would have wanted. The key to Don Snowden's extraordinary career is that he never lost touch with who he was or how it all began. His wife, Mary, said shortly after his death, "Don was really happiest in the Arctic. He loved wherever he worked, but it was the Canadian North that he loved the most."

In April of 1961, Don Snowden and two of his staff met with a small group of Eskimos who had formed the first Inuit co-operative, at the George River, twelve miles from Ungava Bay. It was their second meeting and the groundwork was set then that put Canada's first Eskimo co-operative into business. Snowden kept the meetings going night and day until plans for a settlement, a fish freezer, a store, handicraft industry and a myriad other details were understood by all. At the end of the final meeting, George Annanack, the senior Inuk leader, said unexpectedly to Snowden, in Inuktitut "we will remember you forever and ever." This was followed by a spontaneous shout of "*Nakommiik! Nakommiik!*"—(Thank you! Thank you!)—from all the Inuit who were there. When the meaning of these words was translated for Snowden, he remained silent, but a month later he wrote of that meeting:

"There was never a moment in my life when I was so exposed, or so close to understanding how beautiful it could be to be human. Do you suppose that they would ever understand that in that moment they were telling a man there had been some purpose to his having lived, and for that he owed them a debt impossible ever to repay? I will never forget that moment, or them, as long as a trace of awareness of people is with me."

First published in *Inuktitut* magazine, in Inuktitut (both in syllabic and roman typography), and in English and French, Summer, 1984. Published later in *Arctic* magazine, the periodical of the Arctic Institute of America; in the *Caribou News*; in Yellowknife's *News of the North*; in newspapers and magazines in Labrador; in India; and in *Development Dialogue*, the journal of the Dag Hammarskjöld Foundation in Sweden.

Part Four

◆

CANADA

Prime Minister / Premier Ministre

———————— ✦ ————————

I AM DELIGHTED to have the Profile of Pierre Trudeau appear here. It has never been in book form before, although it has been quoted or referred to in almost every treatise about Trudeau and his era.

It was written during the year after Pierre Trudeau became Prime Minister, primarily for American readers, who were already noticing that there was a charismatic, highly unusual but very intelligent new Prime Minister in Canada. His was such a refreshing personality in politics that we were all curious about what kind of a man he was, so I set off to find out.

The idea for me to write about Trudeau came from Gordon Gibson, Jr., whom I had met when he was with Northern Affairs. He wrote me in March of 1968 that he was working for the man he thought would be the next Prime Minister of Canada, and that Trudeau would make a fine story. I replied that if he was elected, I would be interested.

Trudeau succeeded Lester Pearson as head of the Liberal Party and Prime Minister in April, and after he had won the general election in June, I asked his press secretary, Roméo LeBlanc, if Mr. Trudeau would be able to see me. Roméo said that the Prime Minister was about to leave for a trip across the North, and I would have to wait for his reply until he returned.

"Where is he going in the North?" I inquired, always curious to know where people are going when they head north.

LeBlanc read off the list of northern stops, including Grise Fiord in the High Arctic. "Grise Fiord!" I exclaimed. "I've always wanted to go there!"

"You can't possibly get on the trip," LeBlanc said. "It's a pooled press, and only three men are going, one from the Canadian Press, a photographer, and a CBC correspondent."

I hadn't had any thought of asking to go, but to everyone's surprise, especially mine, I did go on that trip. I had to strike a bargain: that I would not interview the Prime Minister on the trip, that I would never interview members of his family, and that since I would have about eight days to observe him while we were in the North, I would ask for as little time with him as possible when he returned to Ottawa. My only formal interview with him alone took place at one lunch, at which I frantically took notes, mostly under the table.

"Why aren't you eating?" he asked at one point.

"Because I can't do two things at once and I'm taking notes," I had to reply.

Trudeau was at his very best during the Question Period in Parliament, so I spent many hours in the Press Gallery of the House of Commons. There were few women journalists in the Press Gallery at that time, and it didn't help that I was from an American magazine. I felt and was treated like an outcast. One journalist called me at my hotel to shout his outrage when it became known I was going on the trip with Trudeau.

The Profile appeared in July 1969, and that fall, thinking I might write about Canadian constitutional reform, I attended a large conference in Ottawa. When I walked in the room, every Canadian journalist I knew, and a lot I didn't know, came up to congratulate me—even those who had given me a hard time. I treasure that memory.

The Profile of Trudeau was intended to be a character study. When I wrote to Mr. Trudeau to thank him for that lunch, I said that when people examined his achievements and evaluated his contributions as Prime Minister of Canada, I would like them to be able to turn to my piece and find out what kind of man he was. I thought I had done a pretty fair job until Trudeau's application of the War Measures Act during the Quebec Crisis, on October 16, 1970. He had made such a deep commitment to civil liberties and was now suspending them in peacetime: hundreds of innocent citizens were taken into custody and denied bail, their right to know why they were apprehended and their right to counsel. I was appalled.

I was so disturbed that first week that I called a number of my friends in Ottawa seeking an explanation. I concluded, as many people did, that the government had vastly overreacted to a small group of Quebec terrorists, believing that it represented a large underground insurrection. A British diplomat was held hostage, a Quebec government minister had been kidnapped and held hostage (and was murdered two days after the War Measures Act came into effect) and, according to one of my informants, "so-called 'communiqués' were flying around with frequent references to 'political prisoners' and numerous threats against society." My informant added, "The complete background is complex, but indeed it was, and is, an attempt to hold a nation up to ransom."

Who could foresee it? We were moving into the hostage era in modern history.

◆

Pierre Trudeau, the improbable fifteenth Prime Minister of Canada, whose dream is to mold a more nearly perfect government and save his country from dissolving into two separate nations, is a man who likes to have the last word. He has been talking back to people since boyhood. When he is reminded of this, he throws back his head and laughs. "Yes!" he says. "I was impertinent to my father, to my teachers—to everybody. It got me into trouble, but when I was intimidated I had to have the last word. As I became more mature, I would state my case and sit back, which is a form of answering." He has been stating his case since 1950, when, in the first issue of *Cité Libre*, a small, free-spirited French-Canadian magazine he helped to found, he presented his own theory of balanced action between central-government authority and provincial autonomy, in an article entitled, "Politique Fonctionnelle." Last year, with characteristic consistency, he stated his case again, in a collection of speeches and essays called "Federalism and the French Canadians." He wants Canada, whose constitution provides for a form of government that unites the qualities of American federalism and British parliamentarianism, to become what he calls "a brilliant prototype" for tomorrow's world, and, as Prime Minister, he is in a position to try to make this particular dream come true.

Trudeau had few listeners until two years ago, when he was appointed Minister of Justice and Attorney General in the Cabinet of Lester B. Pearson, his predecessor as Prime Minister and as leader of the Liberal Party. Until 1965, when Trudeau joined the Liberals—the first time he had joined any party—ran for public office, also for the first time, and was elected a Member of Parliament from a well-to-do suburb of his birthplace, Montreal, he was almost unknown outside the Province of Quebec. Until he became Prime Minister, in 1968, he was not considered sufficiently important to have a listing in the Canadian *Who's Who*. Just a little more than a year ago, when Marc

Lalonde, a Montreal lawyer who is now Trudeau's Principal Secretary and administrative Chief of Staff, suggested to Jacques Hébert, a French-Canadian writer and publisher who is one of Trudeau's closest friends, the possibility of Trudeau's becoming Prime Minister, Hébert pronounced the idea "wonderful but crazy." Hébert has said since, "I could see ten years ago that he was perfect for the job, but I thought it not at all possible that in a democracy a man so well prepared as Pierre, so unlike the traditional politician, could be Prime Minister."

The aspect of Trudeau's complex personality that has caught the public imagination is his ability to "swing" — to close the gap between his own age, which is forty-nine, and the long-haired, miniskirted generation. When he was a bachelor Cabinet minister, his personal eccentricities fascinated a country that puts considerable stress on the proprieties. He would go to his office in Ottawa's austere Parliament Buildings in sports jacket, ascot, and sandals; he might stand on his head, walk on his hands, dive into a swimming pool fully clothed, or slide down bannisters in public places; he would drive a motorcycle or the latest-model sports car while wearing a leather coat, perhaps in the company of a ravishing beauty of less than half his age. In his term as Minister of Justice, during which he introduced legislation that has broadened the grounds for divorce, liberalized the laws on abortion, and abolished penalties for homosexual acts between consenting adults, he remarked, "The state has no business in the bedrooms of the nation," and the remark was repeated with delight around the world. After he won the leadership of the Liberal Party, in April, 1968, and succeeded Pearson as Prime Minister, Trudeau called a general election for June, in the hope of obtaining a clear working majority in the House of Commons. In the ensuing campaign, his every quip made the headlines, and he was photographed dancing in the streets and kissing his way across the country. Kissing is as common a greeting in French Canada as handshaking is elsewhere, yet Trudeau's charm produced a nationwide reaction so powerful that it was given a name of its own — "Trudeaumania." For many Canadians, stirred up by the grand-scale celebration the previous year of a century of nationhood, Pierre Trudeau personified the centennial spirit and promised a fresh start for the second century of Canadian history.

The countless facets of Trudeau's personality inspire a wonderful variety of reactions. The view of a political enemy: "Pierre is conservative, but in the campaign he was passed off as having flowers in his mouth. He is one of the best-equipped men intellectually, but this is not enough until the ancient dream of a republic of philosophers is realized. His greatest weakness is aristocratic arrogance tied to no experience. He's a dabbler, a dilettante, an easy-going bachelor who likes travelling around the world and will soon get fed up with the job."

An official of the Liberal Party headquarters: "Mr. Trudeau is a contemporary man, who looks, acts, and thinks the way we all believe a man of the twentieth century should. He is an IBM computer. He is hip. He is thoughtful, worldly, exciting, candid. Somebody's going to say someday, 'Will the real Mr. Trudeau please stand up,' and about fifty-eight people will rise."

A left-wing Member of Parliament: "He is cautious and conservative, with nothing new or exciting to offer but his manner, which some people find exciting. He is a suspended brain, not fed much by the spirit, detached and cold. I think he's warm in personal relationships, but he is not sensitive to the needs and stirrings in the lower strata of society."

A prominent civil servant: "The Prime Minister has the most precise and logical mind I have ever worked with, a brilliant and versatile mind. He's a bundle of contradictions, different from what you would expect. He is mentally fresh and young, a superb companion. You might think he's frivolous, but he is intensely serious — a very hardworking person, who seldom takes time off for recreation."

An old friend: "The playboy image of Pierre reflects one-tenth of one per cent of his activity. Pierre is always challenging, provoking, shocking, so that no one can see what he's really like. He keeps us guessing all the time, which is what he wants. He is arrogant with people who don't know anything, and he himself has a passionate eagerness to know, to see and learn. He respects competence. He is an individualist who is always challenging himself, and who will always be lonely. He has one consistent personality trait, and this may be what some people don't like: to go through with anything he starts, and through to the end."

"My life is one long curve, full of turning points. Like Einstein, I feel that space is curved," Pierre Trudeau said recently to a visitor, in one of his rare moments of relaxation on a working day. The two were sitting at lunch in the three-story rectangular gray stone house at 24 Sussex Drive, Ottawa, that is the official residence of Canada's Prime Ministers. It is a modest house in a lovely setting of lawns and rosebushes and petunia beds, with a crab-apple tree in the garden, and there is a view from the enclosed sun porch in the back across the Ottawa River to the Gatineau Hills, in Quebec Province, and a narrow white church spire in the Quebec town of Hull. The furnishings of the residence are those of a middle-class home: black leather

and brown overstuffed chairs in a small, panelled library; chintz couches around a fireplace in a gray-carpeted, gray-walled living room; and, beside a window looking out on the river, a piano, which former Prime Minister Pearson played when he thought nobody could hear him. Mrs. Pearson's taste in interior decorating dominates the rooms; Prime Minister Trudeau has changed nothing but the paintings, on loan from the National Gallery. He shows a marked preference for Abstract Expressionist works by Canadians, and especially for artists who have been his personal friends, among them the late Paul-Émile Borduas, Jean-Paul Lemieux, Alfred Pellan, and Micheline Beauchemin, creator of a handsome tapestry rug that hangs above a curving staircase in the hall.

The Prime Minister had arrived for lunch at one-thirty, half an hour behind schedule, bounding into the room with a broad smile of welcome, looking extremely natty in a well-tailored conservative brown suit, a striped tie, and a blue shirt that exactly matched his eyes. He is a slim, athletic man of medium height. His receding brown hair is just beginning to gray, and there is a small bald patch at the back. His features are pleasantly irregular—high cheekbones, which give his face a faintly Oriental cast; a slightly aquiline nose; and a large mouth with very white, even teeth. His eyes are luminous, and of a blue so brilliant that the effect of his gaze is startling to some people, even a bit frightening. He looks at one with such intensity, seeming to listen with his eyes, that the object of his attention is apt to feel that every word spoken must be significant.

The Prime Minister apologized for his tardiness, and offered his visitor a cocktail. He was delighted when it was refused, "Good!" he said. "Then we can go right in and eat." He sat down at the lunch table and poured chilled dry white wine into small cut-crystal glasses, remarking that he drank very little and didn't smoke at all. "I'm not willing to sacrifice the control of physical and mental ability that drinking and smoking take away for what they give in return," he said. "I used to tell myself that smoking impaired the memory, and in time I believed that it did. I have always thought, Why should I lose even a little bit of my memory, since it is not all that good? Also, in my early boyhood I was frailer than most boys and I thought I had to be more careful. I still have to average eight hours' sleep. I think I just have to have that. I can go for weeks or months on five hours or so of sleep, as I did during the election campaign, but afterward I have to make up for it by sleeping twelve or thirteen hours."

There are many Trudeaus in Canada (more than six hundred are listed in the Montreal phone book), and, according to the Prime

Minister, the first Trudeau arrived in Canada from France in either 1628 or 1632. The Prime Minister's father, Charles-Émile, who died in 1935, was a farmer's son who was trained as a lawyer and became a very successful businessman. Pierre Trudeau's mother, who is ill and lives in retirement in Montreal, was Grace Elliott, the daughter of a Scottish father and a French-Canadian mother. Pierre Trudeau grew up speaking both English and French at home, and is totally bilingual, but he believes that he writes with greater precision in French. In conversation, he is soft-spoken in either language, but he is also a superb orator. He speaks vibrantly in French, but in English, when he is tired, his voice can drop to a lifeless monotone.

Trudeau, whose distaste for growing older runs to a vagueness about his birth date, although he is otherwise precise about detail, was born on October 18, 1919. He has an older sister, Suzette — a shy but composed and friendly woman, who is married to a dentist in Montreal and has three children — and a brother, Charles, two and a

Illustration by Thomas B. Allen

169

half years his junior. Charles is quiet and sensitive, and shares with his brother a deep love of the Canadian wilderness. An architect by profession, married but childless, Charles Trudeau is an expert skier and swimmer, and has become absorbed in art, music, and outdoor living, dwelling in a woodland area in the Laurentian Mountains in a striking modern house of his own design. Pierre Trudeau's most zealously guarded possession, next to his time, is his privacy, which also involves the right to privacy for his immediate family, with whom he has an affectionate relationship. Whenever he can, he slips off to Montreal for a weekend (and he is likely to stay at a different hotel each time) and, after Sunday mass, pays a visit to his mother. During his backbreaking coast-to-coast election campaign last year, he managed to find a telephone every night at seven o'clock and call her up.

Trudeau's father, who is said to have amassed at least a million dollars — now considerably increased — from service stations, real estate, and investments that included an amusement park and a baseball club, was a sporty extrovert, whom everyone called Charlie. Pierre was fifteen when his father died. In the curve of Trudeau's life, his friends believe, his father's death produced a deep sense of responsibility toward his family, which he still feels.

"My father taught me order and discipline and my mother freedom and fantasy," the Prime Minister said, beginning the first course of the lunch — lentil soup. He has an expressive face, and it lights up as he speaks about people he loves. When he can, he likes to lunch informally at a small table in a bay window of the dining room, facing the garden and the view, as he and his visitor were doing on this day. The dining room proper is a large chamber with two huge crystal chandeliers above a long, handsome mahogany table, which can seat twenty-two. The table is frequently filled, because Trudeau likes to discuss the nation's affairs at dinner two or three nights a week.

The Prime Minister finished his soup and, as the next course was being served, said, "My father believed in things done well. My mother was a great respecter of the freedom of her children and was always prepared to take a chance. I suppose that because my father gave us a strong disciplinary base I could make good use of that freedom. If I was going to take off for James Bay, for example, she would say, 'So long. Have a nice trip, and don't get drowned.' She never said, 'Why don't you work or study instead?' She just said, 'I'll expect you back when I see you.' She was like that about my friends, too — never said I couldn't bring someone home. She wasn't always off to parties, didn't break down and weep, never took things too tragically, never imposed her wishes on us. She left her children free. What happened is that my parents probably lived in a way that I found sound and I tended to imitate them. They didn't preach."

For years, Trudeau's mother, small, delicate, elegant, serene, was a *grande dame* to those who saw her at museums and concerts. During the Second World War, when there was not much cultural activity in Montreal, Pierre and Charles Trudeau regularly invited their friends to Sunday-night concerts of classical music from their collection of records. "The concerts were attended by forty or fifty people, or even more, most of them artists and writers," Guy Viau, deputy director of the National Gallery in Ottawa, who has known Trudeau since they were both twelve, recalled recently. "The Trudeaus were fond of music and wanted to share it, although inviting so many people was something quite new for such a reserved family. Guests sat in the basement playroom, where the record-player was, and all the way up the stairs, and in the rooms on the ground floor, where the boys had put up extra speakers. We were all very serious, not social—it was just for music lovers." Another friend remembers that Mme. Trudeau used to remain on the second floor during the concerts but would come down later to say hello. "She would drift through the room, looking as if she weren't listening to the conversation, and then suddenly come out with a remark right to the point," he said. "She was intelligent, very clever, and the most charming person you can imagine. She was something like Pierre. We always suspected that she knew a lot more than she cared to say."

The Prime Minister's mother still lives in the family house, on McCulloch Street, off the broad Chemin de la Côte de Sainte-Catherine, in the Outremont section of Montreal, which is an old, prosperous residential area. McCulloch Street climbs an extremely steep hill, which levels off into a plateau of large houses and spacious grounds. Very few of the people walking or pushing bicycles up the hill seem to know where the Prime Minister's family house is. The Trudeau house is on a narrow lot, and is smaller than the ones surrounding it—a modest structure of brownish brick, with an old-fashioned front porch. The interior is conventional early-nineteen-twenties, except for several paintings on the walls in the downstairs rooms by Georges Braque, a friend and neighbor of Trudeau's uncle Gordon Elliott, a landscape architect who once lived in France. The only decoration that any of Trudeau's friends can remember in his room is a few paintings, and shelves filled with books from floor to ceiling. "A chair, an old desk, maybe a few souvenirs from trips—otherwise books and more books," says Jacques Hébert. Until a year ago,

Trudeau also kept a flat on Sherbrooke Street, in the center of Montreal. It was a one-room kitchenette apartment, and, like his quarters at home, it had a Spartan quality. "A place to go, with a lot of books there," Hébert says. "He doesn't like luxury."

A mile or so from the McCulloch Street house—a short bicycle ride for a boy in his teens—are the big, classical-style cream-colored brick buildings of the Jesuit Collège de Jean-de-Brébeuf, which the Prime Minister attended between the ages of twelve and twenty, leaving with a Bachelor of Arts degree.

"I suppose the man who most influenced me as a student was Father Robert Bernier, a French Canadian from Manitoba," the Prime Minister said, a warm note in his voice. He had just finished second helpings of fish soufflé and of cucumbers with sour cream and was sitting back while the table was cleared for dessert. "Father Bernier was the most highly cultivated man I had met, and he confirms what I am always saying—that you can be a damned good French Canadian outside Quebec. Bernier was the man who talked politics to me. He was my teacher of letters—of French literature. We used to go to school six days a week, and to Mass on Sunday, so school was almost a complete life, even for day students. That Bernier's mind was wonderful! He not only made you study the right works but incited you to read."

"Pierre must have been sixteen or seventeen when he was my pupil," Father Bernier told a visitor not long ago. "It was the academic year 1936-37, and I was twenty-five, in the second year of my teaching." Father Bernier, now fifty-eight, who left Brébeuf in 1939, is a philosopher and political scientist and the author of books on international politics. He lives in Quebec City, where he is the rector of Villa Manrese—a comfortable old house set back from the street behind a curved driveway—which is a Jesuit retreat house and residence for priests. Father Bernier, a quick-moving man with a firm manner, a ready smile, and alert eyes behind rimless glasses, led his visitor to a quiet room in the Villa, and there, after lighting a cigarette, he apologized for his English and settled back in his chair to talk. "Brébeuf was a typical classical school, and my course was belles-lettres," he began. "There were about fifty in my class, and the idea was to train a boy's mind and personality so that he would be ready for anything and would learn rapidly. It was quite a special group, and Pierre was one of the best. I don't present myself as knowing him intimately, but I saw the man emerge from the boy. Nothing in his thinking or acting surprises me. I thought, A boy like that will be a leader. But Prime Minister? No, no, I wasn't that much of a prophet!"

Father Bernier asked if his English was clear enough. Reassured that it was, he continued, "We were very close, the boys and I. Part of the teaching was the idea of meeting a man, of getting to know him deeply. I was young myself, discovering the world of culture and America at the same time they did. We passed books back and forth. Literature, philosophy, music, painting—all went together. We lamented the lack of museums in Montreal, but we got acquainted with Cézanne, Renoir, Degas, Gauguin, Manet, van Gogh, and the ultimate, Picasso—and even the sculptor Maillol—through reproductions in books. In architecture, we bought the books of Le Corbusier. Great music was beginning to be heard in Montreal, with Wilfred Pelletier conducting there. We wouldn't miss any concerts if we could help it, especially if they included our favorites—Fauré, Debussy, Stravinsky. And, of course, there were records. All this was a bit cut off from the atmosphere of daily life, but these were the sons of bourgeois, and didn't have money troubles, so they could throw themselves into art and beauty. Pierre Trudeau was among the most enthusiastic, and, like all intelligent boys, a bit avant-garde. We lived in a little world by ourselves—no television yet, of course, and the social conditioning of the families kept the boys from being much interested in political change. It was an atmosphere of elation, where everything was beautiful."

Father Bernier leaned forward eagerly in his chair. "I also gave them a history course," he said. "I insisted not only on facts and dates but on thoughts: the importance of the democratic spirit and the idea of federalism as a way of having political unity and cultural differences in the same country—a pluralistic society, with a sense of the universal and a love of differences for themselves, where outside all the differences of nation, religion, sex, color, and so on, a man is a man, and is respected as such. I think the boys got something out of it. In addition, I taught them French, Greek, and Latin literature, and although this was a typical modern French culture—oh, a very French atmosphere—it was open to other streams of thought, like Tagore, the Indian poet, and outside of class we would read and discuss, in English, Hemingway, Faulkner, Henry James, Hawthorne, and Thoreau, particularly what Thoreau said about the wilderness, which was very appealing to Canadians. We could enter easily into the mind of Locke, de Tocqueville, Acton, Jefferson. Our little life gave the boys respect for the rational, an instinctive repulsion against the rising Fascism and Nazism. I insisted on a respect for man-made beauty. I insisted on that. They had to understand that our real men are not destroyers but builders—of society, of poetry and of beauty—and that all these things are linked together. I remember reciting a phrase from Paul Valéry's 'Eupalinos, or The Architect': 'I built so much I think I finally built myself.' I used to give the boys Plato as a model of intellectual courage—the man who by himself caused the Greeks to pass from a mythical to a rational mode of knowledge. You could feel that Pierre had this kind of courage. Even as a boy, he would say what he thought anyplace. I would like to use a French word about Pierre—*intelligent*, which is the highest praise. And if I had anything else to note, it would be his deep honesty—*probité*."

There was a knock at the door, and a priest entered with a steaming coffeepot. Father Bernier poured the coffee, then ignored it. His mind was elsewhere. "My father studied law, was stung by the political fly, and passed all his life in the Manitoba Parliament. He was very French, but he read exclusively in English—everything from Newman and Burke to Winston Churchill—and I remember hearing him make a speech and thinking he had a political outlook that was British. Well, Pierre is in advance of most of us. He is a prototype of what the French Canadians can be in a few years, if the extremists don't get the upper hand."

Leaning forward again, his hands pressed together, he said, "I will explain. The social and cultural personality of French Canada has four components. The first is the old, traditional society, whose people have kept many characteristics of Old France but are Canadians first, dynamic and arrogant. After the British conquest in 1763, when economic and political power passed out of French hands, French Canada became a country of workers and peasants under the guidance of priests, doctors, and lawyers, with the church at the center of every small town, and with a strong emphasis on family values. The second component is the contact with modern France over the last fifty years. French Canadians have made trips to Europe and have bought French books, and when Pierre was a boy this cultural impact was great. The third component is the effect of the British, through business contacts and parliamentary institutions. The British type of democracy has affected us deeply, for we are in the system, now more than ever. The fourth component, the impact of the United States, is getting more important every day. American civilization has the power of seduction, and our young people are more and more American in outlook. So, you see, the French Canadian has all that to digest. He wants to be himself in his bones and keep his own values, and he fears that he will lose his personality. Pierre has assimilated and dominated these differences. He has the brilliance of the French intellectual, the grave manner of the British parliamentarian, and the dynamic organization and efficiency of the American. But we know him as one of us, a French Canadian who likes to talk and be flippant when he lets himself go."

Father Bernier now remembered his coffee and drank it. "Pierre has taken on a tremendous job — keeping this country together," he said. "He is placing very efficient machinery in Ottawa, and his great strength in building will to a certain extent correct his own intuitions, which are not infallible. But his values are the same as they always were: a deep respect for the other man, a respect for things beautiful, and a revulsion against anything mediocre. *C'est un homme qui a des grandes exigences envers lui-même* — who asks much of himself — so he has a right to ask much of others."

As his visitor was leaving, Father Bernier said, "Even as a boy, Pierre needed a sense of dedication. To swallow the world takes a long time, and he started by getting an international background — preparing himself for anything and waiting to see where he could best go. I think he really committed himself to Canada with the magazine *Cité Libre*. We had the Duplessis government in Quebec, and the occasion was right. The domination of the clergy over political matters at that time in Quebec was detestable. They had been the most learned men for a couple of hundred years, and everyone had consulted them, but then they became detrimental to liberty and it was time for them to step back into the religious life. Pierre thinks, as a political man should, about the order in this world. Religion is something else; it's what to do to get into the other world."

> *"My teachers used to say that for a Catholic I was pretty much of a Protestant," the Prime Minister told his luncheon companion. "I believed in the Protestants' rule of conscience, and that you must not deliberately hurt others." He had been eating a dessert of stewed peaches, and now he paused with his spoon in the air. "So I try not to hurt people, and when I do I feel it is a sin. That's the only really basic sin — to hurt others. I was very much impressed by what George Bernard Shaw said about Joan in the preface to his play about her. She was the kind of Catholic I probably am. What she called her voices I call my conscience."*

The magazine *Cité Libre*, which usually had a circulation of about twenty-five hundred, was at times the only voice in Quebec openly opposing the corrupt Union Nationale regime of Premier Maurice Duplessis, the local tyrant, whose government was in power from 1936 to 1939 and from 1944 to 1960, a year after Duplessis's death. *Cité Libre* was founded by ten men, Trudeau among them, who in

1950 put up twenty-five dollars each to publish five hundred copies of the first issue, but the guiding hand was that of the distinguished French-Canadian journalist Gérard Pelletier. Trudeau has the capacity for deep and lasting friendship, and his relationship with Pelletier and Pelletier's wife, Alec, a television playwright, is especially close. Nine out of ten times when Trudeau feels a need to be in the company of friends, he goes to see the Pelletiers. Gérard Pelletier is now the Secretary of State—a Cabinet post concerned with cultural affairs, broadcasting, education, citizenship, and elections. Trudeau is said to feel that the success of his Government rests on its ability to reform the Canadian constitution, to include, among other things, a provision naming both French and English as the official languages of Canada. Equal status for the two languages is one of the basic principles of Trudeau's "Just Society"—his favorite, if never precisely defined, phrase for expressing his ultimate aims. Parliament is currently considering the Official Languages Bill, which would give the two languages this status, and enable five million French Canadians in Quebec and a million in other provinces to deal with the federal government in French. The responsibility for applying the law, through language courses for government employees, will rest with Secretary of State Pelletier.

"I was nineteen and Pierre was not yet nineteen when we met," Pelletier told a visitor to his office a while ago. He is a slight, dark man with sharp features and an amused, urbane air, who especially seems to embody three characteristics common to Trudeau's circle of intimate friends: intelligence, humor, and warmth. "He came from Outremont, on the right side of the tracks, with a reputation of being quite a *personnage*," Pelletier said. "Mine was a modest background. My father was a railroad employee, and we were eight children. I was editor of an inter-collegiate youth-movement paper that circulated throughout the province, while Pierre was editor of the paper at his aristocratic school." Pelletier pulled at his ear and smiled. "I wrote an article challenging other student editors to define themselves and say where they were going—whether they were literary or performed a function in their environment," he said. "Pierre, exercising his sense of humor, wrote, 'We went down to the basement, put out the lights, and said, "We don't know who we are, and we must find out!"' I thought this so good that I wanted to discover who wrote it. We met, and I liked him, though his flippancy disconcerted me a little. But he was obviously so intelligent."

Pelletier went to work for a Catholic youth movement, and Trudeau took a law degree at the University of Montreal. He graduated with honors in 1943, and then went south to Harvard for a

Master's degree in political economy. The really close relationship between Trudeau and Pelletier began in Europe, in 1946, when Trudeau arrived in Paris to study at the École des Sciences Politiques. "I sensed in Pierre an intellectual capacity that attracted me very much," Pelletier said. "I think he envied me a certain gift of action. I was more involved, because I had to earn a living, and was working in an international student relief agency. He was studying, and I picked his brains as much as I could, since I had no formal training in economics and politics." The next year, Pelletier returned to Canada, and Trudeau enrolled at the London School of Economics, where he studied political science with Harold Laski.

"What a fabulous memory that Laski had!" the Prime Minister exclaimed. Having finished his dessert, he pushed his chair back a little from the lunch table. "A lot of guys thought that Lord Acton was the great forming influence on me," he said. "The truth is that I liked Acton's approach and several of his essays but probably read less of him than several newspaper people studying his influence on me have read since—and less of de Tocqueville, too. Quite frankly, I didn't read de Tocqueville's entire works, and I was well into my thirties by the time I found confirmation in him of my theories of checks and balances. I am very eclectic. I can quote from Plato and from the theories of de Tocqueville and from Montesquieu's 'Laws,' but it would be a mistake to single any one of them out. I bet many people in my position have read more than I have in the field of history and economics. I have probably read more of Dostoevski, Stendhal, and Tolstoy than the average statesman, and less of Keynes, Mill, and Marx. The point I am making is that I am not a scholar of any of these disciplines. I haven't read as much as a good economist, and, being eclectic, I have done a lot of other reading and travelling."

Trudeau left London in 1948 to take a year's trip around the world—a *cours pratique*, Pelletier has called it. Trudeau made a point of travelling to unusual places, and of melting into the stream of the local population wherever he was. Even Jacques Hébert, with whom he has shared many travel experiences, is continually discovering, when he himself is about to depart for some out-of-the-way place—Malaya, say, or Burma—that Trudeau has already been there and can give him a few addresses. "Maybe the face of the world would be different if Mao Tse-tung had travelled as much as Pierre—if he had, for instance, camped on Vancouver Island or walked in the woods of Vermont," Hébert observed recently. "Pierre made all those trips of his in a very intense way."

Hébert, a lively, generous man in his mid-forties, met Trudeau for the first time twenty years ago, in Montreal, at a gathering of travel enthusiasts who assembled every so often to talk about their trips. He has written many travel books, one of them in collaboration with Trudeau, describing a journey they made together—a sort of guided tour of China, in a Chinese-government-sponsored group, in the fall of 1960. The book, a witty, sharp-eyed account of their travels, entitled "Two Innocents in Red China," has lately been translated into English and reissued. "Our friendship has been of the humorous type, telling each other how awful each thought the other was," Hébert remarked. "I had agreed to write the fancy descriptions and leave it to him to fill in the serious economic and political commentary, but when we exchanged what we had written we found that, for fun, each had written the part reserved for the other. It was a game—so much so that Pelletier, reading the book, said, 'That's Pierre's' when it was mine. I asked Pierre if he wanted to read the proofs when 'Two Innocents' was reissued, and he said no, so I said, 'You are the Prime Minister, and I don't want to take on the responsibility' and he laughed and said, 'It's OK. If I have trouble, I'll say you wrote that part.'"

The Prime Minister's French and English speechwriters have also been among his travelling companions. He met his English-language speechwriter, Tim Porteous, in Nigeria, in 1957, during the course of a seminar organized by a group called World University Service. At the time, Porteous was a graduate student at McGill University, and earlier he had written a revue lampooning the government, which toured the country very successfully. Trudeau's French speechwriter, Roger Rolland, who is a handsome man with a clipped gray beard, was a school chum of his in Brébeuf days, and for many years he was unofficially in charge of the practical joker in Trudeau's nature. "I would initiate the practical jokes, but Pierre has so much humor that he would fall in line," Rolland said. "Actually, I don't know a more serious man. If he dives, he won't dive just for the fun of it but will try to improve his technique. At twenty-two, if we were thinking of skiing, he would first have to discuss the idea with himself and see if he had the time for it. If he is going to enjoy himself, he has to plan for it ahead. But when he relaxes, he surely does relax."

When Rolland and Trudeau were students, they dreamed up an informal association called the Agonizers. In answer to the question, "How are you?" they would say, "Very bad," and fall over backwards, breaking the fall with their hands just in time. This made quite an impression in Montreal living rooms. During the Second World War, Trudeau and his friends uneasily took no part, along with many other French Canadians, in protest against English Canada's broken promises concerning conscription. In Quebec, after the First World War, the Liberals never missed an opportunity to remind people that the Conservatives had forced conscription upon the country in 1917. During the Second World War, after much soul-searching and a nationwide plebiscite, Parliament, under the Liberal Government of Mackenzie King, worked out a compromise whereby a certain number of men could be conscripted for service within Canada but only volunteers would serve overseas. Trudeau—who, his friends say, was longing to fight—felt he could not betray his moral position as a French Canadian. He and his friends used to amuse themselves by donning German helmets, goggles, sabres, and boots and racing through the countryside on motor bikes, scaring people. "Pierre liked to dress up as a German spy from a submarine or as an Army deserter, and he loved to provoke the Mounted Police when they rose to the bait," a friend has recalled. "It was funny once or twice, but I got bored and I asked him why all the fuss. He said he found it a good way to develop confidence in himself and to learn to control the circumstances around him. I think he looked on it as a form of training."

Training for what? Trudeau was following the Jesuit mystique of wanting to have the best mind, be the best athlete, develop the greatest will power and the strongest character. But in his relationship with Gérard Pelletier—a personal application of Trudeau's philosophy of counterbalancing—he was beginning to show purpose. It was Pelletier who involved Trudeau in his first political action, and the two men have been involving each other ever since—first one of them leading, then the other. When Pelletier returned from Europe to Montreal in 1947, he went to work as a reporter for the daily newspaper *Le Devoir* and, while covering a strike, renewed an acquaintance with Jean Marchand, a prominent Quebec labour leader whom he had known as a student. Marchand persuaded Pelletier to work for his Confederation of National Trade Unions, and by the time Trudeau returned from Europe in 1949 he found Pelletier totally involved in a bitter strike by five thousand asbestos workers at mines in Thetford and Asbestos, Quebec. The strike was as much against the oppressive Duplessis government and the repressive elements in the Church as it was against the mines, which were run by a Canadian subsidiary of the Johns-Manville Corporation. "Pierre joined us," Pelletier recalls. "He had grown a beard, which was blond, and the miners christened him St. Joseph. We decided then that something should be done about Quebec, and out of this came *Cité Libre*, in which we hoped to develop our ideas. Pierre, more easily than any of the rest of us, could have escaped and had a brilliant career anyplace as a writer or teacher.

We were the first generation to say, 'God damn it, we'll stay home and change the place.'"

Marchand was impressed by Trudeau, and offered him a job. Trudeau said he did not want to be confined by a permanent job, but from time to time he worked for the union confederation free, representing it in negotiations with the aluminum industry and with the paper and textile industries. Marchand, Pelletier, and Trudeau saw each other constantly for years, and the association finally brought them, with Marchand in the lead, up Ottawa's Parliament Hill, where they became known to English Canadians as the Three Musketeers, or the Three Wise Men, and to French Canadians as the Three Doves, or the Three Virgins of Canadian Politics.

"*Cité Libre* was a curious affair," Pelletier has said. "We would meet every week, and anyone who had written an article read it to the others for criticism. This is why the publication came out so irregularly—just whenever we had time. In 1949, Pierre had gone to Ottawa as an economic adviser to the Privy Council, but he came back to Montreal every weekend for meetings to plan *Cité Libre*, and it was at those meetings that I discovered his ability to communicate his knowledge and ideas to others. He had such a natural superiority over all of us in the international field, and we also discovered how far he had gone in evolving political ideas for French Canada—and for the rest of Canada, too. The meetings were quite informal. We brought our wives, and Pierre brought his girl friends. I would preside, and he would get very impatient if I tolerated any digressions. He is exactly the same at Cabinet meetings now—strict, but in a nice way. He has a particular gift for bringing the conversation back to the subject without offending."

Tact is not always Trudeau's strong point. René Lévesque, a leading Separatist, is a member of the Quebec Parliament who left the Liberal Party in 1967 to help start Le Parti Québécois. Lévesque's group wants to separate Quebec from the rest of Canada, with which it would coexist under vague economic and defense arrangements. "I remember the first time I met Pierre, because I got a bit of the Pierre Trudeau arrogance," Lévesque, who was a well-known journalist before he became a politician, has recalled. "I had come back from overseas and was working for the Canadian Broadcasting Corporation. Pelletier, who was trying to get guys interested in starting *Cité Libre*, introduced us, remarking to Trudeau, 'Maybe we can get him,' to which Trudeau replied, without looking at me, 'Yeah, but can he write?' It would have been better if he had looked at me and said, 'Can you write?' This is part of the trouble with Pierre."

Trudeau is genuinely sorry to have hurt Lévesque's feelings. "I just meant it as a joke," he said recently. "It was my way of complimenting him."

Trudeau spent two years working for the Privy Council in Ottawa. When he had to wait in anterooms of superiors, he would walk around on his hands, for exercise. He was too far down in the bureaucratic hierarchy to be given credit for his work on any published reports, but he did some of the historical research for conferences held to explore ways of amending the federal constitution. He also had an apprenticeship in the complexities of federal-provincial relationships. In a footnote in his recent book, he records that in 1950, at the request of the Privy Council, "I made a summary of existing federal-provincial cooperative arrangements, which covered more than fifty pages."

After leaving Ottawa, Trudeau worked as a labor lawyer, travelled extensively, and wrote for *Cité Libre* and about his travels for the daily press. He also edited, and partially wrote, a book entitled, "La Grève de l'Amiante" ("The Asbestos Strike"), a complete study of the 1949 walkout, a momentous event in Quebec. The book describes how, during the hundred and thirty-five days that the strike lasted, the government, backed by the reactionary wing of the Church, fought a vicious battle against the workers. The strike was a turning point in Quebec history, because, for the first time, people engaged in what came to be known as the Quiet Revolution—the fight for Quebec's freedom—became aware of their identity and their combined strength. "La Grève de l'Amiante," a collaborative effort involving scholars, lawyers, union officials, and journalists—including Pelletier—was published in 1956. Trudeau wrote an exhaustive first chapter, about Quebec's backwardness and immobility, and he also wrote the last chapter, a summing up. That same year, he also helped form La Rassemblement, an organization of people from every political party whose primary aim was to get rid of Duplessis. Le Rassemblement lasted three years, during which it acquired many antagonists, among them members of a Socialist group called the New Democratic Party, or NDP. Although Trudeau has worked closely with the NDP, he partly blames it for killing Le Rassemblement. The NDP men, for their part, regard Trudeau as a deserter, pointing out that in 1963 he was campaigning for a close NDP friend, Charles Taylor, in the very constituency in which, running as a Liberal, he defeated him two years later, and also in 1963 was attacking Liberal Prime Minister Pearson—who had won the Nobel Peace Prize in 1957—as "Le Defroqué de la Paix" ("The Unfrocked Priest of Peace") for permitting nuclear warheads on Canadian soil when he had previously opposed them.

"Quite frankly, I didn't enter the NDP in earlier years because I was not ready to make up my mind, and later I didn't believe in it, because the ideology was wrong," the Prime Minister said. "It was a basic difference of orientation. In those days, the NDP didn't think it was important to do anything in Quebec. They were all for the Ottawa boys, and the Ottawa boys won. We said, 'We have to reform Quebec before going on to Ottawa.' So we disagreed. Ironically, a lot of people who were fighting us then because we gave too much importance to Quebec have since become Separatists, or at least want special status for Quebec. In other words, the swing went full circle."

At the time Trudeau left Ottawa, he hoped to teach at the University of Montreal — a logical but not a realistic ambition in Duplessis's Quebec. Trudeau was barred from the faculty of the university for ten years, or until two years after the death of Duplessis. When his supporters pressed for action, the university authorities always had a handy collection of excuses: they were afraid he might stir up the students to rebellion; that he was a Communist or a Socialist; or that, anyway, he was a dilettante, who would stay for six months and then go off somewhere on a trip.

"It became a cliché to call me a dilettante, just because I didn't live on the same rhythm as other people," the Prime Minister said impatiently. He was clearly annoyed; his eyes were icy blue. "Just because I wasn't in court or teaching every day, people didn't realize that I worked. Many of my friends didn't even realize that I had an office. I would be working for a trade union, or I would go off for six months, and they didn't know I had written three articles, or a third of 'L'Amiante,' while I was away. I wasn't married and settled down, and I wasn't showing up to toot my horn. I was working much harder than any of the people who called me a dilettante. If a person works in an office from nine to five, plays golf at a country club, and spends his weekends in the country, he is not a dilettante. But if he is reading or writing sixteen hours a day and not doing things that people can see, he is a dilettante. They say this about artists, who do not go to work. They imagine them up in an attic sleeping with the models, when actually they may be painting ten or twelve pictures."

After the end of the Duplessis regime, Trudeau was invited, with what he has described as "almost indecent haste," to become a member of the Montreal faculty. Two departments wooed him — Political Science and Law. Jean Beetz, a professor of constitutional law, who is now dean of the Law School and one of the Prime Minister's principal advisers on constitutional reform, had at the time just become director of a new Public Law Research Institute, and Trudeau was one of his first appointments. "Another department wanted him, too," Dean Beetz said, "so we both *did* approach him with haste. He chose to come to the Faculty of Law." When Trudeau was asked to list his academic credentials after joining the faculty, he wrote down, among other things, "Brown Belt"—the award given to judo students who achieve the second-highest degree of proficiency.

Trudeau enjoyed teaching, although he has described the university atmosphere as "rather sterile." He is still technically on leave, and listed in the university catalogue as associate professor of law and member of the Research Institute. In his field, which was human rights, he was a provocative lecturer, and he encouraged students to come to his office before and after lectures to talk. As Prime Minister, he thoroughly enjoys question-and-answer sessions with university students, and will more readily make that kind of public appearance than any other. He was a demanding teacher, challenging his students and growing impatient with any who hadn't done their homework, and he was a controversial figure on the campus. Many students at the university are radical, which in Quebec means Separatist. The non-conformist aspect of Trudeau's personality placed him to the left of center in some people's eyes, but because he was a federalist, who wanted Canada to remain united, the out-and-out Separatists regarded him as a reactionary.

Actually, Trudeau's political philosophy is thoroughly pragmatic, and whenever a need or an opportunity arises to practice what he teaches he jumps right in. Never does he do this more eagerly than in defense of an old friend. In 1956, Jacques Hébert, who is a passionate civil-libertarian, became convinced that a Canadian named Wilbert Coffin had been unjustly executed for the murder of three American hunters, killed in 1953 in the Gaspé region. Hébert set out to prove Coffin's innocence, and wrote a book in which he accused the Quebec government of murdering him. The government responded by setting up a Royal Commission of Inquiry. Hébert voluntarily spent five days a week for a year before the Commission in Quebec City, but it issued a report unfavorable to him, whereupon he was charged by the government with contempt and was suddenly clapped into jail. Trudeau, who had given him legal help during the inquiry, got him out on bail, and Hébert eventually won his case. "It was a crazy thing for me to do, to start a fight without money or means," Hébert said recently, sitting in a small upstairs office of his publishing firm on the Rue Saint-Denis, in the old part of Montreal. "Pierre's office was nearby, and we used to eat in a very simple restaurant on the corner—

really quite a poor one. You certainly wouldn't take a girl there — certainly not. Well, Pierre is the kind of man who won't pick up the check for his friends — even if it is only a dollar and a half — because it would destroy a kind of dignity in their relationship. But when one of those friends is in real difficulty, he will discreetly lend him thousands. Pierre was the first to offer his services, even though he was not altogether happy about some of the things I had put in my book, because they were difficult to prove. When I went to Quebec City for the inquiry, he said, 'I want to represent you, but I am a civil, not a criminal, lawyer, and your case won't be completely secure with me.' For my part, I didn't want him thrown out of his teaching job after he had waited so long for it, so we engaged a very fine criminal lawyer. Even so, Pierre came as often as he could to Quebec City the first month, and his presence gave me quite a lot of prestige. And, on the last day, he came and sat down with me, to show the Commission, and the public, he was there. When I was thrown into jail in Quebec City, Pierre came running after me, right up to my cell door. He laughed and said, 'Look at you here, in your jailbird costume!' He helped to plead my case before the judge during both the government suit and my appeal, and he was marvellous."

Most French-Canadian intellectuals would rather meet than sleep — or, possibly, eat. Their solution for any pressing political problem is immediately to call a meeting. In 1963, sporadic bombings by Separatists in the streets of Montreal inspired Trudeau and six younger men, who were groping for a constructive approach to the growing Canadian disunion, to hold a series of Friday-night meetings. There were, besides Trudeau, three university professors, a psychoanalyst, and two lawyers — one of whom was Marc Lalonde, now the Prime Minister's chief aide and principal political adviser. Lalonde had met Trudeau briefly in 1949, when he sought advice from him on whether to study law or social science, but he did not really come to know Trudeau until 1960, which was when Lalonde began writing for *Cité Libre*. The Friday-night meetings produced a four-page document entitled "Manifesto for the Nation," which was published in the Montreal *Star* on May 14, 1964. A rebuttal of the Separatist position, it was a scathing denunciation of economic and political conditions in Canada. By the time the "Manifesto" appeared, Marchand, Pelletier, and Trudeau were already considering their triple march toward Ottawa.

Trudeau's ascendancy was a political accident. It came about because Marchand declined to run as a candidate for the leadership of the Liberal Party when Pearson announced his intention to resign, in December, 1967. Marchand's prestige in Quebec as a labor leader had brought him to the attention of the national leaders of the Party, who were looking for a French Canadian capable of holding the country together after Pearson stepped down. If he had chosen otherwise, Jean Marchand might very possibly be the Prime Minister of Canada today. A slight, gray-haired man of fifty with a small mustache and glasses, he is gentle-looking, despite his reputation as a tough labor leader. He is a worldly, humorous person, very Gallic and down-to-earth. In Trudeau's Government, he is Minister for Regional Economic Expansion, which means that he is in charge of plans to bring Canada's depressed areas into Trudeau's Just Society. In his office, Marchand recently traced for a visitor the events that brought him and Pelletier and Trudeau to national prominence. He seemed noticeably fatigued; his health is said to be precarious.

"Pierre and Gérard were not very well known, and they insisted I be the one to make the decision to enter politics," Marchand began. "They said they would follow if I made up my mind. In the general election of 1963, Pearson wanted me to run for Parliament. Things in French Canada were becoming worse and worse, and we thought it essential for the new generation of French Canadians to become involved in federal politics. I made it a condition that Trudeau and Pelletier join me. Pearson and his people were a little reluctant, but they agreed. I was convinced that one French Canadian in Ottawa alone would be destroyed—that there needed to be several of us. And I think it's still true."

Marchand shifted in his chair and sighed. "We three were opposed to having American nuclear weapons established in Canada. A few weeks before the election, Pearson changed his mind and announced he would accept such weapons on Canadian soil, so we refused to run. The Liberals were elected as a minority Government, and everything seemed to be disintegrating. In November, 1965, there was another general election. Again Pearson insisted that I run." Marchand closed his eyes for a second, then continued, "The nuclear warheads were no longer a public issue, so I made the same condition. I said, 'I'll run if you accept Trudeau and Pelletier.' Pearson's people were again reluctant, but finally succeeded in getting them ridings—constituencies in which to run. For Pierre, they chose Mount Royal, a suburb of Montreal. We were all elected. Right away I became Minister of Manpower and Immigration. I started working at once to get ministerial offices for the others." He paused and took a sip of water. "So in January, 1966, Pierre was appointed Parliamentary Secretary to the Prime Minister," he continued. "This was a very difficult step for Pearson to take, because Pierre had been so critical of him a couple of years earlier, and the reaction in the caucus of the

Liberal Members of Parliament was violent. Some of them said that Pierre was not a Liberal and the Party shouldn't have accepted him. Well, in the spring of 1967, the Minister of Justice retired, and I thought that afforded a good opportunity to put Pierre in the Cabinet. After a few weeks, Mr. Pearson agreed, and there was a second violent reaction in the Liberal caucus." He smiled. "In December, the Prime Minister told his Cabinet that he intended to resign as soon as a qualified successor could be chosen. A few friends in the Cabinet had been meeting together, including Trudeau and me. We were looking for a prospective leader. They were unanimous that I should run. No one mentioned Pierre Trudeau's name." He laughed softly. "That December, Pierre introduced his bill on divorce in the House of Commons, and made such a big case for it that almost overnight he became a public figure. I had always been the prospective candidate, but I had always refused. I am deeply rooted in Quebec, and I see that fact as deeply dangerous, because as Prime Minister I would have to represent the whole of Canada. So I had a conversation with Pierre. I said, 'The situation is changing, and you have become a potential candidate.'" Marchand stirred restlessly. "Pierre refused," he continued. "He said, 'It's not the reason we came — to take over the Party and the government,' and he said we had plenty of time. I said to him, 'In politics, there is the opportunity, and if we miss it it may not recur.' Pierre left for Tahiti over the Christmas holidays for some scuba diving with Tim Porteous, and I left for a vacation in Florida. I came back before I had intended, to gather support for Pierre. Then Pierre had a second chance to reach the Canadian public — as Minister of Justice at the first of the federal-provincial conferences on constitutional reform. He performed there particularly well." Marchand smiled and appeared to relax. "There was no doubt in my mind then that he was a serious candidate. What he had been lacking six months before he now had. Besides, he was intelligent, a good lawyer, a good economist, perfectly bilingual, healthy, rich, young, and a bachelor. The Liberal Party in Montreal was still hesitant, but the 'Draft Trudeau' movement increased in strength. Pierre formally became a candidate on a Thursday night in February when a group of us met in his office in the Parliament Buildings. Pierre took out a large trick coin and flipped it, and then, without looking at how it had come up, said, 'OK!' And we started the show."

Marchand went on, "Pierre makes a very good Prime Minister. He works very hard and is very responsible, and he's got a lot of support among the people. That surprised me at first. But I think he performed well on TV, and I think he has a personal magnetism we didn't notice, because we were too near him. The goals we wanted to attain when we came to Ottawa were to integrate Quebec into the federal government and show that French Canada can achieve something with Ottawa if everyone works hard and consents to play the game, to get rid of dangerous regional disparities, and to have some kind of civil-rights bill enacted. Well, it's still not certain we can achieve all of them. But Pierre is tougher than Pearson. He's highly disciplined. He's refreshing, too. After the Liberal Party Convention, we went to Florida to work on the reorganization of the Cabinet, and he said, 'Let's go for a swim.' He started diving—he dives very well—and people asked, 'Who's that man?' And I said, 'The Prime Minister of Canada,' and they said, 'Ha, ha!' They didn't believe a Prime Minister could be such a good diver."

"I began to think about the Liberals as a possibility when we founded Le Rassemblement, and a few years later I was urging people to vote Liberal," the Prime Minister said. "Friends made an effort to have me accepted as a parliamentary candidate of the Liberal Party in 1960, but the leaders didn't want me. Later, Lévesque entered the Party and tried to draw in Marchand, Pelletier, and me. The Party told him no. The main reason was our attack on Mr. Pearson's reversal of his nuclear stand in 1963. I happen to be against the proliferation of nuclear arms. If we permit them, why couldn't the Cubans have theirs—and everyone else who desires them? The Liberal Party had committed itself to no warheads since 1958, and Mr. Pearson reversed their stand without broad consultation within the Party. I was strongly opposed to the way he did it. As for Pearson's nuclear policy, in time he and I put our differences aside. We both felt that now he was taking me and I was taking him for better or worse. This was true of the Liberal Party, too." He added, smiling, "The coin I tossed was a great big green-and-red one given me by Pearson's Secretary of State, Judy LaMarsh, in a Cabinet meeting. It said 'Yes' on the green side and 'No' on the red one. She was telling me to make up my mind to run or not to run. But at the meeting where I tossed the coin I had already made up my mind. I had done that a day or so earlier, while walking around the Parliament Buildings until two o'clock in the morning. How did I make up my mind?" He stopped smiling. He seemed to forget that anyone else was there. Then he answered himself rapidly, in a low voice, "I was pushed."

Probably the first person to think seriously that Pierre Trudeau could be the next Prime Minister was Marc Lalonde, in the spring of 1967. Characteristically, he held meetings every Saturday with two friends to plan a course of action. Lalonde, the son of a politically-minded Quebec farmer, is a determined, methodical French Canadian with a seemingly unlimited capacity for work. Well over six feet tall, he towers over Trudeau, and, when the two are together, gives the impression of standing protectively on all sides of the Prime Minister at once. All documents that go into Cabinet meetings cross his desk, and he is one of the four people who see the Prime Minister every morning. He first broached to Trudeau the question of the leadership of the Liberal Party in November, 1967, and when Pearson announced his intention to resign Lalonde started trying to pin Trudeau down. Trudeau would say yes and then say no, but more often it was simply no. He said he wasn't ready, wondered if they were being influenced by the press and fake publicity, worried about Party support and the possibility of an ignominious defeat, in which case their reasons for going into Parliament at all would be destroyed. When Trudeau went off to Tahiti, Lalonde thought he would still say no after his return. Then came the night when Trudeau donned a large coat made of wildcat fur, which is one of his favorite possessions, and took his long and lonely walk around Parliament Hill until 2 a.m. Trudeau had promised to meet Pelletier and Marchand for breakfast in the parliamentary restaurant that morning. Marchand and Pelletier were there first, and when Trudeau arrived they immediately began talking about inconsequential matters. Trudeau finally said, "Aren't you interested in my decision?" To which one of them replied, "So much so that we are afraid to mention the subject." "I'm running," he said, and by eight-fifteen he had notified Lalonde.

Another early Trudeau backer was a thirty-year-old English Canadian named Gordon Gibson, who was the son of a wealthy logger and politician from British Columbia. In the spring of 1967, Gibson — who, although he was then serving as Executive Assistant to one of Pearson's Cabinet ministers, didn't know Trudeau — started, as a sort of mental exercise, trying to figure out who the next Prime Minister should be. He decided that only a French Canadian would do. At about this time, Gibson's attention was caught by a newspaper article about Trudeau, accompanied by a photograph of him in a yoga pose wearing a turtle neck sweater. When Trudeau was appointed Minister of Justice, Gibson began watching his performance in the House and reading his remarks in *Hansard*, the official daily record of debates. "I was thinking of public acceptance, and he looked good," he said. Gibson is an earnest-looking blond young man who, at first glance, seems a little bit wide-eyed behind his shell-rimmed spectacles but is extremely keen and hardheaded, with a matter-of-fact view of life and a Master's degree from the Harvard Business School. He knew Lalonde, but he did not know that Lalonde and Trudeau were friends.

"One day, I was having a drink with Marc and I said that the only man who could be the next Prime Minister was Pierre Trudeau," Gibson said. "He told me a small group was interested in backing this delightful but unlikely person, and even before Pearson announced his resignation we started small, secret meetings. When I had been working on the plans so long that I felt I ought to meet Trudeau, I called on him at his office and told him he was more acceptable to English Canadians than any English Canadian and, as far as French Canada was concerned, he was the only game in town. Then I wrote him a fifty-page memo about why the country needed him." Gibson stopped and scratched his head. "He didn't give me any encouragement. I asked him after he came back from Tahiti in early January about opening an office, and he replied, 'Do what you think right, but don't tell me.' We kept working, kept holding meetings. Then finally we opened the office, paying the rent with a thousand dollars one of Trudeau's young legal assistants, Eddy Rubin, put up."

At the Liberal Party Convention on April 6th, Trudeau had to impress on the Liberal politicians of the ten provinces of Canada the fact that he possessed the ability to run the country, and he did. For the general election on June 25th, he had to convince people from one end of Canada to the other that they should send Liberal representatives to the House of Commons. In these efforts, his record as Minister of Justice helped. Early in February, the three-day conference on constitutional reform—where, as a legal scholar put it, "Canada began doing in midstream what the United States had done in Philadelphia in 1787"—brought the ten provincial premiers to Ottawa, two months before the Liberal Convention. Beforehand, Prime Minister Pearson had been persuaded by Lalonde and Gibson that Trudeau should pave the way—for the constitutional reforms and for his candidacy—by taking a cross-country trip and meeting with the premiers. Pearson had also suggested that Carl Goldenberg, a leading constitutional lawyer, accompany him. Trudeau made an excellent impression on most of the provincial politicians, once they had figured out which of the two men who debarked from the plane at each stop was the Minister of Justice. Goldenberg, a youthful sixty-one, is small, gray-haired, and dignified, and wore a black hat and blue topcoat, so that he looked like everyone's idea of a Cabinet minister, while Trudeau had on a short leather coat and a fur cap. Goldenberg has said, "Trudeau always insisted I walk out of the plane first, and then he'd follow, carrying the bags. So naturally I would be greeted as the Minister of Justice. When we got back to Ottawa, he was still carrying my bags, right into the hotel where we were staying, and the clerk gave him a very simple room. When Pierre saw mine, he was astonished. 'I didn't know they had rooms like this!' he said."

Several spectacular television appearances probably had more to do with Trudeau's meteoric political success than even the speeches he eventually made at shopping plazas, street corners, and public rallies during the election campaign. Not long before the federal-provincial conference, Trudeau gave an impressive television interview to two prominent CBC newsmen, Norman DePoe and Ron Collister, and on March 26th he turned in a dazzling performance at the St. Lawrence Hall, a historic building in Toronto, where he was introduced to the TV audience in one of a series of programs devoted to Liberal candidates for the leadership. Fraser Kelly, the political editor of the Toronto *Telegram*, asked him what he would think of a politician who, as Prime Minister, might come into the Province of Ontario advocating a constitutional policy opposed by its premier, by its other leading politicians, and by its press, and who was himself opposed by most of the Church in that province. It was obvious that this was a precise description of Trudeau's situation in Quebec, where many Separatists and a large segment of the press had denounced him, some going so far as to call him a traitor. Trudeau replied without hesitation, and with a smile, "I'd say he had a lot of guts"—a remark that brought down the house. The program was again stopped by wild applause after a CBC interviewer, Warner Troyer, paraphrased a quotation to the effect that public men who most want to be leaders try much harder to do a good job than those who don't, and asked Trudeau, "How badly do you want to be Prime Minister?" Trudeau replied, "Not very badly," and went on, "But I can give you another quotation, from Plato—that men who want very badly to head the country shouldn't be trusted."

On the evening of April 4th, two nights before the voting at the Liberal Convention that was to make him Party leader and Prime Minister, when all the delegates had arrived in Ottawa, and many were sitting around in their hotel rooms watching TV, an interviewer, Patrick Watson, talked with Trudeau for an hour on a local station. The show was full of closeup shots of a very warm, human, and thoughtful Trudeau, making the gestures with which the country is now familiar: shrugging his shoulders or using his hands to emphasize a point; making a motion when he explained an idea, almost as if he were physically unwinding it; sighing or pursing his lips when thinking through the answer to a question; smiling courteously or looking at the camera with his amazingly bright eyes, appearing to give the listener the same full attention he gives in a private conversation.

According to Canadian election law, all broadcast electioneering must cease forty-eight hours before the voting, but many people think that a brief drama caught by television cameras the night before the general election in June substantially increased the majority of Prime Minister Trudeau's party. The occasion was the great annual parade in Montreal of an old and influential French-Canadian group called the St. Jean Baptiste Society. At the time, anti-Trudeau sentiments among Quebec Separatists were so strong that pamphlets had been circulated likening the Prime Minister to Machiavelli's Prince and to Mao Tse-tung. (Trudeau's amused friends bought them as souvenirs.) Because there were fears of trouble at the parade, word was passed to its organizers that the Prime Minister did not want to be invited. But, months before, the Society had announced that the Prime Minister *would* be asked, so an official invitation was tendered. Then the Separatist leaders publicly said that it was a shame that Trudeau, a traitor to the French-Canadian cause, should be a guest at the parade. Trudeau, who had meant to decline the invitation, was now challenged and felt he had to accept. The organizers, frightened of a possible disturbance, went to Pelletier the day before the parade and asked him if he could keep Trudeau from coming. Both Trudeau and Pelletier thought it impossible now for Trudeau to appear to be refusing to come, and he is said to have felt that yielding to the Separatists' threats would give them such a feeling of power that Canada's democratic system would be seriously threatened.

The parade began passing the reviewing stand at nine-thirty in the evening on June 24th, and Trudeau was sitting in the front row of the stand, on Sherbrooke Street before the Municipal Library, with Mayor Jean Drapeau of Montreal, the late Premier Daniel Johnson of Quebec, their wives, and a number of other dignitaries, including Archbishop Grégoire of Montreal. There were half a million people at the parade, and clashes between Separatist rioters and police had already led to some violence, although the paraders themselves were orderly. An hour or so later—it usually takes a couple of hours for the floats and bands, the flag-bearing troops, and the various French-Canadian detachments to go past the reviewing stand—bottles suddenly soared over the Prime Minister's head and crashed against the library portico behind him, in full view of the television audience. Everyone in the stand rose in surprise, ducking and covering their heads with their hands. Then a second flight of bottles crashed on the portico, and Trudeau was pushed down by a bodyguard. He immediately rose, shook his fist angrily at the guard, and sat down again determinedly at the front of the stand, leaning forward intently over its bunting-draped edge to watch the paraders below. Meanwhile, the other dignitaries left the stand, many of them pushed by the police, and for a moment the television viewers saw Trudeau sitting alone, with only his bodyguards behind him. Mayor Drapeau, after leading his wife out, returned almost immediately and sat down in the empty seat at Trudeau's right. Trudeau could then be seen smiling, almost laughing, and at one point clasped his hands together in a relaxed gesture of salute. The other people gradually returned to the stand. The whole incident appeared on TV screens for a matter of minutes, but that was enough for viewers and people who saw the newscast later that night across Canada to be thoroughly impressed. A Trudeau supporter who was standing in front of the grandstand later reported that a Separatist said to him, "My God, now in addition to everything else you're going to say he's got courage!" Trudeau himself, talking about fear a few weeks later, remarked, "It takes up too much time, being afraid."

The voting age in Canada is twenty-one, but so many young people flocked to Trudeau's side during his campaign that at one point the average age inside the campaign organization was twenty-two. Publicity and much of the arrangement of rallies were actually put in the hands of teen-agers. Trudeau has frequently made the point that if he lacks experience, so much the better; he can then face old problems with a fresh approach. The very fact that the young people didn't understand why new things couldn't be tried was considered an advantage; the country was eager for a change. Wherever Trudeau showed up, he was flanked by miniskirted volunteers who were remarkable not only for their good looks but for their ability to answer questions about the candidate, about his policies, and about why they were for him even if they couldn't vote. "The climate was right," one of the campaign officials has said since. "If you started tomorrow morning with the same tactics, you'd fail. We happened to come along and gauge it right. We just offered the man. It was amateurish and convincing, and that was it." But the truly remarkable quality of Trudeau's unconventional campaign was that he got elected without having made any commitments to the Party, to any particular provinces, or to any individuals.

"If you make promises, that gives you obligations that you have to carry out," the Prime Minister said quietly. "I was afraid of those obligations. You mortgage yourself and lose the freedom of decision. Justice is the problem — the one about which I have been concerned the most, stated the most, thought the most. I guess most of the authors I've read crystallize my particular idea of virtue — that justice is a cornerstone of the society I live in, the basis of all human relations in the family or the state. I was not dreaming the Just Society up as a

catchword or cliché, and I shrink from the thought now. To me, it summed up the total of the relationships in a society of free men. The Just Society is the kind of society freedom would establish. Looking ahead, I don't think a state can say, 'Here's a state, a package imposed on you.' A Just Society is one toward which every citizen must work, and the first condition of such a society is that of respecting the liberty of individuals."

Trudeau moved formally into the Prime Minister's residence with one large dark-brown suitcase, one small tan one, and some sports jackets and suits over his arm. The only really personal objects in his principal office, in the East Block of the Parliament Buildings, are a *bilboquet*—an Oriental game of skill in which the player tosses a wooden ball about four inches in diameter into a cup to which it is attached by a string—and a battered filing cabinet with his name on it in big letters. When Parliament is in session, he moves a few hundred yards to a more formal, elaborately panelled second office, on the third floor of the Centre Block, where the House of Commons is situated. The Prime Minister's East Block office is an old-fashioned room with Gothic windows, white walls, green hangings, leather furniture, a fireplace, and a large octagonal table-desk. Only the pictures on the walls have been changed by Trudeau. Traditionally, a portrait of Sir John A. MacDonald, the first Prime Minister and a Conservative, hangs over the fireplace if the incumbent is a Conservative, and a portrait of the great Liberal Prime Minister Sir Wilfrid Laurier hangs there if the incumbent is a Liberal. Pearson was the first Prime Minister to keep both portraits in his office. When someone teasingly suggested that instead of the portraits Trudeau should have paintings more in style with his personality, he spent about five minutes pondering how the public would take this before he had the portraits replaced by the type of Abstract Expressionist work he prefers. He likes to have fresh flowers in his office, and usually wears a rosebud or a small red carnation, symbol of the Liberal Party, in his buttonhole.

The ministerial privilege that Trudeau enjoys the most—he told a colleague before he was elected that it was one of the few things worth waging an election for—is Harrington, the country house provided for Canada's Prime Ministers. It is twenty-one miles from Ottawa, situated on a two-mile lake in a national park in the Gatineau Hills, and although Harrington has been described as "a collection of boards nailed together," it is actually a rambling twelve-room cottage, very plainly furnished, in a beautiful area of woodland. The Prime Minister goes there frequently for weekends, and occasionally on a quick overnight trip during the week. Trudeau always has chosen sports at which he had to work hard to achieve excellence, and at Harrington he is still presenting himself with challenges, in the form of three-hour walks over the roughest routes, to test whether he is in good physical condition. Having a house is a new experience for him, and he enjoys showing friends around, but he is not a comfortable host. He goes through the motions, carving meat at the sideboard and sitting at the head of the table, but he has never been much on small talk, and the silences can be monumental. It often takes until the end of dinner, when his guests are about to leave, before he unwinds. "He tunes out quite frequently in the middle of everything," one frequent guest has said. "When he does, he sits absolutely motionless. Then all the men feel that they must say something profound, and since all of them are sitting around trying to have a fantastic thought, the women try to fill in. His mood is purely a matter of luck. You're OK as long as you don't overstep a couple of boundaries. He doesn't like to be interrupted, and he hates to be driven into a corner socially. If he gets cornered at someone else's party, he's apt to leave immediately."

Trudeau's first semi-vacation as Prime Minister took him far from the Gatineau Hills, on a week's trip to inspect new development areas and some old settlements in the North—to the Yukon Territory, across the High Arctic, and down through Baffin Island in the east to the Labrador Peninsula. Since boyhood, Trudeau had taken carefully planned wilderness trips on foot and by canoe through the Canadian North, but he was the first Prime Minister to make an extensive tour through the Northwest Territories, which comprise a third of Canada. On this trip, he followed a rigid routine aboard the plane that carried him and his party of seven: ten minutes or so looking out the window; next, pulling out his briefcase, putting on his glasses, and burying himself in state papers; then, perhaps, a catnap. When the scenery was irresistibly magnificent, as it was above the deep-cut fjords of Ellesmere Island, or when the route passed over the Barren Lands of the Mackenzie District, through which he had once travelled by canoe, he stopped his work entirely. Above the Barrens, he gazed lovingly across the rolling empty land. "Not a tree, not a stick of wood," he murmured. "They are very attaching." Trudeau has a pilot's license, and he eagerly accepted a suggestion that he fly the chartered plane, an old amphibious Canso, a durable but clumsy aircraft. At towns and settlements where the plane landed, he shrugged off his informal holiday air and became the Prime Minister, as if, in slipping on his jacket to face the welcoming crowds, he was also donning a mask—a pleasant, courteous, smiling countenance that endured a barrage of picture-taking with no visible change of expression. "It's all part of the game," he said over and over again, as if to remind himself of what he was about. Visiting an Eskimo settlement, he asked about everything: the housing, the industry, how many shots it took to kill a polar bear, what kind of music the Eskimo girls preferred (rock and roll). At a new asbestos mine, his range of interest covered every aspect of technical operation, labor, and living conditions.

Last summer, Trudeau returned to Lake Ouareau, in the Laurentians, where he, Pelletier, and eight other friends bought a piece of land in 1958 and put up small places, visiting back and forth, climbing, swimming, improvising plays. Trudeau has sold his portion, because not long ago he bought a large tract of land with its own small private lake near his brother at Saint-Sauveur, an hour and a half north of Montreal. He spent last Bastille Day with the Pelletiers, as he has done since 1950, at their log cabin at Lake Ouareau. This was three weeks after the election and the St. Jean Baptiste parade, and already his friends thought he had changed in ways hard to define. "Pierre wants it to be the same, but you sense that he is alone now," an old friend who was present said. "He's there, but somewhere else at the same time, even though he is acting very much as he did before. All the children know Pierre—he loves children—and they were excited about his coming in a helicopter, and the bodyguards, and so on. The kids kept throwing him into the water and calling to the bodyguards, 'Come and get the Prime Minister! Save him! Somebody wants to drown him!'

"Later, at midnight, we were swimming and heard shooting across the lake. So Pierre took someone's flashlight and tried to see what it was. We shrugged our shoulders and said, 'So what?' But we knew his life was in danger. We weren't afraid, but the Kennedy assassinations had made us conscious of the danger."

All kinds of systems and flow charts showing what is happening have been installed in the Parliament Buildings to sort out the demands on Trudeau's time. Gordon Gibson is his Executive Assistant, with an office immediately adjacent to the Prime Minister's, and is in charge of his daily schedule both in Ottawa and when he travels. Unlike Pearson, who has lived a life full of political crises, Trudeau cannot switch off and look at a baseball game for relaxation. Like all bachelors, he is a bit fussy. He has described himself as a "clocked person," who does not like surprises. Even his well-tailored casual clothes are an expression of his studied approach to relaxation. Although the pressure of time makes it essential for him to have speechwriters, he finds it difficult to use other people's words even after extensive consultation during the speechwriting. When he is bored with the text, his delivery is deadly dull; on the other hand, when he is pleased and the structure suits his own rational mind, he may surprise listeners with the drama and excitement of the speech. He is himself an agonized writer, who weighs every word. In speaking, he often departs from the text, to the relief of his writers, who think he is much better then, and in fact his best speeches are spontaneous, which is why he prefers any question-and-answer type of meeting. Hard questions stimulate him, and he is apt to complain later if the questions were too easy. He is, even now, a painstaking correspondent, keeping up written contact with hundreds of people he has met all over the world. In many cases, he gives his private secretary, Cécile Viau, a general idea of what he wants to say, and she drafts the letters that he signs.

Time to think—this is what Trudeau requires above everything, and, theoretically, a full two-hour period during which nobody is permitted to see him is kept open whenever possible (although this is fairly constantly invaded), and an attempt is made to keep at least every second weekend free for catching up on paperwork. He expects anyone to whom he delegates authority to take full responsibility, and if something goes wrong he wants to know why. If the same thing goes wrong again, because of the same person, that person's days are probably numbered, no matter how close to Trudeau he may have been. Trudeau is decisive once he has made up his mind, but he makes up his mind slowly, considering alternatives as long as he can and continuing to question himself until it is time to choose one course of action over another. For him, a tight schedule is an entrapment, and where another man might do his best when pressed, Trudeau rebels. When he gets irritated and explodes, he usually feels quite sorry afterward, since is he really concerned about his staff and sensitive to their feelings. "The most important thing I do is to try and give him time to maneuver," Gordon Gibson has said. "Whenever I can, I postpone pressing him to do things as long as possible, so that he can do them voluntarily. It's not as tidy planning, but it gives him more freedom and flexibility."

Trudeau's working day starts at nine o'clock every morning. When Pearson walked into his office in the morning, his staff waited to say hello until they had gauged his mood. Trudeau always walks in with a hello and a smile for everyone. A daily early-morning staff meeting lasts anywhere from fifteen minutes to an hour, depending on the number of questions each person raises. Only four people besides the Prime Minister attend: Marc Lalonde; Roméo LeBlanc, a former CBC correspondent, who is Press Secretary; Gordon Robertson, the Clerk of the Privy Council and the Secretary to the Cabinet, which means he is the highest-ranking Canadian civil servant, who is sometimes referred to as the Keeper of the Secrets; and Robertson's assistant, Marshall Crowe. Certain appointments are inflexible. Every Monday afternoon, from four to six, there is a long-range-planning meeting with members of the staff. Tuesday mornings, Trudeau has a planning session with Cabinet ministers, and Tuesday afternoons he meets with other Cabinet members on Canada's most pressing current problem, federal-provincial relations. Every Wednesday morning at ten-thirty when Parliament is in session, the Liberal Members have a caucus that the Prime Minister attends, and at six that evening he goes to see the Governor-General, the Right Honourable Roland Michener. On Thursday mornings, or more often when necessary, the full Cabinet meets, either in a room near the chamber of the House of Commons or in the East Block's Canadian Gothic Cabinet Room.

When Parliament is in session, a large portion of the Prime Minister's life revolves around one appointment in the House of Commons, the Question Period — that daily display of parliamentary responsibility in government wherein the Prime Minister and his Cabinet are exposed, without previous notice, to questions from the House. It begins promptly at two o'clock every weekday but Friday, when it is at eleven in the morning, and customarily lasts from forty minutes to an hour. The severity and extent of the questioning is peculiar to the Canadian Parliament. In the British House of Commons, prior notice must be given of a question, and the Prime Minister need not be present more than once every few days, whereas in Canada the Prime Minister is present every day. This places a heavy burden on Trudeau, who is expected to somehow have all the answers. The Question Period has two purposes: to obtain information about how the Government is operating, and to embarrass the Government by springing questions that make those in power look foolish. A highly sophisticated game, it is the dramatic climax of the parliamentary day. Everybody comes to the show, and Trudeau is an expert, witty, and sometimes irritable performer. He is not upset by fair questions, and is exhilarated by really tricky ones, but shows his annoyance plainly when questions are silly, stupid, terribly general, or have already been asked and are repeated by backbenchers who have been absent and not done enough homework.

The assignment of keeping the Prime Minister on top of this seemingly impossible duty has been given to Ivan Head, an outwardly serene professor of international law from western Canada, who was once in the Foreign Service. He has full access to Trudeau at all times, by telephone or in person, and comes very close to being an indispensable man. "You gain a kind of sixth sense of how to do it," Professor Head says. "Civil servants back you up with information. Ordinarily, if the Government is defeated on a major money bill or a plank on government policy, it is a signal for it to resign, so, although nothing requires the Prime Minister to answer, if he doesn't the Opposition will assume he either doesn't know something or is hiding something."

Professor Head's office is a step away from the Prime Minister's. "Although quite often he gets here just as the bells are ringing for the session to start, I am supposed to see the Prime Minister for half an hour immediately prior to the Question Period and brief him on events that, in my view, might be reflected in questions," he says. "A quantity of material has to be passed to him on the go. We're in tune on the vocabulary and the essentials, and he's on top of the job now. After the House meeting, we have a debriefing, and decide which matters have to be followed up and what has to be done. I have had all kinds of relationships with ambassadors and heads of state, and so on, but I have never worked with anyone who so stimulated me as Trudeau. You determine your intellectual investment in accordance with the task, and the investment required with him is just total. He has an immense grasp of detail, and a functional mind. He will not tolerate slipshod work or indefensible opinions. He's not the kind of fellow who makes you nervous, but he has a commanding presence. He's in control, and he's open-minded, too. He'll say, 'What would you say about that?' I find him incapable of insincerity or deception. The fact is that he has such high intellectual standards that he won't permit himself to be deceptive, and that fresh, open approach is one of the factors that have made him so appealing. The kids recognized it, a hundred per cent."

Other experienced government officials who work frequently with Trudeau regard his mind as the best they have ever dealt with. All three Liberal Prime Ministers in the past half century have been men of topnotch intelligence, capable of arriving at good conclusions on complex questions. Pearson was vague and intuitive, his associates say, but his reactions were predictable, and usually the results were good; he was not actually the open man he seemed to be, and most of his staff felt that they never quite knew him. Louis St. Laurent was a relatively uncomplicated French Canadian, with a clear, logical mind, like Trudeau's. Mackenzie King, another bachelor, and a political genius who lasted more than twenty years, had a subtle mind that went off on tangents, but he came to conclusions, although it was never quite clear how he managed to. He himself said he always knew what to do but not always why. Trudeau is mysterious to his associates, and something new about him seems to show up every couple of days. His emotions are not readily apparent, and his reactions seem to be totally intellectual. According to those who know his mind best, Trudeau arrives at a conclusion by logical, precise thought. As a lawyer, he thinks and requires others to think in a rational, constructive way; if they do not, he becomes annoyed. One of his colleagues, describing him, said, "While he keeps his perspective on the whole picture, he wants to tie a bow on each point and move on to the next one. He has a distaste, almost a repugnance, for taking things in the wrong order, or getting facts associated in an illogical way. You can practically see him recoil. If there are three lines of consideration for an aspect of policy, Trudeau will start on the first one. If someone moves over to the second before they have finished with the first, he just won't do it. It's not a confinement, it's a method. It's not a plodding one, two, three, but a streaking brilliance. The intervening steps might not be touched upon, but you know they are there. If all the information isn't there, he finds it better not to decide, and will go back, if he has given something the wrong weight, and re-examine it. He will also remember exactly where a view was at variance in a previous conversation, and you have to justify your shift."

The Prime Minister's popularity has waned a bit, and there are complaints that he is not doing enough. More than most people, Trudeau is aware of the inconstancy of the public mood, and his apparent indifference to public affection or alienation is probably based on his attitude that whatever happens in political life is part of the game. In his own life, he does not neglect any part of what he thinks he can be or do, and by extension this is what he now wants for his country. During this past year, especially in the last six months, he has been rearranging the government of Canada in ways that do not necessarily show: bringing the creaky machinery of Parliament up to date, by such measures as reducing the time required for ministers to be in the House during the Question Period, so they have more afternoons to work, and strengthening the House committee structure to handle increasing work loads; modernizing the government by means of a whole array of new rules and financial arrangements, especially with the provinces, to cope with an increasingly complex society; having fewer meetings of the large, unwieldy Cabinet and more of Cabinet committees; and establishing an office for the Prime Minister, with staff members covering various areas of responsibility and providing him with a separate reservoir of advice. The development of a Prime Minister's office, somewhat paralleling in concept the White House office of the President of the United States, challenges the whole system of Canadian government. Until now, no Prime Minister has had such an extensive staff of his own with delegated authority, and Pearson functioned with only about a quarter of the staff that Trudeau now has, obtaining his advice primarily from his ministers and the civil service. Canada had prided itself on being the rugged frontier country that, until recently, it was, operating simplistically, hesitant to face its own increasing maturity. But now, beyond the beauty and grandeur of the land and its lavish supply of resources, it has huge gleaming cities, an expanding industrial economy, its own distinctive and exciting culture, and highly complicated social problems. The changes Trudeau has quietly made already, although they may appear minor, have impinged enough upon time-worn customs to produce shouts from the Opposition about the "destruction of the democratic way of life" and complaints from Trudeau's own constituents that the government is letting them down. Trudeau's philosophy of counterbalancing is so much a part of him that it follows naturally that, after a flamboyant campaign, he began the actual process of governing in the low-keyed manner he chose, following some inner and compelling blueprint, carefully testing the way and moving meticulously, as he does with everything.

"I have felt that the government of Canada was breaking down in the last few years," the Prime Minister said. "It was breaking down under the pressure of the provinces, when we had a minority Government in Parliament. We had a hell of a lot of catching up to do before we could operate, and I wasn't sure whether it wasn't too late already. We needed all kinds of reforms — in Party organization, the civil service, federal institutions, finance. We weren't able to plan our government or our expenditures, and to govern we had to solve all this. Then the government might become a ship we could steer. We are pushed by Parliament, we are pushed by international events, but I have not been in a hurry to produce any revolutionary ideas. First, we had to get a runaway federal government under control. In the last six months, we have succeeded beyond our dreams. It is working now, and I feel that there is little chance today that my government will break down."

The Prime Minister took a last sip from his coffee cup. He looked out the window toward the garden. "The federal and provincial governments were stumbling over each other, completely out of kilter, like characters in one of those Chinese plays," he said. "Conceivably, the country could have foundered, and the people probably sensed this. The forces of disruption and chaos are so great in the world that I am not afraid of erring on the side of machinery. Most important is the reform of Parliament and the Cabinet committees, of election laws."

He rose from the luncheon table, looked quickly at his watch, and continued talking as he walked to the front door and climbed into a black chauffeur-driven limousine that was waiting to carry him to the Parliament Buildings. Trudeau changes rapidly. He can be dashing and youthful, full of vigor, a severe and proper public servant, or suddenly tired, as he seemed sitting back in the car, with deep circles under his eyes. "My next appointment this afternoon is with VIPs, which I don't enjoy because I need that time for repose, to think things out," *he said.* "I have a lot of fun, even in Parliament, and I am beginning to be a little less impatient, but I tire physically."

At the Parliament Buildings, he got out of the car and ran rapidly up the steps, taking them effortlessly two at a time. In his oak-panelled formal office, four large brown leather dispatch cases covered chairs behind him. "Full of documents, all of them to be signed," *he said with a sigh. It was a hot day. He took off his jacket, rolled up his shirtsleeves, sank into his chair, and put his feet up on the desk.* "I dream. I dream all the time," *he said.* "I've always dreamt of a society where each person should be able to fulfill himself to the extent of his capabilities as a human being, a society where inhibitions to equality would be eradicated. This means providing individual freedoms, and equality of opportunity, health, and education, and I conceive of politics as a series of decisions to create this society. We in Canada have a chance that other nations do not have of attacking and solving problems. We should be devoting ourselves to finding the way. We should be experimenting with institutions, penal reforms, uses of freedom, the scope of permissiveness. We live in a society that is peaceful. We have no violent revolutions, we haven't been touched physically by war. We really are most favored for developing conditions under which the man of tomorrow can experiment. I dream of a Canada that can be doing those things."

He loosened his tie and ran his finger around his collar. "I don't want to sound as if I've got a vision or that Canada has a vision," *he said.* "I'm not a crusader, and I don't feel we are charged with a mission by the Holy Ghost. But progress is a very large word for man's movement toward freedom for the individual. On the constitutional side, when you have a federal form of government you need and want a constitution to define the rules of the game. In the British system, where you assume the sovereignty of Parliament, you don't need a written constitution, because Parliament can change the rules of the game. For the British, Parliament is supreme, and for the United States the constitution is supreme. We're in between; we have retained elements of the sovereignty of Parliament, which can change all our statutes, but to an extent this is limited by our constitution."

He dropped his feet to the floor and got up. "When I talk to students, I tell them we shouldn't think of Canada as one of the big important nations. We can't tell the rest of the world what to do and force our ideas on Africa and Asia. We must be more modest in our ambitions, and not carry the burden of the world on our shoulders. If we don't solve our own problems, other people will — and the world of tomorrow belongs to the people who will solve them."

He smiled. Standing in his shirtsleeves, tie loose, eyes shining, he looked young and full of energy. He quickly rolled down his sleeves, put on his coat, and straightened his tie. "I see Canada as a land of tremendous opportunity in terms of jobs, in terms of its natural beauty and wealth and its three oceans, its temperate climate, its standard of living, its system of education, its technical knowledge," he said, walking with his visitor to the door. "I enjoy being Prime Minister. I am pleased to be part of this society. I see Canada exploring its past, experimenting with its future — playing its political role — first at home, and then in the world."

First published in *The New Yorker*, July 5, 1969. Published in the *Vancouver Sun*, August 1–5, 1969.

The Strangers Next Door

———————— ✦ ————————

WHEN I RE-READ THE ARTICLE I wrote about Canada, "The Strangers Next Door," which appeared in *The Atlantic Monthly* in 1973, I was astonished to find how contemporary it seemed. While factual details have changed, the social and political atmosphere and some of the economic pressures do not appear to be all that different, eighteen years later.

In that same year, 1973, I crossed the country to visit Vancouver for three months, to see if I liked living here well enough to stay. I had written so much about Canada that in the process I had fallen in love with it. My idea was to spend six months of the year on each side of the border, because I am American, and hold dear my own country too. Then in the fall of 1973, while I was giving Vancouver a try, I met and was entranced with a Canadian fisherman, John Daly, and that settled where I would live: in Canada. Since his death in 1978, I spend two or three of the darkest winter months in New York, visiting with my oldest friends and working, with side trips to my family in Ohio, but I always come back to what is now home. I am very much a part of my community in Pender Harbour. I cherish my house, John's house, to which I keep adding rooms that to me mean roots, and I have acquired by osmosis the national passion for politics.

If I were writing the *Atlantic* piece now, I would add several Canadian idiosyncrasies that I admire, and it is a great relief to write them here. I have been wanting to write them somewhere for a long time.

For one, almost every Canadian woman I know, and many men, make their own bread. This may be because I live in the country, but I don't have a friend or family member my age in the States who is a breadmaker. For another, everyone I know in Canada, absolutely

203

everyone, takes off their shoes when they enter a house in winter, and often in summer too. I suppose it's because longer winters make for muddy shoes; muddy shoes, if permitted indoors in BC, also deposit alarming quantities of pine needles. Finally, every house in Canada appears to be equipped with an electric kettle, in constant operation. I have never seen an electric kettle in use in the States, or maybe never seen one at all in the States, and oddly enough when I am there I never use one either.

On a deeper level, I am dismayed at the way situations I observed in 1973 have evolved. Despite an enormous effort for two decades, especially on the part of taxpayers, to keep Canada united, the possibility of Quebec separation is more real than ever. We could wake up any morning to find it has happened, and all the king's horses and men might not be able to put Canada back together again.

Equally critical is the overwhelming intrusion of the United States into the economic and cultural life of Canada, with eager assistance from the Conservative Prime Minister and his government. It is far worse than it was when I wrote the piece: then it was a threat, now it is a reality.

After living in Canada for the past eighteen years, and paying taxes in both countries, I feel half American, half Canadian. The Mulroney government, with its misnamed Free Trade, combined with its birth-to-the-grave Goods and Services Tax, and its policy of privatizing and/or starving out the public institutions in Canada that have bound it together and made it great, has embarked on a program that threatens to dismember the country permanently.

Anyone in doubt should count the industries and business organizations that have moved across the border to the United States and the ominous unemployment and bankruptcy statistics since Free Trade and the GST have been in place. The concept of public service has vanished in our postal and transportation systems, once the pride of Canada, which have deteriorated through privatization. Enormous funding cuts to great public institutions like the National Film Board and the Canadian Broadcasting Corporation have left them gasping for life, without the means or energy to lead the world as examples of national cultural excellence, as they formerly did. We have to wonder how long Canada, whose medical plan, social welfare systems and old age assistance programs are still the envy of the world, can survive.

There is no reason to applaud what is occurring in the United States, either, where uncontrolled greed and worship of the "bottom line" profit motive march hand-in-hand with poverty and homelessness. The country has chosen to let the democratic system erode under three presidents: a shady character who resigned under threat of impeachment; a plastic movie actor who became a joke around the world; and an ex-CIA chief without a heart, who tilts more dangerously to the far right every day. One wonders how long real democracy in the United States can endure.

Democracy does provide a solution that works: the vote, and participation in government. I guess that's what it's going to take to restore government to serve the people, not to fleece them, and the level of statesmanship my generation once knew.

I debated whether to include this article after so many years, but then I read it again and the distress I feel for both my countries began to roll onto the paper. I thought, maybe we should all be reminded now that on both sides of the border, there are still "Strangers Next Door."

✦

Directly above the United States on the map is a huge landmass called Canada frequently colored pink to distinguish it from us. Most Americans have no idea what goes on up there or what constitutes the Canadian character, but assume that there are so many of us and so few of them, two hundred million to twenty-two million, that they must be just like us.

Why not? The Canadians whom Americans meet, unless they venture into French Quebec, speak English, see the same television programs, and read *The Reader's Digest*. Americans as schoolchildren don't find much about Canada in their history books. Those who are aware of Canada's natural resources have a comfortable misapprehension that the country is a storage room we can draw from when we run out of precious minerals, oil, and water. We also have a dim idea from the periodic violence that erupts in Quebec that a French-speaking minority in Canada threatens to set up a separate government. But even those Americans who use Canada as a vacation land are remarkably ignorant of the Canadian personality; of the ten provinces and the territories beyond, comprising the second largest country in the world; of a parliamentary system in a federal arrangement that gives Canada's government a distinctive form somewhere between that of Great Britain and the United States, but not like either one; and of the people, who are rapidly developing a new self-esteem and a desire to control their own destiny. With increasing emotion, Canadians are coming to think that they have a country whose special qualities are worth defending. Nonetheless, the United States blindly continues to regard Canada as a gangling hayseed who admires our sophisticated ways, gratefully accepts our culture and the golden fallout from our economic superiority, and loves us no matter what.

"We like you Americans very much on a person-to-person basis, but let's face it, as a nation the United States is unlovable, and we certainly don't want to use it as a model," a Canadian recently confided to an American friend. The Canadians know a great deal about us, thanks to our television programs, the flood of movies and periodicals that engulf them, and to the stark fact that roughly 75 percent of Canadian industry is American-owned and oriented. Once, the United States was the mecca toward which ambitious young Canadians were aiming. Now for the first time there are more Americans emigrating to Canada than there are Canadians coming to settle in the United States. The "brain drain" of Canadian scholars and scientists into American universities has stopped. The Canadians are realists, however. They don't like the American domination of their economy, but they know what will happen to their already high unemployment and their excellent standard of living without it. They want some form of control over foreign investment but not so severe as to jar the economy.

More and more, Canadians refer to the United States in that cold term, a "foreign country." They are a peace-loving people and the Vietnam War and our conduct of it shocked them. The name *johnconnally* has become a single dirty word in the Canadian lexicon. The bullying behavior of President Nixon's economic emissary, with his threats of retaliation if Canada should hold back raw materials that the United States needs, does not suit the reserved Canadian temperament, but nothing has shocked our friendly neighbor as much as the unexpected imposition of a 10 percent tax on Canadian imported goods in 1971. Although that tax was rescinded fairly soon after it was imposed, Canadians remember the date the tax was announced, August 15, 1971, and refer to it as a day of infamy. It exposed them to their own vulnerability, and they regard the fact that it could happen at all as a betrayal and warning. When Canadian Prime Minister Pierre Trudeau visited Washington a year later, he was introduced to John Connally, then Secretary of the Treasury, who was moving down the receiving line. President Nixon said, "And here is the terrible Mr. Connally," and Trudeau and Connally shook hands. After Connally had moved on down the line, Mr. Trudeau was seen looking at his back, and then the Prime Minister began openly counting his fingers.

Many Canadians think that the need to defend themselves against encroachment by the United States is what has kept them together.

"Logic would have made our maritime provinces in the East allies of Boston, and western Canada a part of the West Coast of the United States," a western Canadian newspaperman observed in a letter to an American friend not long ago. "If Canada has survived, it's because of the existence of the United States. I am certain that if the American portion of North America were to sink fifty feet below the waves, Canada would divide into several independent states: the Atlantic provinces, Quebec, our wealthy industrialized heartland of Ontario, the prairies, and British Columbia. The North, custodian of the national dream, might be too expensive for anyone to keep, but would probably be colonized by one or more of the five states."

Canada is not yet a unified nation. It is a disjointed federation of regional groups, the provinces—federal states loosely tied into a central government in Ottawa, the capital city. Ottawa is in Ontario for convenience, but the provices have enough mutual desire for unity to engage in a remarkable sharing process known as equalization grants. Three so-called "have" provinces, industrialized Ontario in the East, oil-rich Alberta at the western end of the prairies, and British Columbia on the Pacific coast, share their riches with the seven "have-nots": the Atlantic provinces of Newfoundland, Nova Scotia, New Brunswick, and tiny Prince Edward Island, plus Quebec in the East, and the central prairie states of Manitoba and Saskatchewan.

Scratch the surface of the country and what do you find? A population which is a third French in heritage; a third British from Scotch, Irish, and English forebears; and the rest a mixed congregation of immigrants who have arrived by hundreds of thousands since 1900, from Europe, chiefly, but in substantial numbers from China, Japan, and a rainbow of other countries. Canada is no melting pot. Canadians cling proudly to their origins, not only the French in Quebec, but others who continue living in their own settlements and speaking their own languages in the new country. There are large French communities in New Brunswick and Nova Scotia, where they are called Acadians, and in Manitoba, on the central prairies; and Ukrainians in Alberta think that if there is a second language, it should be Ukrainian. Census takers beg people to trace their lineage to the country they came from and this is duly recorded in the *Canada Year Book*. There are probably more than a hundred thousand blacks, Asians, and West Indians now in Canada. Ten thousand descendants of a few escaped slaves during the Civil War live in a community just outside Halifax in Nova Scotia, mostly on welfare. French-speaking Haitians are settling in Montreal, and so many West Indians have come to the Toronto area that an annual Caribbean Festival takes place there every summer.

There have been a few racial skirmishes between blacks and whites, but the war is between the English and the French, between Quebec and the rest of Canada, which Canadians themselves invariably refer to as British or English Canada. Six million French-speaking people in Quebec, many of whose ancestors predate the British conquest of Canada and the American Revolution, sincerely regard themselves as second-class citizens, in an inferior economic position to the British Establishment. The official policy of bilingualism, which was begun under the late Lester Pearson when he was Prime Minister and which has been implemented by Trudeau, a French Canadian, is a belated effort to correct one of the major irritants. The Official Languages Act passed in 1969 requires by law that people be able to talk with their government in whichever of the two official Canadian languages, French or English, they may choose.

Previously, virtually all federal government business was conducted in English, even in Quebec, where a large proportion of the population speaks only French, although business is British-oriented. The burden for providing communication in either language in government offices now rests on the government, and a bilingual board recommends which districts should be bilingual, depending on whether the local population is French, English, or both. The government has no intention of making everyone learn both languages, a basic misconception held in the far West, where a French Canadian is a rare bird indeed. In a place like Kelowna, British Columbia, for example, where the population is entirely English-speaking, a French-speaking Canadian seeking assistance in a government office would be hooked up by telephone to Vancouver, where there would be two or three civil servants who could speak French. In the French-speaking town of Rimouski on the south shore of the St. Lawrence River in Quebec, the same thing would happen in reverse.

In the East, anti-French prejudice was responsible in the General Election last fall for the loss of at least two Liberal seats in Parliament to the Conservative Party in Ottawa, where English civil servants frequently feel that French-language requirements threaten their jobs and career advancement. Anti-French sentiment is also evident in such places as Moncton, New Brunswick, where the English-speaking mayor has enraged the large Acadian population by denying them the right to have a sign at the door of the new City Hall in French as well as in English, although the building was rented from the Assumption Society, an Acadian investment co-operative.

The Official Languages Act applies only to federal institutions, and the provinces are free to do whatever the population requires at the provincial level. Education is a provincial responsibility. Canadian citizens can receive their education in French and continue speaking nothing but French, or the reverse, but most schools provide facilities for a working knowledge of the other official language, and in some provinces, teaching or taking the second language is compulsory. "Right now, we are deciding whether to make our son's education in English or French," a French Canadian father of a three-year-old boy recently explained to an Ottawa visitor. "In the capital here, of course, there are both English and French schools. I'd like my son to be in a French one, but then I pause and say to myself, 'If he is bright, why not open him to the whole American continent instead of just one part of one country or even just one country?' Let's say he wants to be a nuclear physicist. Why then, it's better to be educated in English, with French as a second language. I don't want to close that door!"

Canadian people are basically middle-class. They like surface conformity and although they may smile on erratic behavior, even scamper out briefly on an adventure, they run quickly back to the safety of the familiar, the comfortable, the proper. Canadian cities are handsome, clean, and some of the architecture is among the most exciting in North America; people are highly motivated, full of energy. Social experiments are daring and innovative, but too much originality at any one time, too great a deviation for too long, gets people nervous and edgy. Canadians are not opposed to change but they like to tiptoe in cautiously, without jolting their settled-down psyches. "Permissiveness toward his children, weekend family life, and TV" is the description a Canadian has given to the homelife of an average man of Canada. "When I go to a saloon, called a cocktail bar [expensive], or a beer parlor [cheap], or a private club [cheap but exclusive], I prefer the exclusion of women and children," he said. "I like to talk about hockey and Canadian football while I am drinking, and I like to talk about oil strikes in the High Arctic. More and more I find myself conversing about American domination of our economy, American arrogance, and American ignorance. I am fairly typical." On weekends during the winter everyone who can get on a pair of skis or skates heads for the hills or a sheet of ice. One of the largest ski clubs in the world is Camp Fortune, thirty minutes out of Ottawa. It has about twelve thousand members, and on a cold Sunday this past winter sixty-four thousand skaters were reported to be gliding up and down on the longest man-made skating rink in the world, the four-and-a-quarter-mile Rideau Canal that bisects the capital. Civil servants keep a pair of skates in the corner of their offices so they can take a quick turn on a nearby outdoor ice surface during their lunch hour. Almost every Canadian city, town, or village has a curling club.

Curling, a Scotch game, resembles bowling, but the alley is made of ice and a heavy stone is used instead of a ball.

Whole families curl, but the national Canadian sport is ice hockey, with football coming on as a close second. Officially, the national sport is lacrosse, a game invented by North American Indians, but that game has lost out in the scramble for TV coverage. Saturday night hockey on TV, sponsored since the early days of radio by Imperial Oil, is a religion and tops all the ratings. Canadians are passionate vicarious sportsmen, and the biggest event since Expo was last year's international ice hockey tournament between Team Canada and the Soviet Union. The tournament was a tie until the last thirty-eight seconds of play, when the Canadians won the series, and the people back home, all glued to their television sets, went wild with joy. Only three of the sixteen teams in the National Hockey League are Canadian (Montreal, Toronto, and Vancouver); all of the rest are American, but three hundred and eleven of the three hundred and twenty-three players in the League are Canadian. Four of the twelve teams in the new World Hockey Association are Canadian, and there is a similar imbalance of nationality in players.

The Canadians have put a quota of 50 percent on the number of Americans allowed on their football teams. This figure may foreshadow the allowable percentage in other Canadian enterprises fighting for identity. The Canadian football field is ten yards longer and twelve yards wider than the American, which makes other differences possible. In three-down Canadian football, the punt is returned twice as often from a scrimmage. "Football fever" is a familiar Canadian ailment, which reaches its peak on the last Sunday in November when the entire nation watches the Grey Cup on television. The gift of Earl Grey, a Governor General of Canada in the early 1900s, the Grey Cup is the trophy awarded for the Canadian Football League championship.

Summer is national fishing time on both coasts as well as on the lakes and rivers. A glance at the roads in summer makes it seem as if all of Canada has left home on wheels, in campers and cars, trailing a boat or a camping outfit behind. Fall brings out the hunters, for duck and partridge, and in the north of all the provinces, for bear and deer. But what Canadians cherish most, whether they are hunters, fishermen, sports fans, or none of these, is the idea that the outdoors is so close at hand, with wilderness just beyond.

There is an old way of Canadian living that can still be found, in the quilting bees in the Atlantic provinces, in the wood carving in small Quebec towns, in bingo and contract bridge anywhere. What is new is the culture revolution, the fantastic growth of art, music, and theatre that has given every sizable city a civic center where these interests can thrive in a professional setting, instead of the public school auditoriums used previously. There is still plenty of home-grown culture—almost every community has an amateur theatre group, orchestra, and art club or classes—but formal culture used to be confined to "celebrity concerts" six or eight times a year. Now three world-renowned ballet companies flourish, in Winnipeg, Toronto, and Montreal; there is a liberal scattering of regional professional theatres, of which the Shakespeare Festival at Stratford, Ontario, is the best known; and there is a growing number of excellent civic orchestras. Everybody still loves country music, especially in the hands of a Western singer named Tommy Hunter, who twangs his guitar each week for an hour of prime time on TV. Something new, however, has come into the cultural life of the Canadian viewer: the Baby Blue Movies, also known as the skin flicks, soft porno seen on Channel 70, the new Toronto Cable TV Station on Friday nights when the kids are supposedly in bed. *Last Tango in Paris* has been playing in legitimate theatres in Canada in both French and English, but *Deep Throat* was recently shown in Montreal on eight-millimeter videotape in a special studio to avoid the commercial censors. Back-room movie houses are taking their place along with noon-hour massage parlors and topless or nudie nightclubs.

Television viewers have two Canadian networks to choose between: CTV, a centralized private association of affiliates, like CBS or NBC, and the Canadian Broadcasting Corporation, CBC, a Crown corporation, publicly owned and subsidized, but partially independent in that it accepts advertising from private industry. CBC operates four national networks, two, English and French, on radio, and an English and a French television network. It is committed to reaching even the Indians and Eskimos in the farthest outposts of the North. The Canadian equivalent of our Federal Communications Commission is the Canadian Radio-Television Commission, and CRTC requires that at least 60 percent of its programs on both networks be Canadian in content. American programs like *All in the Family*, *Mannix*, and the Flip Wilson and Carol Burnett shows and perhaps a dozen others get prime time on Canadian as they do on American TV, but occasionally there is a slight change in format. In a show called *Red Pony*, starring Henry Fonda and Maureen O'Hara, not long ago, the complete birth scene of a pony was shown in Canada, but it was cut out in the United States.

A young American actress working for four months with a school tour troupe at the Manitoba Theatre Centre in Winnipeg expressed amazed delight at the high quality of Canada's television programs.

"The French programs are the best," she said. "Why, one channel had a French children's very sophisticated *commedia dell'arte*, beautifully done, with one harlequin playing different musical instruments. And the fine rock shows! And the professional artists they had! All wonderful!" She had watched a lot of British soap operas, BBC offerings on videotape, and had enjoyed the English life they portrayed, especially a cockney lady who operated a hotel. Her viewing included country music, a regular variety show out of Winnipeg in an English pub-like setting called *Pig and Whistle*, and the public affairs programs, *Encounter* and *Weekend*.

Canadian viewers close to the border at points like Vancouver, Winnipeg, Windsor, and Toronto tune in on American stations. Station KVOS in Bellingham, Washington, apparently exists only to serve the Vancouver area and makes its money from Canadian advertisers. Several years ago a special committee of the Canadian Senate studied the mass media and the resulting Davey Report recommended that this sort of "piracy" be controlled in the same way that Canada has controlled the invasion of American publications on the Canadian magazine market, by refusing to permit Canadian advertisers in American publications to write off money spent on advertising as a business expense on their income taxes.

Not even tax deterrents can keep American publications from the Canadian market, in such overwhelming numbers that only the strongest Canadian periodicals can survive. "Somehow or other, we've arrived in the peculiarly Canadian position where our most successful magazines are American magazines, and we're moving inexorably towards the day when they'll be the *only* magazines we have," said the Davey Report. "This makes sense in terms of economics; on any other basis, it's intolerable." Some Canadians would like to see the exceptional status removed that was granted two American publications, *The Reader's Digest* and *Time*. Section 12A of the Income Tax Act of 1964, which still prevails, permitted them to pass as Canadian magazines, because at the time they had some editorial staff, and were partially edited, in Canada, and had been printed and published there for more than a year. *The Reader's Digest* publishes some articles especially for Canada in both English and French editions. *Time* is published only in English, in the same format seen in the United States, but with a Canadian section added at the beginning, and occasionally a different cover. Only Canada's *Chatelaine*, a general women's magazine with an English and French edition, has a bigger circulation than *The Reader's Digest*, with *Maclean's*, an excellent general feature Canadian monthly published in both languages, in third place, and *Time* in fourth. Canadians read *Saturday*

Night, a journal of opinion, but *Vogue*, *Ladies' Home Journal*, *Playboy*, *Cosmopolitan*, *The Atlantic*, *Harper's*, *Scientific American*, and *The New Yorker* are popular too, and the sight of so many American periodicals on a Canadian newsstand makes the visitor wonder which country he is in.

The book publishers in Canada are struggling with the same syndrome. *Jonathan Livingston Seagull*, an American book, topped the fiction list, and of the other nine fiction books, only two were by Canadian authors, Robertson Davies and Margaret Atwood. On the other hand, six of the ten nonfiction writers on the best-seller list were Canadians, with the late Lester Pearson's memoirs the favorite, and Farley Mowat's *A Whale for the Killing* in second place. Canadian readers have a taste for adventure, but the books they select are likely to be from American publishers. In the Canadian book publishing world, only a handful of publishers manage rather frantically to keep above water. With huge American concerns like Doubleday, Macmillan, and McGraw-Hill establishing separate Canadian companies, it's no wonder, and the federal and provincial governments have begun offering subsidies to indigenous publishers to keep them in business. The sale of the United Church of Canada's Ryerson Press to McGraw-Hill was protested in Parliament not long ago, but not in time to stop the transaction.

Canada still has the two-dollar bill. Canadians observe with detachment American excitement over the changing value of the US dollar. Recently the dollar has been at par, but when Americans used to get eight or nine cents more for their dollar in Canada, they usually found this an attractive incentive to spend money locally. What has annoyed Canadians for years, and still does, is that American dollars are viable any place in Canada, but Canadian bills in the United States are looked upon as "funny money" and can be changed only at official exchanges or banks.

An economic happening the Canadians would like to see unchanged is the 1965 auto pact agreement made between the United States and Canada when Lyndon Johnson was President and Lester Pearson was Prime Minister. Last year a quarter of all United States exports went to Canada, and a little more than a quarter of its imports came from Canada, quite a sizable chunk of the American economy. Yet the 13 billion dollars' worth of American exports represented only 4.2 percent of the American gross national product, whereas the 14 billion dollars' worth the Canadians exported to the United States was 20 percent of Canada's. The largest single item in our trading relations was motor vehicles. We sent 1 billion dollars' worth of cars to Canada, but 2 billion dollars' worth of these commodities crossed from Canada to us. Before the auto pact, American-owned automobile plants in Canada had been producing all their car models for a Canadian market of 22 million people, resulting in short runs and inefficient use of capital. The pact permitted automobiles and parts to move free of tariffs between the two countries, allowing the manufacturers to "rationalize" their production for greater efficiency. The pact also included temporary safeguards to protect and stabilize the Canadian end of the industry, requiring that a substantial percentage of parts be Canadian in relation to the Canadian market, that the volume of production in Canada not be allowed to fall below the volume of Canadian purchases, prohibiting the importation of American used cars for sale in Canada, and continuing a 15 percent unilateral tariff on new cars brought from the United States by individual Canadian citizens.

After the pact, the automobile companies started manufacturing some parts and cars entirely in Canada, in smaller plants and with longer runs. The automobiles they decided to build there were Mustangs, Mavericks, Pintos, and Dodge Darts, which turned out to be such big sellers generally that the differential swung over to a billion-dollar advantage for Canada.

The United States government would like to see the pact's temporary safeguards removed, especially the unilateral tariff. "There's no doubt Canada has benefited well beyond the level of the safeguards," a Canadian businessman said recently, "and if *johnconnally* hadn't been such a bastard, they *might* have been removed. As it was, our people just got up and walked out of the discussions."

A new cause for alarm in Canada was sounded last year on the storage of confidential information about Canadian citizens in data banks in the United States by American-based credit card agencies and credit bureaus. A government report made a worried statement that "a great deal of personal information about Canadians, much of it highly sensitive, is stored beyond Canadian borders and therefore out of reach of Canadian law," and urged monitoring this flow and the encouragement of data banks in Canada instead.

Canadians sit tight on their money. They play it safe with savings accounts and bonds and let Americans invest billions in the capitalization of their country's industry. Canadian promoters have big ideas for getting oil and gas from the Mackenzie Delta, and for the largest hydroelectric scheme in North America at James Bay—but a shortage of funds for capitalization. Is it worth the price of American capitalization to get Canadian development going now? Many Canadians are beginning to wonder, along with economist Eric Kierans of McGill University, who resigned from Prime Minister Trudeau's last cabinet in protest against continued American subsidy of Canadian industrial development and resource exploitation. They ask if it wouldn't be better to wait a while until the Canadians need the development enough to finance it themselves.

"What choices have we got to keep our national identity?" a new member of the House of Commons asked an American visitor at a dinner table in the Establishment Ottawa suburb of Rockcliffe. "We can buy the country back and go broke, or we can gradually move into the sections that are vital to our future and say to the United States, 'You can't remove materials in the raw state, but must process them to a certain degree and manufacture some products, in Canada.'"

The young wife of a Western politician was listening. "I keep remembering a remark made in Colorado before an American audience in 1970 by our Cabinet Minister for Energy, Mines and Resources at that time, Joe Green. He said that the American dream has turned into a nightmare. A lot of us feel that's what you've got in the States now, and we're learning our lessons from you. We realize now that your fuel's running short, and that we have a bit still. This makes us feel rather smug, and gives us a new feeling of identity. Our cities are safer than yours too. They are still small enough so that we think we can correct our direction in time. We have major problems but we feel that a choice is still open to us. We have sun still, so we won't put up skyscrapers and when we saw what the superhighways were doing to your country, we stopped the Spadina Expressway from being built through Toronto and said, 'This city is for people.' I used to think I'd love to live in the United States, but not anymore. We don't have your numbers yet, so we can stop in time."

Sometimes when Canadians brood about United States dominance they describe themselves, with some bitterness, as the fifty-first state. But a look at the capital, Ottawa, should reassure them. Stability and permanence is the message in the buff-colored sandstone Gothic buildings that stand high above the Ottawa River on Parliament Hill. They house the law-making body, the House of Commons, and the Victorian, red-upholstered chamber of the Senate, a body appointed by Prime Ministers and consisting of a hundred and two members with so few duties (other than the production of some very fine reports) that political reformers perpetually campaign against it. A prominent forty-nine-year-old Senator, John Nicholl, recently resigned from the Senate, saying he had other things to do, an act without precedent. Perhaps a visitor cannot truly understand the country until he has traveled from the genteel poverty of the Atlantic coast with its picturesque fishing villages and stiff towns through the

Frenchness of sophisticated Quebec cities and rural landscapes, past the vigorous bustling Ontario municipalities and industrial vistas, over mile after mile of wheat fields between prairie settlements into the lush and spacious beauty of British Columbia; but he must also visit Ottawa and the House of Commons. Ottawa the stuffy, with its dull-looking houses, its blistering summer heat, its gray rainy afternoons; Ottawa the beautiful, on a snowy day when the government buildings stand tall and protective, warmly solid above the white landscape; on a sunny spring afternoon with the cool river winding below, and people moving easily through the clean streets, purposeful but not pushed. Even during the morning and evening traffic rushes, Ottawa seems to remain sane.

A Prime Minister who forgets the fiercely independent character of the country or neglects it, as Pierre Trudeau did before the last election, is in trouble. The Prime Minister is not chosen by country-wide vote but indirectly, through a filtering process that begins in each of two hundred and sixty-four election districts. Canadians vote for a Member of Parliament to represent the riding in which they reside, and, as in Britain, the political party sending the most Members to Parliament becomes the government. The leader of that party becomes the Prime Minister, but he must be elected to Parliament from his local riding. Riding by riding, a government in power is put to the test, two hundred and sixty-four times, of whether it has satisfied the needs of the separate countries inside Canada.

The answer in last October's election, which gave the returning Trudeau government a plurality of just two seats, was the closest vote in Canadian history. One hundred and nine Liberals were returned to Parliament to face one hundred and seven Progressive Conservatives sitting in green leather seats behind handsome, burnished wood desks, across the long, narrow dividing space where the Speaker presides in the House of Commons. With an almost even split between the two old parties, the mildly socialist New Democratic Party, the NDP, netted six additional seats from the election to wind up with thirty-one Members, and the balance of power.

Most Canadians, especially those who were undecided until the very last minute or voted Conservative or NDP as a protest, believe that Trudeau's government squeaked through only because there was no interesting alternative. Robert Stanfield, the Opposition leader, a patient, high-minded man, is about as exciting as the long underwear manufactured by his family that gave him the sobriquet of "Mr. Underwear."

"This is my tenth Parliament and there has been no other like it for uncertainty and constant negotiating in the open," an NDP veteran exclaimed recently. "We are wooed constantly. This is the most bedfellow session there has ever been!"

At its best, a session in the House of Commons is a lively and witty spectacle, a lesson in alert democracy; at its worst, it is a sleepy display of long-winded speechmaking to empty seats, with only a handful of official listeners in duty attendance. Minority government raises the level of parliamentary performance to a fairly even high. Previously, ninety to a hundred Members might be absent, especially on Thursday evenings, when Members began leaving for the weekend to go to distant ridings. Now, however, the loss of one Member could bring down the government, or conversely, give the Conservatives their chance for power on a suddenly called vote of no confidence, so attendance in the House has been very high.

Since 1957, there have been five minority governments and only two majority ones, but this is the first time that the NDP has been able to swing the vote on its own. There is so little difference between the two major parties that dissimilarities are largely a matter of emphasis, reflecting the basically middle-class character of the country. The Conservatives lean toward free enterprise, but accept the controls of social legislation; the Liberals happily mix a potpourri of social legislation and tax incentives for business, but any lack of difference in basic philosophy is made up for by sharp verbal attacks on one another, which can be brutal and even personal.

Most of Canada's social legislation has been accomplished during minority governments: Medicare, which pays doctors' bills; pensions that automatically start at sixty-five; amendments to the labor code that brought vacations with pay and statutory holidays. The NDP is a scratchy bedfellow, but it has more faith in the Liberal than the Conservative Party. "The Liberals are prone to concessions," said Stanley Knowles, NDP House Leader, a gaunt former printer and minister, known as "Standing Order Knowles" for his mastery of parliamentary procedure, who came to Parliament from Winnipeg in 1942. "The Liberals will go into public ownership and social legislation," he said, "not because they believe in it, but when they have to. We *do* believe in it, so if they don't deliver, we'll throw them out and put the Tories in, and treat them the same way!"

"We can't become the government, but anybody concerned about political gamesmanship has the duty to make minority government work, or it would be chaotic," David Lewis, the leader of the NDP, remarked to this writer. He is a short, stocky, vigorous man in his sixties with graying hair, glasses, and a firm chin. "We have no more confidence and respect for the Liberals than we do for the Conservatives. It would be utterly irresponsible for us to bring down the government, but we want it to know exactly where we stand, because if it miscalculates our position it might go down sooner than it expected to. We want equity for the tax system, old-age tax relief, a deeper concern about foreign ownership, things like that. I am not persuaded that Trudeau has learned anything from the last election. At all events, time will show. If they don't produce, *down* they go!"

Published in *The Atlantic Monthly*, July 1973.

Part Five

HOME TO BC

"Capi" Blanchet

◆

My FAMILY AND FRIENDS began visiting me in Canada after I married John Daly, and the contrast between my life in the United States and my existence in Pender Harbour seemed to overwhelm them. My son, Richard, for instance, arrived at ten one night after a three-hour bus ride from Vancouver, and I was waiting at a dusty road corner beside a gas station as he stepped off the bus. He staggered toward me, his arms outstretched as if he were groping his way, crying out, "Where am I?" That pretty well expressed what everyone else was feeling, only it took them a day or two to say so.

Since John was fishing when most of my early visitors came, I couldn't show them the grandeur of this coast by boat, which is the correct way to see it. I did the next best thing: I gave them Mrs. Blanchet's *The Curve of Time*.

Invariably, I would be asked, "Who is M. Wylie Blanchet?" I didn't know, although I was curious about a woman who had the courage to take five young children by herself on a small boat for a whole summer. I found out about her when I stayed at my all-time favorite hotel, the Sylvia in Vancouver. An elegant middle-aged woman stepped out from the office behind the front desk one morning, introduced herself as Kathleen Caldwell, and said, "I see you are carrying Capi Blanchet's book. She was a friend of mine." So Kathleen became a friend of mine, thanks to Mrs. Blanchet.

It turned out that a lot of people wanted to know more about the author, including Howard White, the editor of *Raincoast Chronicles*, who asked me to find out. It was the first time he had invited me to write for the *Chronicles*, a publication I greatly admire, so I was happy to take on the search, which also uncovered a children's book by Capi Blanchet — *A Whale Named Henry* — that was subsequently published by Harbour Publishing. My neighbor down the coast, Hubert Evans, knew Capi Blanchet well. My quest also took me to the home of David Blanchet, Capi's youngest son, a brave and gallant man confined to a wheelchair by polio. He died in 1981. His widow, Janet, and I continue the friendship that commenced with my writing this piece for the *Chronicles*.

◆

When I came to live on the British Columbia coast I was given as a sort of spiritual introduction a remarkable little volume entitled *The Curve of Time* by M. Wylie Blanchet. The book was a particularly appropriate choice: my summers were spent on a fishing boat, the *MoreKelp*, with my husband John Daly, a commercial salmon troller, and the area he regularly traversed partly followed the path travelled by Mrs. Blanchet and her five children on their tiny motor launch, the *Caprice*.

The five Blanchet youngsters, led by their indomitable mother, spent four summer months for fifteen years — the older ones less time as other commitments pressed in — on a twenty-five by six-and-a-half foot boat made of half-inch cedar, travelling around the west coast of Vancouver Island and as far north up the Inside Passage as Cape Caution. They explored the inlets and bays, sometimes following the trail broken by that earlier intrepid mariner Captain George Vancouver, with whom they felt a great empathy, their experiences finally written down in a series of sketches that encompassed all the years of their journeys as if they were one. The title *The Curve of Time* refers to the capacity of any one of us to stand on the highest curve of the Present in Time and look back into the Past, forward into the Future or to wander at will from one to the other. Which is precisely what M. Wylie Blanchet did in this brief account that has triumphed over Time to become one of the classics in British Columbia literature.

Until *A Whale Named Henry* was published posthumously, *The Curve of Time* was M. Wylie Blanchet's only book, originally published in 1961 when she was seventy years old. That same year she died of a heart attack, sitting at her desk where she was found slumped over her typewriter. She had lived just long enough to enjoy being a published author with a small reading public that wrote her admiring letters.

M. Wylie Blanchet. At first, she tried using just "M. Wylie." M was for Muriel, the author's given name, which she hated; *Wylie* was borrowed from a grandparent; and *Blanchet* was acquired by marriage. Altogether it was the impersonal sound that she intended; she hoped the author would not be recognized by the people up the coast about whom she was writing, who knew her simply as "Capi" Blanchet. As to the nickname—wasn't she the Captain of the *Caprice*?

In the last chapter of the book, entitled "Little House," Mrs. Blanchet comes off the *Caprice* to write about the family's land base on seven secluded acres of Vancouver Island's coast, from which they departed each June and to which they returned in October. For an ordinary family this would have meant cutting two months from the school year, but the Blanchet children received their early education at home under their mother's guidance. In the first edition of the book, Mrs. Blanchet confined herself in this final chapter to a poetical narrative evoking the wild and beautiful setting of Little House. Later editions include the beginning of a second unfinished manuscript and add mysterious shadows, with the suggestion of personal tragedy in a cryptic statement, "the legacy of death often shapes our lives in ways we could not imagine." *The Curve of Time* manages to be sentimental, imaginative, and often strays into whimsy, but it is reticent about hard facts; it reads like an impressionist painting. Its characters, whose physical appearances are never really described, are shadowy figures against the lush and brilliant scenery of the British Columbia coast. We know what they do and how they feel but not what they look like or who they are other than a mother and five children, three girls and two boys, the youngest around three at the time Mrs. Blanchet chose to locate her story.

Despite the reticence we do know the important things about this remarkable woman. She comes through as extremely courageous and innovative and as a kind of mechanical wizard compared to most women. Without formal training or experience she could make an engine that failed at an isolated anchorage start chugging again. She could steer a small craft over shoals, through narrows and rapids, read charts correctly and arrive where she intended to be, while she was providing food, proper shelter from whatever winds were prevailing and adventure for her children. Yet readers close her book with a scratchy feeling of curiosity. Who *was* M. Wylie Blanchet? What was she like?

Her Canadian publisher Gray Campbell, a fellow British Columbian who was both neighbour and friend, has described her as having "a delightful shyness," as a serious person with "a delicious, dry sense of humour." Campbell first became acquainted with her when the *Caprice* was berthed next to his boat at Canoe Cove, a short distance from the Blanchet house, which was five miles from Sidney. He too was writing, and Capi Blanchet used to sit in the cabin of his boat and read the chapters of his uncompleted manuscript. He has said since that it was the lack of success of the first edition of *The Curve of Time*, whose English publishers never bothered to see that it was stocked in bookstores either in Victoria or Vancouver, that helped to convince him that there was a need for regional publishing. Only six or seven hundred copies even got as far as Toronto. The author had to loan a local bookstore the money to get copies of her own book for her friends.

Muriel Blanchet was born Muriel Liffiton in 1891 in Lachine, Quebec, into a well-to-do family with High Anglican principles. The Liffitons were English but the Snetsingers, on her mother's side, were pre-Revolution Dutch settlers in the Hudson Valley. They crossed the border into Canada during the American Revolution, settling in the St. Lawrence valley with a land grant well located downstream from the town of Cornwall. Grandfather Snetsinger was a warden of Cornwall and Member of Parliament for the area, and left a considerable inheritance whose final distribution was made only a year ago. The ancestral home is now under sixty feet of St. Lawrence river water and all the original land has been sold.

Muriel was the middle one of three sisters and something of a tomboy. She customarily carried squirrels and mice around in her pockets, to the horror of the girls' tutor, described as "a kind of retired clergyman." Their father was a prosperous customs broker who announced from time to time at breakfast that he was departing and would then disappear for a year or so. The only hint of his whereabouts would be a casual remark later when he helped his daughters with their geography lessons, that he had just been in Alexandria, Egypt, or once, in Timbuctoo. Later he sent the three girls to St. Paul's private school for girls near Montreal, where Muriel developed a strong sense of competition with her sister Violet, five years older and a prize-winning scholar. Muriel set out to surpass her in the same determined manner with which she later approached the mysteries of the gasoline engine. The results of this four-year scholastic campaign are still evident in a row of small red leather Temple volumes of Shakespeare in the library of Mrs. Blanchet's youngest son David (called John in the book). Each volume was given her as a prize for top honours in a different subject, and she never stopped until she had the whole set, inscribed to Muriel Liffiton in the heavy black script of R. Newton, Rector of St. Paul's, and bearing the motto *Non Sans Droit* with the school's coat of arms. Between 1905 and 1908 Muriel Liffiton repeatedly captured first prizes in Latin, French, spelling, astronomy, history, geography, geometry (Euclid), algebra and English, beginning with a modest two her first year and winding up with six at graduation. One year she was awarded a special prize (*Antony and Cleopatra*) for top excellence in "All Subjects." Her older sister Violet, known in the family as "Auntie Teake," subsequently married a banker, was widowed, and at ninety-six lives in a nursing home in Windsor, Ontario. Until very recently she still continued a lifelong habit of writing letters all night to the family. The youngest sister Doris, remembered by her nieces and nephews for her charm and erudition, studied at Oxford and the University of Rome, converted to Catholicism and became a nun, entering the Order of the Sacred Heart. When she was Mother Superior of the Sacred Heart Convent on Point Grey Road in Vancouver the two oldest Blanchet girls, Elisabeth and Frances, attended high school there for two years.

With a scholastic record like hers Muriel Liffiton was expected to go on to university but instead at eighteen she married Geoffrey Blanchet, the brother of a school friend — a decision she is said to have regretted later. The first Blanchet in North America arrived from France in 1666 but Geoffrey, although bilingual, was only about one-sixth French. He was from Ottawa, the youngest of eleven children, and his father was a minor civil servant.

Geoffrey and Muriel Blanchet started married life in Sherbrooke, Quebec, where he was a bank manager. Later he was placed in charge of foreign exchange at the Toronto headquarters of the Bank of Commerce. He was a clever, somewhat artistic man with a highly emotional, nervous temperament. In his early forties he became ill and took early retirement. The family by that time included four children, and when he had sufficiently recovered he packed them all into a Willys-Knight touring car which, according to one of the children, "had flapping curtains and a great top that folded like an elephant sitting down," and started driving across the country looking for an island to live on. They drove and drove until they came to Chicago, where the Blanchets parked their car on a city street while they all slept. David had not been born yet and Peter, then aged three-and-a-half, remembers sleeping in a hammock strung from the roof of the Willys-Knight. A policeman woke them up and they continued across Canada and the States until they came to Vancouver Island.

Peter Blanchet, whom the family calls by his middle name, Tate, is now a grey-haired geological engineer in his late fifties. Sitting in his office in Vancouver, he can still remember clearly how they found their new home. "We came to a locked gate with *Clovelly* written on it, got out of the Willys-Knight, climbed the gate and had supper on the other side," he recalled. "Intrigued, we packed the gate off its hinges and drove a quarter of a mile to a house built of log slabs with the bark still on it." Clovelly, named by a previous owner after a place in Cornwall, became Little House, purchased by the Blanchets in 1922. It had been empty since 1914, part of a one-hundred-acre real estate scheme that collapsed during World War I. The Blanchets were able to buy seven acres at the extreme tip, Curteis point, overlooking the Gulf of Georgia, and they kept it until Mrs. Blanchet died in 1961, although Little House was torn down in 1948. It was an unusual house, a strangely mystical English cottage covered with ivy, with a big fireplace and a billiard table on the first floor and four bedrooms up a rickety flight of stairs on the second floor. "It was designed by a celebrated architect, Sam McLure, and built by a crook," said David Blanchet, who was born there. "It was a beautiful design on wretched foundations and full of dry rot." By the time he and his mother tore it down after World War II the foundations were so far gone that the house had a tremendous list and dining room chairs were sliding every which way.

Their boat the *Caprice* was purchased in 1923 for six hundred dollars. It had been built the year before, a cold year, and the Brentwood Ferry, near which it was anchored, managed to shove a cake of ice into the side of the *Caprice*, sinking it. It was hauled out on a nearby dock and the Blanchets bought it on the spot, with water still dribbling out of it. "This was probably when my mother learned to deal with engines," David has commented. "It had to be cleaned out immediately, once it had been in salt water. We had that same engine for twenty years, until it was changed in 1942."

Peter Blanchet remembers the first time his mother took the *Caprice* out on her own. It was in March, on his sixth birthday, and she had promised to take him to Shell Island, a favourite spot where she liked to say she would spend her hundredth birthday. She and Peter got in the boat, which they kept at Canoe Cove, and "she cranked and cranked that darned engine, and still it wouldn't start," Peter recalled. "She could see my father sitting on the Point watching to see if we would get off and she had to go and get him, which really irked her. Then she and I went fishing for the day off Sidney Spit. We caught a couple of fish which we cooked over a fire on the beach at Shell Island. It was very good salmon!"

Geoffrey Blanchet died in 1927. He had gone off on the *Caprice* by himself for the day, stopping at nearby Knapp Island, where he anchored and set up his cookstove. He was never seen again, but his boat was found by a Chinese gardener working for the Harvey family, who lived on the island. Blanchet had had heart problems and was presumed to have gone for a swim, had an attack and drowned.

The second summer after his death, Mrs. Blanchet rented Little House and took the children off on the *Caprice* for the first of the venturesome trips that as a composite memory became the substance of *The Curve of Time*. With the money she received from renting Clovelly in summer to a wealthy family from Washington and her own small income, she was able to manage. The two oldest girls,

Elisabeth and Frances, missed several summers on the boat when they were sent east to live with an aunt and uncle on their father's side in Ottawa; and later when they went to the convent in Vancouver, their holidays were shorter, eventually shrinking to two weeks when they both studied nursing. Elisabeth started nursing on the BC coast, married and went to England, where she still lives. She became a freelance journalist and the successful author of over thirty published books. Her mother's attitude towards her writing was a mixture of pride and a tendency to regard her daughter's books as pot-boilers. Most of them are novels with a documentary background, often based on Elisabeth's hospital experiences, and many are still selling. Frances married two years after she started nursing, and she and her husband, Ron King, raise Hereford cattle on their ranch near Golden, BC.

The three younger children, Joan, Peter and David, were educated almost entirely at home, by correspondence, by their mother, and by a Scottish engineer who was a mechanic at the Canoe Cove boat works, who taught them math, chemistry and physics. Joan, known as the rebellious member of the family, went to art school in Vancouver and then continued her art studies in New York. When she left Vancouver, she bought an old Indian dugout canoe for five dollars and paddled home. It took her five days, and she crossed the Gulf of Georgia at night, to avoid traffic and heavy seas, a remarkable feat since it required at least nine hours of steady paddling. Frances King vividly recalled hearing about her sister's arrival. "When she rounded the point in her dugout, wearing an old red sweater, Capi and the boys were sitting on the bluff, wondering who the Indian was!" Joan had expected some commendation, and was amazed at Capi's anger. "Just because I'm a fool doesn't mean you children have to be!" Capi said. Later the boys reported that Capi laughed herself to sleep. Joan later confided to a friend that she was testing herself; she felt if she could cross the Gulf of Georgia alone, she would have the confidence to face New York. She subsequently married Ted McFeely, from whom she is now divorced, and lives in a remote spot on the already remote Queen Charlotte Islands.

Peter, who had an inventive mind and was working on a memory rod before he ever heard of computers, entered the University of British Columbia at sixteen, and managed one more summer on the boat before the pressure of adult life took him away. David, who inherited his mother's imaginative sensitivity, after one year in a local school and a year in university joined the army when the Second World War began. After the war he returned to Little House, which by now was literally falling apart. He and his mother proceeded to tear it down, starting at the top, and together they designed and built her an attractive white bungalow directly overlooking the sea. David went on to construct another house for a friend and began one for himself, meanwhile returning to university to study architecture. By then he was married to Janet Patterson, a handsome woman of great character and the daughter of writer R.M. Patterson. They had one child, Julia, and when she was four David was stricken with poliomyelitis, which left him partially paralyzed, confined to a wheel chair. They live now in North Vancouver.

In appearance, Capi Blanchet was of medium height, with very fine blonde hair brushed upwards so that it formed a kind of haze around her head. She had a strong rather than a pretty face, round and pleasant. Her normal attire was a pair of khaki shorts, an Indian sweater and sneakers that sometimes had holes in the toes. She had begun wearing shorts in the nineteen-twenties, long before they were fashionable, and her daughter Elisabeth has recalled that a journalist writing about people he had met on the BC coast in the *Saturday Evening Post* "commented on her shorts and how suitable they seemed for what she was doing—running a boat." In 1957 Capi went to England to visit Elisabeth, bought a Land Rover, and the two women went camping. "We were shopping in Chartres, France, and she was wearing blue jeans, clamdigger length," Betty said. "A white-haired Frenchman walked slowly around her, smiled and bowed. 'Très chic, Madame!' was his comment." What impressed Mrs. Blanchet, however, on her trip was the lack of wood on the beaches, since this was her main source of firewood at home.

Mrs. Blanchet's children and friends were enormously fond of her, somewhat in awe of her all-around competence, and thought her fair-minded but domineering. "She was a challenge for any child, but slightly dampening," her eldest daughter has written. "She could do almost anything that men did, and still be feminine."

"She had a lot of courage or self-confidence, but she did not overestimate her mechanical ability," a writer friend, Hubert Evans, has said. "On a run from Sidney to Vancouver, the *Caprice* was overtaken in the Gulf by a late season southeaster, and the little boat took quite a dusting," he related. "Capi had several children aboard. 'I told the Lord I could take care of the boat but would he please keep the engine running,' she said to me afterwards."

Capi Blanchet does not seem to have been particularly light-hearted or spontaneous, and she was somewhat arrogant about anyone she considered her inferior. "Like many English of a certain class she had a stiffness and tended to classify people," another friend has remarked. "She had a slightly Church-of-England attitude, even talking to fishermen, who were never sure how to take her. She had a good sense of humour but a rather studied laugh. I think there was a good deal of repression there. Even when David was desperately ill she never permitted anyone to see her upset, and said to her daughter-in-law, 'Oh heck, he'll get better in no time!'"

A description from her daughter Frances exemplifies the quality of character her children and friends remember best: "She was capable of handling any situation. If she was worried she didn't let us know."

On the boat Mrs. Blanchet was even tempered under what must often have been trying conditions at such close quarters; her method of discipline was to separate her children, not argue. David remembered his mother losing her temper with him only once, when he was about twelve. "It was some silly mistake, something about an anchor, that I did my way instead of what she wanted," he said. "Normally her eyes were brown, but suddenly they were a turquoise colour and blazing. It was unbelievable!"

She was one of those rare women who are mechanically inclined, and enjoyed tinkering with engines and working with tools. Every so often she took apart the *Caprice* engine, a four-cylinder Kermath, cleaned and painted it and put it back together again, grinding the valves herself. Frances King remembers the first time she took her husband to meet her mother. The morning after their arrival he found Capi in her workshop. She had taken the old engine out of the *Caprice*, had ground the valves and was putting in new rings and checking the timing. "Having worked in a garage, Ron could appreciate with amazement what his mother-in-law was doing, whereas this was everyday stuff to me," Frances said.

An intimate friend of Mrs. Blanchet's, Kathleen Caldwell, has described her as "not excessively domestic, but interested in people and politics, which she loved to discuss. Her house was comfortable and pleasant, and Capi could produce a beautiful meal with what looked like no effort." In their close circle Capi was renowned for her roast beef, Yorkshire pudding and mouth-watering pastry. Oddly enough, although she liked to eat fish, she never cooked it except outdoors on a beach because she couldn't stand the smell.

Mrs. Blanchet liked to draw sea creatures in pen and ink, and once illustrated a fairy story she wrote with drawings in the margin. She was also a fair pianist, and in later life enjoyed playing a violin that her grandfather gave her when she was twelve. It now hangs on the wall of David's living room, but his mother used it often; she had joined a small orchestra at Deep Cove, playing second violin, reputedly a quarter-tone flat.

Children found her very understanding. She treated them like adults, and when David contracted polio she took care of their daughter Julia for two years while he was in hospital in Vancouver and Victoria and his wife Janet worked. Grandmother and grandchild got on very well, and it was a mutually beneficial relationship; by then Capi had become somewhat reclusive—having Julia with her forced her to go out.

David fell ill before the interior of Mrs. Blanchet's new house was completed and it never seemed to advance beyond that half-built stage. She lined the whole interior with vertical cedar planks herself, but doors were a late addition to the bathroom and kitchen and knobs usually came off in hand. Her firewood was never quite dry and Kathleen Caldwell once delighted her by bringing a gift of Presto logs. When Capi's doctor prescribed a drier climate for a cough that later developed into emphysema she ignored him and instead sat with her head as far into her oil stove as she could get it for twenty minutes a day. "That's my high, dry climate," she said. She had an ingenious system of heating water in the morning before she was ready to light the oil stove. She turned an electric iron upside down, supported it with stones, set it at its highest heat, put a pan on top of it and boiled her water for breakfast there.

As for the *Caprice*, it was never meant to have any other owner than Capi Blanchet. After the war she planned to build a new boat and sold the *Caprice* for seven hundred dollars—a hundred more than she had paid for it—to the owner of a boat works in Victoria, who hauled it up for repairs. While it was on the ways, the entire boat works burned down, including the *Caprice*. Mrs. Blanchet did have another boat after that, the *Scylla*, but she never really used it.

Mrs. Blanchet's children, now older than she was when they made their wonderful odysseys along the coast, look back on that faraway time with wonderment and affection. "They were exciting; something we looked forward to," Peter commented. "It was a fairly normal life for us, however, because we always seemed to be doing it."

"I loved the summer journeys but I doubt if any of us appreciated quite how unique our childhood was. We just knew Capi was doing something unusual," Elisabeth writes from England. "She used to get a bit tense if we were taking green water over the bow or wallowing about in a following sea or running the Yuculta Rapids. Otherwise she took everything in her stride—whether crossing the Straits of Georgia at 4 a.m. to beat the sou'wester or exploring new territory."

"Only fools seek adventures," David has remembered his mother as saying at one time or another. However foolish Mrs. Blanchet's adventures may have seemed to her (which is doubtful), they have a dreamlike charm for an increasing number of readers. *The Curve of Time* has had a separate and ongoing life of its own, achieving its own small immortality.

Published in *Raincoast Chronicles #8*.

Seven Stones

◆

WHEN I FINISHED the Profile of Pierre Trudeau in 1969, I treated myself to a trip with my sons through British Columbia, which I had been longing to visit. Before leaving New York, I called Don Snowden in Newfoundland and asked him what we should see in British Columbia, since his parents lived there. "Don't miss Simon Fraser University," he said.

The first thing we did when we arrived in Vancouver, was to rent the station wagon, three sleeping bags, three air mattresses, and the air pump we thought we should have for our camping trip. Twenty minutes later we were driving up Burnaby Mountain. It was a perfect summer day, clear and sunny, and when we drove around a bend, there, hugging the ridged summit of the mountain, was Simon Fraser University. The three of us were dazzled by that stunning set of buildings flowing together, and we had to know at once who the architect was.

"Arthur Erickson," was the reply at the information desk, and I wrote it down on a scrap of paper and tucked it into my purse. Sometimes you get a feeling, a kind of sense of the future; I knew right then I was going to write about him. Jay, Richie and I then started off to see the rest of the province, touring 3,500 miles in two hilarious weeks.

Seven years later, after I moved to BC, I called Arthur Erickson and arranged to go to his house to start our interviews. Before our first appointment, I decided it was time to modernize my equipment, which consisted of a pen and a lined notebook. I arrived at his house with a tape recorder I had just purchased, complete with a full set of batteries. I had rehearsed with it once with my husband John, on his fishing boat, but the rumble of the engine had made too much noise.

Arthur and I, and my new machine, and my ninety-minute tapes, got off to a fine start. I had gone through several tapes when all of a sudden the recorder went *click!*, and everything stopped.

Arthur, who was getting his first view of a tape recorder at close range, said, "What do you think is wrong?"

"I don't know," I said. "It's not supposed to do this."

We both examined the tape recorder. "I'm terrible at this sort of thing," Arthur said. "I can barely drive a car."

We concluded that the tape recorder's batteries must be dead. I asked him to excuse me while I rushed off to a hardware store for more batteries, and when I got in my car I was mortified to discover the battery in my car was dead too. Arthur had to give me a good push to get the car started, and I came back with new batteries all around.

That night I called Howard White, who was my consultant on Trouble, long before he was my publisher. "What?" he exclaimed. "Don't tell me you didn't know *that*! The tape recorder plugs into the wall."

At my next interview with Erickson, I said, "You will never guess what I have found out about the tape recorder," and I plugged it into the wall.

I finished interviewing Arthur on tapes, seven of them, but on my next story I went back to my notebook and pen, which had worked perfectly well for years and years.

John died soon after I completed the Profile. After it was published, Howie White and I were talking about Erickson, and he asked me if I had any more material than I had put into my *New Yorker* piece. I said, "I certainly do, and there are all those beautiful buildings to see in photographs, too."

We agreed that I would write a book about Erickson, and after a few months, Howie came to see why I wasn't doing it. "I can't write in my study," I said. "It's on the other side of the wall from John's workshop, and I keep wanting to talk to John."

"I'll fix that!" Howie said, and ran down to John's workshop, pulled a sheet of plywood out from underneath and started hammering. In a very short time he came up the hill with a fine looking table and set it up in the living room, put my typewriter on it, and said, "Get to work."

That's how my book, *Seven Stones: A Portrait of Arthur Erickson, Architect* came about. Following are excerpts from the *New Yorker* Profile, "Seven Stones."

◆

Arthur Erickson is a witty, semi-mystical, not at all humble Canadian architect who has performed the sizable feat of adorning the North American landscape with some of its most admired structures. A youthful man of fifty-four, Erickson says, "Where I am or what I am is no concern of mine. I am concerned with what our civilization is all about, and expressing this in buildings. Everything I do, everything I see is through architecture. It has given me a vehicle for looking at the world. I am not involved in the aesthetics of architecture or interested in design as such. I'm interested in what buildings can do beyond what they look like, and how they can affect whole areas and people's lives. I have never done a building where I didn't at least attempt to see it in a new philosophical or social way. I could have asked questions in any field, but I am doing it through my buildings. What panics me is how little time I have. Now I want to build with all details suppressed, to make what I build look as if it had just happened—as if there were nothing studied, no labor or art involved. Architecture is no different from any other art process. It is like poetry, in which you compress everything into a few words. To achieve that economy takes a lifetime."

A colleague who was asked to classify Erickson's architecture exclaimed, "Why, Arthur doesn't even follow himself!" Erickson's architectural style has been defined as lyrical, cool, daring, romantic, monumental, contemporary, classical, derivative, original, neo-Inca, timeless, modern—and sometimes as just breathtakingly beautiful. There are recognizable Erickson devices: strong horizontals; wooden lattices to soften solid wall mass; high fences or plantings for privacy; skylights; flooded roofs or ground pools to catch reflections; the illusion of infinity; a mound of earth outside (which Erickson calls "my signature"). But by and large his most consistent trait is inconsistency, professionally and personally. This has produced a deliberate method of living, which he thrives on, and which Geoffrey Massey has described as "consistent chaos."

Erickson says that designing space for human beings to use—preferably clusters of buildings and the land and water around them—occupies almost all his conscious moments, and he believes that it absorbs an even higher percentage of his unconscious, or what he refers to as his super-conscious, thoughts. In the Canadian *Who's Who*, he once listed architecture and travelling as his "recreations," and he has not stayed more than ten days in one place since 1965. Travelling enables him to check up on every type of building constructed by civilized man, and possibly by earlier human species, going back to Paleolithic man. "North America is in a very primitive

Illustration by Burt Silverman

stage, because culture takes hundreds of years to evolve," Erickson has said. "I am fortunate that I can stand in Canada, a country without a culture, and look at the world. When I am given a project such as a university or a courthouse or a museum, I can detach myself from the patterns of learning about that type of structure in North America, because I know the solutions at Oxford, at the El Azhar mosque in Cairo, or at a temple in Thailand. I can say, 'What is its essence? How can I extract something pertinent for today?'"

Erickson, sometimes in partnership and sometimes alone, has designed and built apartment houses, schools, office buildings, banks, three prize-winning international-fair structures, a Sikh temple, a plastic swimming-pool cabana, a visitors' pavilion made of recycled newspapers for a recent United Nations Habitat Conference in Vancouver, two subway stations in Toronto, and more private houses than he can remember. In the new Vancouver civic center, he has introduced not only indoor and outdoor gardens with orange trees and flowering shrubs, three waterfalls, and a miniature forest but a small cinema, a day-care center, shops, restaurants, an ice-skating rink that converts into a marketplace in summer, and an exhibition hall and conference center, next to provincial offices partly submerged below the street. A radical new courthouse was built, and the Vancouver Art Gallery occupies the remodelled old neo-classical courthouse building. The hundred-million-dollar, three-block complex is transforming downtown life in British Columbia's largest city.

Many of Erickson's commissions were won in competitions, and he has lost count of the awards and medals he has acquired—two or three dozen. In 1978, the American Institute of Architects, whose Hawaii chapter had previously given him an award for "singular individuality and excellence in design," made him an Honorary Fellow, and in 1971 an award of fifty thousand dollars and a gold medal was given him by the Royal Bank of Canada. This is a distinction conferred on one Canadian annually for contributions "to human welfare and the common good."

The essence of Erickson's consistent inconsistency was expressed in a speech he made to the Canadian business establishment at a sumptuous banquet held in his honor on the occasion of the Royal Bank award. He is a sophisticated observer of the power structure, who knows where the vast sums must come from to make an architect's designs materialize. Yet he scolded the assembled businessmen for the "ruthless economic competition" in North American cities, which expresses itself in streets that are "wastelands of parked cars...grim, sunless spaces between towering edifices...showing our priorities for services, roadways, and real estate." He defined the bulldozer as the "symbol of North America." He asked for a shift of "mind set"—his term for rigid values that control the future development of ideas—away from "aggressive independence and self-sufficient individuality" and toward a "balance between economic profit and social well-being." He posed the question "Should not the land come under public ownership so that the ultimate control is in the public's hands?"

At the 1974 International Congress of Architecture, in Iran, he pleaded with Third World countries to preserve their own cultures, to avoid the Western solution of freeways and high rises—"all the trashy neon and plastic glitter"—and added that what the West has "thrown on the waters of the world drifts back to us on a tide of cultural pollution appalling to behold." In 1975, at a meeting of the International Union of Architects, in Madrid, he pronounced Western architectural techniques "stifling" and begged the assembled architects to adopt urban forms consistent with their own diverse cultures rather than simply to follow the lead of the West. He recommended that they suspend rational thought to achieve "a floating, unselective frame of mind...in order to receive information from all sources unconditionally." To put it in Zen terms, he said, "it is only the empty vessel that can be filled."

Erickson feels that differences between the architecture of the East and that of the West are a result of opposing attitudes towards man's importance: in the West, man is at the center of everything, while Eastern concepts make him a part of the larger scheme of nature. At a meeting of the Institute of Canadian Bankers in 1972, Erickson compared the imposition by tourists from the West of their own values on other cultures to "an infectious disease decimating whatever values existed before." Their egocentricity, he said, makes them "incapable of measuring things except in their own terms;" they regard ancient living cultures as "undeveloped" and their current practitioners as "non-achievers." After this warmup, he attacked the World Bank specifically, for funding a "multistoried, monster" hotel in Afghanistan, in "one of the most beautiful valleys in the world," and a three-thousand-room hotel development in Bali, "whose impact on that island will be terminal." He said, "You, as bankers, cannot afford to be concerned with only the economic aspects of projects that you finance. There may be serious implications. . . which at some future time may even be considered crimes against mankind."

Commenting later on his address to the bankers, he remarked, "I felt that it had to be said, but I expected a disaster and was amazed at the applause." He noted that the bankers published this speech in their journal and gave it their award for the best talk of 1972.

In October, 1978, at the World Congress of the International Union of Architects, in Mexico City, he attacked tourism again as an industry that has "gone wild," comparing package tours to plagues of locusts that "arrive, destroy, and leave conscienceless from the havoc they have wreaked." Referring to the new hotels in Bali and Afghanistan, he continued, "Architects and international agencies have conspired in this. . . desecration," producing "overcrowding and sleazy developments. . . As the number of empty or deteriorating hotels has increased, the tourist agencies have looked elsewhere for a virgin place ripe for raping. . . In America, a new kind of anonymous city was born—Anywhere, USA—to spread everywhere in the late sixties and seventies, as unchallengeable American expertise became in universal demand, giving birth to Anywhere, The World."

He said afterward, "The audiences I speak to are the people with the power to make changes. You don't want to flatter if things are not as they should be. I repeat and repeat and repeat in my speeches. All one can hope is that what I say will have some meaning to someone and may influence his life and, through his, influence someone else's. I am completely apolitical, but I am pro people. If I can get away with what I say in the circles I speak in, it's because I am considered a member of their group. It is important to upset them."

♦

Erickson was born in Vancouver and spent his first twenty years there. It is still his home. The forest clearing that Erickson created for that home is on a sixty-six-by-one-hundred-and-twenty-foot city lot in a neighborhood of small houses fronted with patches of lawn. His house, however, has a high cedar fence around it and, like the majority of the dwellings he has designed for others, it is almost invisible from the street. Bushes and trees peer enticingly over the fence, and an odd-shaped roof with skylights is barely discernible through the foliage. Two garages and a lean-to were at the back of the lot when Erickson bought it, in 1957, for eleven thousand dollars. The previous owner had lived in one garage and the lean-to, reserving the second garage for a car. Erickson doesn't own a car; he ordinarily rents cars, and uses a lane at his back door for parking—a practice that is frowned upon by the city, as are high fences. His house now consists of the original garages and the lean-to, which has become part of a small, skylit connective structure, containing the bathroom and kitchen: a total area of twelve hundred square feet. His living room has the unmistakable rectangular dimensions of a narrow, one-car garage, and so does his bedroom-study, but in each the wall facing the garden has been replaced by sliding glass.

The visitor to Erickson's house, upon opening a gate in the fence, enters a magical realm of trees, bushes, and wild grasses surrounding a small body of water that appears to be a lake; at the far end of this garden, there is a small mountain. The lake is actually an artfully placed pond deep enough to contain fish, and the mountain is an eight-foot mound of earth, but illusion is everywhere: spacious, lovely country landscape continuing into the beyond. From the gate, the visitor follows stepping stones through this sylvan scene, crosses a wooden deck, and steps down to a brick patio, where a glass door set into an off-white travertine-marble wall appears to arrive at the visitor's feet rather than the other way around, or so it seemed one day when I visited Erickson. I could see him through the glass, coming to the door with a rapid, lithe step: slim, of medium height, casually dressed in tan slacks, a black-and-white checked sports shirt, and a tan cardigan sweater. He has short, curly gray hair flecked with brown and some white; his eyes are a friendly blue. He has sometimes been mistaken for a dilettante because he enjoys the company of wealthy and famous people; in the East, he gravitates toward the international jet set, dropping the names of members into his conversation, as if their acceptance of him surprised him. He is a gifted raconteur. In Vancouver, he relaxes within a small circle of artists, writers, and teachers, among whom old friends predominate; or with his mother and his brother, Donald — a talented writer and teacher, who is four years younger — and Donald's family, to all of whom he is devoted. In company, Erickson almost always seems to be smiling or laughing, but his outwardly easygoing nature disguises a compulsive worker who is somewhat solitary. The unsmiling Erickson has a long, serious face and determined features that all seem to be pointed: peaked hairline, aquiline nose, wide but tapered mouth, and firm, pointed chin.

Erickson told me he had just returned from a business trip that took him to Toronto, New York, and the Middle East, and allowed him a day of skiing in the Swiss Alps, which included glacier-hopping by helicopter — a new variation for him of the only sport besides scuba diving in which he indulges. Erickson's enthusiasms translate into verbal extravagance, some of his favorite words being "extraordinary," "spectacular," "incredible," and "absolutely." He described the experience of being dropped by helicopter on "a little handkerchief of ice," then skiing five thousand feet to the bottom of a valley and being picked up there by the helicopter and transported to the top of another glacier to ski down as "absolutely incredible."

It was ten on a Sunday morning, and Erickson had just prepared his breakfast — a blended liquid of fresh orange juice, milk, wheat germ, vegetable protein, and vitamins. He started coffee in a glittering miniature espresso machine on a teak kitchen counter, and while the coffee gurgled and hissed we stood looking into the garden from the living room. It is a small room with a velvety carpet, low sofas around small tables, and walls lined with five-inch squares of Italian suede — all a soft-beige contrast to the off-white of the drapes, travertine floors, fireplace, and tabletops. Erickson used to sleep in the living room on a couch made of straw streetcar seat backs, but recently he was persuaded by Francisco Kripacz, who advises him on interiors, to adopt this more elegant simplicity, and to create new sleeping arrangements in the other garage building. Except for a slim, delicately carved eighteenth-century Japanese goddess of mercy on the mantel, several small pottery pieces on clear Plexiglas shelves around the fireplace, and two Oriental figures on pedestals, the art that he has collected in his travels has been consigned to teak cupboards. Simple statement extends even to the kitchen, where formerly open shelves have disappeared behind teak panels. In the bathroom, fixtures are of black porcelain, and almost invisible.

Outside, a typical Vancouver rain squall started, transforming the garden into a glistening jungle. "For years, I was going to move to a view of open water, but this place is so convenient, because I can shut it and leave," said Erickson, drinking his breakfast as he talked. "Besides, I have to have a limited, closed view, so I can withdraw into my own world. When I moved into this house, in 1957, I was teaching architecture at the University of British Columbia and collecting pottery. The things that surrounded me were more important to me. That pot is upside down!" Interrupting himself, he walked over to a shelf where a small brown square pot with a slim neck stood, broad end down. He turned its neck to the bottom, and laughed. "It's by a well-known English potter, Hans Coper, and every second week, when my cleaning woman comes, she turns it upside down." He took a soft-green plate off another shelf. "I love this piece — it's a version of Sung celadon, and I got it in the Celebes," he said. "I have always been fascinated by pottery. It gives you such an intimate relationship with the person who did it." He ran a finger along the fluted edge, stopping at a flat spot. "This potter made the edge with his fingers, and you can see where he had his doubts and failed to do it!" He touched some tiny pinpricks in the middle of the plate. "In classical pottery, there should be two fish in the center. I don't know what this is, but it's off-center. Imagine a Chinese potter in the outer provinces who knew of the great Sung pieces trying to duplicate one from memory on his own wheel!"

He put the plate back. "In 1965, when I started travelling every week to Montreal to work for Expo on Canada's Man in the Community pavilion, everything changed. I loved my little house, but suddenly possessions had no importance. I realized I could live happily out of a suitcase, and didn't really need even that, and I had a freedom I had never had before. Architecturally, this house is terrible, but it serves as a refuge, a kind of decompression chamber. The nice thing about the garden is that I started it and it's been doing its own thing ever since."

The rain stopped suddenly, and the sun made a trembling attempt to enter the garden through the dripping trees. "I bought this house for its wonderful garden," he went on "A charming Englishwoman who lived here had a white picket fence, phlox, delphiniums, lupines, Shasta daisies, a rose arbor with a strawberry-and-vegetable garden behind it, and a lovely lawn. I thought the place could be self-sufficient, but the catch was that someone had to take care of all that. The second year, it became like a deserted garden. It was terribly romantic, the kind of secret garden that children love — saturated with weeds but with the flowers still growing and the grass a foot high.

The third year, the weeds took over entirely, so I got a bulldozer and told the operator to bury the garden, dig a hole, and make a hill high enough so I couldn't see the house across the street. I didn't have this high fence then, and I *had* to get rid of that view. Everybody in the neighborhood thought I was excavating to build a house, and chatted with me over the picket fence, very happy to believe that they were no longer going to have a nonconformist garage dweller among them. I hired a student to line the hole with roofing paper and fill it with water, and I have never touched this pond since. I got grasses and rushes from the Fraser River, dug plants and the pine trees from the forest, put in ten different species of bamboo, the ten-foot-high zebra grass you can just see, and those very rare Himalayan rhododendrons. The dogwood, apple, pear, and plum trees are from the old garden, and I put in the persimmon tree. Then I just let the whole thing go."

How had he achieved such an impression of depth and space, I asked.

"You put in as many horizontal planes, one in front of another, within your field of vision as possible," he said. "Your eye has to take in the whole series, and reads that as greater space. If you put in water, psychologically you have to cross it, and the resulting sense of remoteness extends the visual effect to another land. If I have a lavish party, I put musicians across the water, and it's as if they were playing from an island over the sea. Actually, there are twelve planes: the deck right out here, the low hedge, the brick terrace beyond the hedge, the marble slab that sticks out over the pool, the water, the edge of the rushes and grass, the gravel beach on the other side, the pine trees, the juniper that grows horizontally on the mound, the bamboo, the dogwood and fir, and those poplar trees at the fence. Everything is starved for water in the summer, but it's planned so as to keep a certain discipline. Otherwise, it would do too well the rest of the time in this wet climate. The charm of the garden is that everything has survived, because it is in its natural habitat. I have a gardener in just twice a year, and I am an observer, not an intruder. It is endlessly fascinating to see what it will produce."

◆

Former students of Erickson's at UBC remember him as a profound teacher. One of them, Bruno Freschi, describes Erickson's teaching method as "a Socratic, sort of open-ended Zen approach," and explained, "His objective was to turn the person on. Modern architecture is immersed in detail and restrictive therapeutic approaches, whereas Arthur is concerned with design that reflects what he calls timeless dimensions of human behavior. He has a humanist's perception of space, introduces metaphors and symbols into buildings, and tries to define the rhythm of human patterns." Freschi continued, "One of the most poetic problems he created was called 'Seven Stones.' He said to the class one day, 'The assignment is to choose seven stones, and present your project in three weeks.' It was terribly generative. Some students danced with seven stones, some glued them to a piece of cardboard, and one got seven beautiful stones from the beach and presented them in a velvet box, clanking them together for everyone to hear. It was a little performance. Arthur looked and said, 'Why are you wearing a blue sweater?' The kid was dumbfounded and replied, 'That has nothing to do with the problem!' And Arthur said, 'No. It's a performance, and your clothing is part of it.'"

I asked Erickson about all this. "I liked teaching, but I could never carry on a career and teach, too," he said. "Teaching takes everything out of you. I always made a point of teaching the first-year students, to try and break down the hypocrisy of high school and North American middle-class upbringing." He paused. "I wonder what it is about the middle class I hate so much? Conventions, I think. Everything is done for reasons other than intrinsic worth. In a creative field, one has to battle this.

"As far as I am concerned, the Socratic is the *only* method of teaching. All my exercises were to force the students to probe their own resources for the meaning of things and not do anything by habit or convention. None of us knew what the problem was, and the whole exercise was to find out. The assignment just to 'choose seven stones' puts students in a state of confusion—a state where there are no answers, only questions. Whenever they come up with what seems like a solution, you take it away, so they have to search deeper and deeper for reasons for their behavior. The choice of the number seven was purely numerical. With *seven* stones, you immediately have questions of grouping, shape, mass, size, color, and texture, and whether to subgroup within the seven. Students climbed to the top of mountains and dived to the bottom of the sea to collect stones. I got in geologists and mineralogists so that we could understand the context of stones as essential ingredients of the earth—which gave them still a different meaning. Suddenly, the stoniness of stone became a fascinating exercise in the history of the earth and of this region. The possibilities were endless, and the students began to realize that with seven stones one could convey practically anything."

Erickson got up and stood with his back against the sink, looking into the garden, as he went on, "During their first year, when I was trying to get them to explore all aspects of their sensitivity, I would arrange a carefully designed dinner, usually Chinese, and then set a problem of designing an unconventional feast, for which they would have to consider light, enclosure, and ambience. I also let a dancer take over the class, to make then aware of their bodies in space, to show how they could explore anything in architecture by movement. One exercise was to draw themselves in a position of movement and then provide a device to support that position out of plastic, wood, paper, or metal. At the end, I pointed out that they had been designing furniture. If I had said, 'Look, we're going to design a chair or a bed,' they would have explored design on the basis of previous memories of chairs or beds. By approaching the model from the opposite, and essential, direction, I was able to make them realize the vital aspects of furniture."

He sat down, "Now, how does all this lead to building? I was trying to set up a discipline of approach, so that the students would give any problem the same questioning. This is my own approach to an architectural problem. The method doesn't work on many people. All you can hope to do in teaching is to touch one person — perhaps two — in a class, who begins to realize the force of the elements he is dealing with. Architects are so rarely aware of their own powers of communication, and therefore most of what we see is indifferent building, which nevertheless affects us by its indifference."

◆

Erickson taught architecture until 1964, a year after he and Geoffrey Massey, a Vancouver architect, won first prize in the Simon Fraser University competition, and formed a partnership that lasted eight years. They were supposed to submit a design for a typical American campus, with a separate building for each teaching discipline. "When Gordon Shrum, the first chancellor of Simon Fraser, announced our names as the winners, we almost fell over," Geoffrey Massey told me when I saw him and his wife at his home. He is a tall, dark-haired man who bears a close resemblance to his father, the actor Raymond Massey. "We had ignored the requirements, because we thought the university should be a tight complex of elements for use, not of disciplines — with offices, laboratories, and lecture halls arranged in juxtaposition to one another conveniently, to save travel time. We thought we might get a pat on the back for having a good scheme, but we didn't have a hope of winning."

That was in July, 1963, and Gordon Shrum, who was then chairman of the giant British Columbia Hydro and Power Authority, was following the provincial premier's orders to select a site, hire architects, build a university for six thousand students, and open it by September, 1965. Shrum, now a hyperactive eighty-three, has since been given the assignment of overseeing the construction of another Erickson-designed project—the new Vancouver civic-center complex. His main chore is to keep a tight hold on the purse strings, since Erickson, like most architects, sometimes has an aptitude for overspending.

Shrum recalls the genesis of the university design very precisely: "I flew in a little BC Hydro company plane over the Fraser Valley and decided that the imaginative thing was to put the university on top of Burnaby Mountain. I arranged a competition, open only to BC architects. They had to submit three drawings: a plan, a perspective, and an elevation, which is a facade of the building. Any architect, or a firm, could enter, and the first five winners would each take a five-thousand-dollar prize or build one part of the university. Three-quarters of the architects in BC worked on it, and we eventually had seventy-one entries. There was a seventy-second, but his wife went to the hairdresser on the way to deliver his drawings and missed the deadline. *I* was completely dizzy, with two hundred and some drawings, but my international panel of judges was unanimous on one set—Erickson and Massey's. Their drawings were so plain that they would never have caught my inexperienced eye. Erickson had built houses and was an associate professor at UBC—not even in business. But if we had chosen anyone else's design, people would never have come from all over the world to see the university." He scratched his head, and his eyes gleamed behind his glasses. "You drive along that mountain road and don't see a thing. Suddenly, there it is! Dramatic!"

Each of the four runners-up in the Simon Fraser competition chose to build one of the five original units within the over-all design of the winning architects. Thus, with Erickson and Massey in charge, four essentially rival architecture firms worked on the theatre and gymnasium, the library, the science block, and the quadrangle of offices and classrooms. An Erickson mound crowns the grassy courtyard of the quadrangle—the only detail that makes Shrum nervous. "I would have preferred a formal garden, like the one at Versailles," he says.

The winners chose to build the mall—actually a three-story building—because it linked everything together. Erickson has designed several smaller buildings for the university since, and is consulted now whenever construction is anticipated, but during a period of strained relations two structures were put up over Erickson and Massey's opposition—a men's residence, Shell House, which sticks out at right angles to the rest of the design, and a prominent gas station, the funds for both having been provided by the Shell Oil Company.

The students and faculty of Simon Fraser like the place when the sun shines, but rain and fog produce a gaggle of complaints. "Knocking the university is the 'in' thing to do," remarked a student hitchhiker whom I picked up on my first visit there. In wet weather, which prevails twice as often on the mountaintop as in the city of Vancouver just below, the gray concrete has a depressing effect, and the mall becomes a wind tunnel in gusty weather. Everyone grumbles about narrow underground corridors, many of them inserted later by the administration, and small classrooms. "Magnificent to look at but not to work in," says a professor who has been there since the university opened; he feels that the quad offices combine a lack of privacy and a sense of isolation. There have been chronic problems with leaks, and for these the speed with which the concrete was poured has been blamed. Some people complain about the swallows and pigeons that nest under the overhang where the pre-cast cement walls meet the roof. The space-frame roof over the quarter-mile-long mall, containing an acre of glass in a daring innovative design by Jeffrey Lindsay, a Los Angeles-based architectural research-and-development specialist, was plagued with construction difficulties. The contractor ordered the wrong glass, and, after an unusually heavy snowfall in 1969, forty-five per cent of the panes broke—1,900 out of a total of 4,224. The mall was boarded over for a few months, and twice as many panes—half the original size—were installed. A complicated series of lawsuits over who was to pay the bill for repairs ensued among the architects, the original roof designer, several insurance companies, and the university; the suits were settled out of court in 1975, and Lindsay was paid.

"Our instructions were to build as economically as possible, and that's why we went to concrete," Erickson says. "It was supposed to be covered with vines, and when it's wet it's awfully dark gray, but the better mixes that are available now would still be too expensive. I really *like* concrete. It's the marble of our time—the stone of our century—and it's a natural material of the earth. As for whether the students like the way it is up there, Simon Fraser was a center of unrest in the sixties, but I knew there wouldn't be serious damage and they would solve their problems, because there was no escaping them. The concentration of people may not be pleasant, but it's important, because it's the reality of life. The basis of culture is the city, and a university should be like a miniature city, to develop an interchange of ideas. What Simon Fraser lacks is a real community, an all-student resident population. Most of the students now commute. The university has temporarily abandoned the idea of more residences, but I'm not going to let them abandon it for keeps!"

Erickson has compared his second university, Lethbridge, a long ribbon of concrete which seems to span the valley from one ridge line to another among the Alberta wheat fields, to an enormous ocean liner. Like Simon Fraser, it is a single complex, but its central focus is an outdoor assembly area on top of a boiler house. "I had remembered a Chinese student placing the furnace of her house in the middle of her living room because, she rightly claimed, it was the heart of the house," Erickson wrote in the text accompanying a dramatic photograph of the university in his book, *The Architecture of Arthur Erickson*, published in 1975.

◆

When I visited Erickson at his office, I was directed to wait for him there, and while I was looking at a framed blue cancelled check for fifty thousand dollars from the Royal Bank which was propped up on a shelf, Erickson walked in. "I didn't have enough money to pay for parking my car when I went into the banquet for that award," he said, laughing. "I told the garage attendant, 'If you'll just wait until I come out, I'll have fifty thousand dollars.'" He sat down, turned his chair toward me, and leaned back in his favorite position, hands behind his head, feet on his desk, and shut his eyes. I thought, He has gone to sleep or into some kind of a trance, but he opened his eyes and said, "We don't have a design methodology and we *do* have a design methodology. I suppose a certain amount of order is good, but I've resisted it." He sighed. "I'm the worst-organized person. I have no memory of what happened the day or week before, and have to have a note whether to turn right or left or where to go or why or whom I am meeting. Physically, I don't think I can keep it all in my head, so I have found the best method is to keep nothing in my head and be briefed. I have asked myself, 'What does a client want? For me to work on his project? Or to be at all the meetings where I am not really necessary?' What my clients are asking for is my design input, and by avoiding other involvement I save myself for that. The day of the person who has a central idea and enforces it is over, although there will always be a demand, in a rather limited area, for the architect who is an artist with a unique vision. For any large project, we build a model of the site, and I usually find my ideas crystallizing in a conversation with somebody. An idea that has been cooking on a back burner comes forward in a challenging situation. Studying ahead of time closes my mind, which needs my whole life experience to be kept open. If you burden your mind with facts, you narrow down your field of information — eliminate all the input that could come from your superconscious. In any basic effort today, you need a full complement of minds. I am aware of the visual effect of every detail, and I happen to have the kind of mind that relates details to a larger context, so I hire someone who sees the grains of sand on the beach. I often tell my people I can't read, because I have a completely visual memory. I do think when you develop your visual sense the others atrophy. I ask that things be presented to me visually and that detailed information be reduced to simple statements illustrated by diagrams. When all the statements are brought together, you begin to absorb the sense of an over-all design."

He brought his feet down, and began twirling a felt pen on his desk. "I suppose I learned from my mother and grandfather and from my travels, which gave me objectivity, not to accept any status quo, so I can remove something from its cultural context and see it alone. I challenge everything. I do the conceptual sketches, and we work a lot from models. The people here in my office study things thoroughly, so if I'm off base they can correct me. Although the system may seem chaotic, things are very much under control, with the office having priority on my time. I am deeply involved in all the projects and give decisions at every level — from construction principles involving millions of dollars to someone's bathroom tile. Sometimes I realize an hour later that I haven't thought about something carefully enough, and have to go back. Most firms analyze a client's needs and arrive at a solution quickly. I always start out with the approach — which is Oriental — that we have no ideas about *anything*. If anyone said to me 'I have an idea for a building,' I would immediately be suspicious, because in my terms that's not architecture. You can't transplant solutions from one place to another. Buildings are a response to specific requirements, among the most fundamental being the requirements of the locale. Ideas almost always arise in consultation with the client, and the design is a slow process of evolution. We keep all possibilities open until practically the last moment — a frustrating, sometimes terrifying experience for the people working for me. Sometimes it even makes *me* nervous. But somehow it always comes together."

◆

I stood up to go, and as we walked through the door, Erickson said, "Each year, when I go on one of my journeys, I discover something important to my understanding of my work, my values, and my life.

Three years ago, I returned to paradise—to Bali. I visited a remote village consisting of one wide street. Down its center ran a series of beautiful pavilions, each with a ritual function—one for old men, one for women, one for children, and so on—where the folklore was handed down and the culture was perpetuated. On either side were the houses where the families were born, grew up, and died. I visited one of the houses, with a courtyard, a household shrine, a room for musical instruments and masks (because everyone takes part in music and dancing), a kitchen, a shrine for the kitchen, rooms for the family, for the newly married couples, even a room for birth and a room for dying. What impressed me was that the house not only proved useful for living but celebrated all the basic events of life; and in the center was the beginning and the end. The continuity made an extraordinary impression on me. My question to myself is 'How can I put the same strength of meaning, that profound symbol of existence, into whatever I build?'" As I turned to leave, he added, "It may take years for me to absorb and translate this."

Excerpted from "Seven Stones,"
published in *The New Yorker*, June 4,
1979. Published in different form as
*Seven Stones: A Portrait of Arthur
Erickson, Architect*, 1981.

Hubert Evans

———————— ✦ ————————

I FIRST HEARD ABOUT HUBERT EVANS from his son, Jon, when we were travelling in the North at the same time. Jon mentioned that his father was a well-known writer and lived in British Columbia. When I moved to the Sunshine Coast and married John Daly, it turned out that we lived not far from Hubert, and John knew about him already.

Hubert was eighty-one when we met, and it was as if we had known one another a long time. We went to see him often in his snug house by the sea, and sometimes John would tuck a small salmon under his arm before we left home, and cook it for supper when we got there.

Right after John died, I went to see Hubert. He was eighty-five by then, having trouble with his eyesight, and not feeling all that chipper either. He put on his old Mackinaw and a sort of tam he wore, picked up his white cane at the door and said, "We're going to see a friend of mine you will like." We walked down the beach to the home of his close friend, Maximiliane von Urpani Southwell, who was Viennese, and in her seventies. She had been born into the Austrian nobility and maintained her aristocratic demeanor with great humor, although she didn't have a dime to her name.

Everything about Maxie was beguiling: her wit; the elegant way she dressed, making a virtue of simplicity; her home, warm and full of soft colours, overlooking the beautiful Gulf of Georgia; the classical music that drifted through the living room while we talked by the fire; her superb little library of carefully chosen paperback books.

The three of us had a bread-and-butter tea that day. When I was saying goodbye at the door, Maxie said, "Have a good time," and when I looked at her in amazement, she smiled and added, speaking slowly, with her Viennese accent, "It is poss-eeble."

From that day on Hubert and Maxie watched over and nurtured me until they died, Hubert at ninety-four and Maxie at eighty-two. I am forever grateful to have known them.

My strongest memory of Hubert—and he intended it to be that—is of the night he stood by his door in the pouring rain as I was leaving, and lectured me because I wasn't spending enough time writing. He was afraid I would never finish my memoir about John, which became *Fishing with John*. He leaned against the door, because by then he was in his early nineties and very tired, and in his reedy voice, he repeated once more the story I had heard from him so often. It's about the useless adipose fin on the salmon, which I wrote down in the following article about him.

———————— ✦ ————————

One of Canada's most valuable assets is the writer Hubert Evans of Roberts Creek, British Columbia, whom I am lucky enough to have as a neighbor.

We both live on the Sechelt Peninsula, isolated from the rest of the mainland and Vancouver. I met him seven years ago, when he was 81, so I've never known him to be any different than he is now: a small man, lithe and very thin, with sharp blue eyes, a surprising amount of very white hair, a barely visible moustache and an expressive face that is rarely still. In photographs he appears frail and elderly, although the better ones reveal a vivacity that is at the core of his remarkable nature. He is certainly frail, and when he falls ill, as he periodically does, the phone is stilled until he signals his recovery by a cheery request that visiting recommence. He has shown those who know him how to grow old with extraordinary grace, even prodding us, his much younger friends, into increased creativity by the example of his own energy. He has an incorrigible optimism that makes each day its own reward, a day that commences with a brief fling at housework, cooking, washing his clothes, followed at mid-morning by several hours at his typewriter and a rest. Then he is ready for the visitors who come to enjoy his philosophic insights hinged to the imaginary world in which he has spent his writing hours.

"I do not think of myself first and foremost as a writer, but as a man who chose a varied life, mostly outdoors, loved it, and wanted to write about it," Hubert once told me. "I'd sooner be physically active, building boats and gardening, but I'm more or less housebound now, and writing gets me up in the morning and gives me something to think about at night."

Four years ago, at an age when most men have been retired for nearly two decades, he broke the long silence that began after his wife's death in 1960 to produce two new volumes of poetry— *Whittlings* and *Endings*. The poems were so well received—Margaret Laurence, the writer, has called them "sheer wisdom in a lunatic age"—that Evans, regaining confidence, completed a novel that had been simmering on what he refers to as "the back burner" for almost 50 years. *O Time in Your Flight*, published last year, was acclaimed across the country for vividly capturing the quality of life at the turn of the century as seen through the sharp eyes of a nine-year-old small-town Ontario boy. "He's the same little twirp I wrote about in stories for *Maclean's* in the 1920s," Evans says, "except that his name was Chester, and now it's Gilbert Egan and Chester is his younger brother."

George Woodcock, reviewing *O Time in Your Flight*, wrote, "Evans, 87 years old and almost blind . . . looking back with the luminous vividness of what seems an almost total recall . . . is innocence seen with extraordinary mental lucidity through the eyes of experience. And the childhood of the writer takes on an even wider dimension when one realizes that Evans is also writing about the childhood of Canada . . ."

Margaret Laurence made Hubert Evans's acquaintance when she wrote him a fan letter six years ago, after reading *Mist on the River*, the earlier novel that made him famous. They have continued to correspond but have never met. In a full page review of *O Time in Your Flight* in the *Toronto Star*, she said, "The book makes marvellous reading. . . It is a long, rich novel, capturing that era vividly, always from the perspective of the boy and yet with the selective and gently irony of the old man that boy became. There is about it a sense of wonder, a special kind of grace."

His earlier novel, *Mist on the River*, published in 1954, has become a classic. Evans had been living in northern BC among the Indians of the Skeena River, and he wrote then from his immediate experience about the problems of young Indians caught between their old culture and the new world of their white peers. His understanding of that touchy subject was commended by several discerning critics, including the anthropologist Harry Hawthorn, a specialist on Northwest Coast Indians. Reissued in the New Canadian Library series of classics in 1973, *Mist on the River* is now taught in Canadian schools.

Hubert Evans dates his first period of professional writing from 1926 to 1954, but he became a newspaper reporter well before, in 1910. The oldest of four boys whose father was a high school teacher in Ontario, he was the only son who didn't go to university. All had distinguished careers: the second brother, Charlie, was a geologist; the third, Dr. Gerald Evans, who is 80 and lives half a mile along the beach from Hubert, was chief of the department of laboratory medicine and pathology at the University of Minnesota until his retirement; and the youngest, Bill, was a structural engineer.

"My father would have mortgaged his home to have his first son go to university, but I was full of O. Henry and Bohemia. I didn't want to be a rah-rah boy and wear a coonskin coat like most of my chums, and I wanted to see life. I sure saw it!" He started writing at 18 on his hometown newspaper, the Galt *Reporter*, and then worked for the Toronto *Mail and Empire*, the Toronto *World* and two newspapers in BC. Next came two years and three months as an infantryman in the trenches in France in the First World War (he was wounded at Ypres). His first novel, *The New Front Line*, published by Macmillan in 1927, was, in his own words, "about a guy just out of the trenches and his return to civilian life; sort of naïve and autobiographical, but it had a flavor to it." He married a teacher, Anna Winter, in 1920, and they settled in BC, where he became variously a prospector, salmon hatchery superintendent, trapper, first-aid man to Indian communities, beachcomber and hand troller for salmon.

"I made more money writing about the trades I was in than doing them," he recalls. He was one of Canada's most successful authors, with more than 200 published short stories, 60 serials, 12 radio plays for the CBC and seven books of fiction. He was known primarily as a writer for teenagers; Evans says that a series about Derry, an Airedale dog, and the youth who owned him "bought the property I am on and built the house I inhabit. I lived off that dog for four or five years." Fine writing and an impeccable eye give his juvenile books a timeless quality. What he produced 50 years ago remains a fascinating portrayal of Canada's wilderness life in the 1920s and '30s.

Paradoxically, Evans was better known in the United States than in Canada. "I could never have made a living in the Canadian market," he explains. He appeared regularly in leading American and British juvenile magazines, and his books were published by Westminster Press in Philadelphia and Dodd, Mead in New York. Having written so much for American readers, Evans determined in the mid-1950s to create a book specifically for Canadian youth. The result: *Son of the Salmon People*, the story of a young Indian who defends his village against an avaricious white developer. But Evans was unable to find a Canadian publisher for what may be his best juvenile work. The content is so contemporary—village environmentalists stand in front of bulldozers to protect their salmon streams from loggers—that it is hard to believe the book was written a quarter of a century ago.

Published in the US in 1958, it was reprinted in a special edition for American schools. This fall, reissued by Harbour Publishing, *Son of the Salmon People* has finally become available to the audience for which it was intended. His five other novels, including *The New Front Line*, remain out of print.

Visiting Hubert Evans is always an adventure. When I came in the late afternoon he had just finished writing chapter 8 of a new novel. Before I could knock, he opened the door of the modest white frame house he built 53 years ago, where he lives alone. He was dressed as usual in a blue open-neck, Chinese-style cotton jacket, grey pants and worn tan moccasins. He waved me to a seat on a wooden frame couch at a window overlooking a little stream that still nurtures spawning salmon and fingerlings, and beyond, the Gulf of Georgia, on whose broad waters tugs, fishing vessels, cruise ships and small boats are in constant motion. With only peripheral vision, Hubert can see more clearly at the window, and it is a cosy place to talk.

We were discussing his long professional silence after his wife's death: "Between you and me, I got on the Old Age Pension and found I could eat without writing, so I went off in my boat and knocked around on the lower coast," he said. He removed his glasses, dangling them over his crossed knees, leaning with the other arm on the window frame. "I'm working now on the first draft of a new book," he continued. "It's going to be long and will take three years to finish. It's about a funny old guy, a composite of several I knew, a slightly retarded camp cook who comes from Ontario, is a bit of a drifter and not very sophisticated. He's taken advantage of, but the beauty of it is that he doesn't know it."

Hubert rubbed his forehead and laughed. "There's a medieval story of a court jester who went through fire unscathed because he didn't realize it," he went on. "People called him God's Fool. The man I'm writing about is so simple he's beautiful. I am weaving contemporary history into this character because it should be recorded. There was a way of living out here prior to 1930 that has practically disappeared, that very few people are old enough to remember. But I am. In years to come, *O Time* will contribute to the history of the times, like Mark Twain or Bret Harte did. I am sure it will, from the letters people write to me saying I captured an era. The book I'm working on now is going to do the same thing for BC from the turn of the century to 1930. British Columbia is almost as different today in the attitudes of the people as Ontario was."

We got up and moved into his yellow low-ceilinged kitchen, built of V-joint timber, for a cup of tea, passing the cobblestone fireplace that Hubert built himself in the living room. During the winter I like to attend what Hubert describes as an evening of "old coffeehouse, freewheeling sort of philosophic talk about writing, painting—nothing technical but very good." The other regulars around that fireplace are Robert Jack, the artist-illustrator of Hubert's three recent books, who lives down the road and started the custom by dropping in casually every Tuesday evening; Howard White of Harbour Publishing, Hubert's imaginative young publisher; Mike Poole, the CBC television producer; David Kidd, a sculptor; and John Faustmann, a freelance writer.

While we were sitting at the broad old kitchen table waiting for the tea to steep, Hubert Evans, who makes emphysema and the pacemaker that enables him to survive with an ailing heart seem like minor inconveniences, said, "People are going back to what they can read and enjoy, but I am writing to please myself and nobody else. I love my subject, and I like writing. I've got this thing about writers being creative people; that creativity came in a package the night I was conceived. Maybe it was something my mother had for supper. If writers don't write, they'll be like the adipose fin on the salmon. At one time it was quite a big thing, but the salmon didn't use it, and now it's no bloody good to him."

Published in *Today* magazine,
December 20, 1980.

Bill Reid

$\blacklozenge$

WHEN I CAME TO BRITISH COLUMBIA, I knew absolutely nothing about Northwest Coast Indian culture, and I felt I was missing something very important. This was especially so when Arthur Erickson and I went to the Museum of Anthropology he designed for the University of British Columbia, where I was surrounded by some of the finest examples of Northwest Coast Indian art. In order to design the Great Hall, where the huge ancient totem poles stand, Arthur had to sense the mystery and the power of that art. He explained that you have to get inside the minds of the people who made them, and experience their fears and superstitions. For the first time I really *looked* at Northwest Coast art, with my eyes and my mind open.

I decided to take what was for me the most direct route possible to learn about Northwest Coast Indian art: to write a piece about Bill Reid, the great Haida carver and goldsmith. His jewelry—gold boxes, bracelets and necklaces—and his superb carvings attest to his role of leadership among Northwest Coast artists. I soon learned that he is as fine a writer as he is an artist, he is a delightful public speaker, and he is considered to be the person most responsible for the resurgence of Northwest Coast art.

I had already met Bill and his captivating French wife, Martine, an anthropologist who came to Canada to pursue her interest in Northwest Coast Indians. Like her husband, Martine is an original: a multi-gifted person, a student of Northwest Coast Indian culture who has curated a number of art exhibits in this field, in addition to her writing and teaching.

With the guidance of these two remarkable people, I began an enthralling journey into the world of Northwest Coast art, and into the cultures behind it. I was Bill Reid's pupil and he the teacher, with a powerful assist from Martine, when I prepared the following article.

◆

Bill Reid, the legendary carver and printmaker and the driving force behind the resurgence of Northwest Coast Indian art, is a Haida, a member of the vibrantly artistic Northwest Coast Indian nation that traces its origins back to the inquisitive activity of the Raven.

Reid's mother, who came from the Queen Charlotte Islands, married a white man, so Reid was brought up in Victoria, BC and not on her reserve at Skidegate. Nevertheless, in 1978 Reid was honoured at elaborate festivities at Skidegate. A new band-council building was opened and a magnificent totem pole Reid carved and presented to his mother's reserve was raised. At a fabulous potlatch-type feast for 1,500 people, he was presented with a ceremonial button blanket, made by Skidegate women, the greatest gift he could receive. In 1980, his massive *Raven and the First Men* carving was unveiled in a rotunda designed for it at the new Museum of Anthropology at the University of British Columbia. A sizeable contingent of Haida came down from Skidegate and the larger reserve of Masset on the Queen Charlotte Islands and honoured Reid with a Haida name from his mother's family, Iljuus.

Reid says he does not go along with current efforts to "re-invent the old Indian culture." Yet he donated nine months over two summers on the Queen Charlotte Islands to carve his new totem pole for the Skidegate reserve, on which only one teetering, century-old pole remained. His new totem was "intended as a memorial to the Haidas of the past, not as a device to turn the clock back. Since I make my living by flogging the bones of my ancestors, I wanted to recompense them," he explained. "Besides, I did not want my mother's village to be without a pole."

He started his habit of visiting the Queen Charlotte Islands in his early twenties; about then he began his intensive study of the works of his ancestors in the museums of North America and Europe, where so much of the art is sequestered. He talked to the old people and the anthropologists, and read everything he could find about the culture, especially the writings of John Swanton.

"When I came back to Vancouver from Toronto in 1951, with brand new jewellery-making skills, I started exploring the structure of Haida art," he said. "That meant copying old designs from books just becoming available — provincial museum pamphlets, and the publications of Marius Barbeau about totem poles, Haida myths, and carvers. None of these was great scholarship, but they provided photographs of Northwest Coast art which I and a few others could pore over for hours and attempt to reproduce. Eventually we unlocked the secrets of the ovoids, form lines, and so on, which Bill Holm codified and described later in his classic study."

Holm, whom Reid affectionately refers to as "that Swedish-American Indian from Seattle" (he's a professor of art history at the University of Washington), has become such an authority on native arts that he was able to participate with the Kwakiutl in their own dances. His book *Northwest Coast Indian Art*, written originally as a graduate term paper, dissects the complex native drawings so well that the vocabulary he invented—"form lines" to define the basic structure of the design, and "ovoids," which encase sockets or joints and are used as eyes and space-fillers—has become accepted terminology.

Reid's creations meet the standards of the great Haida artist Charles Edenshaw, who lived from 1839 to 1924, and from whom most of the contemporary Haida artists, Reid included, are descended. Reid is similarly dedicated to passing along his knowledge and passion to the next generation; he is in touch with younger artists such as Bob Davidson and Jim Hart, both from Masset, the great-grandson and great-great-grandson of Edenshaw, respectively. At the age of sixty-two, Reid is striving harder than ever to discover and share the full meaning of the old Haida culture.

Northwest Coast drawing is filled with mysterious puns and tricks, ingenious freehand variations to make the empty spaces within traditional forms as interesting as possible. Nothing is as it seems: interlocking figures unexpectedly appear around the fin, say, of a killer whale, or in the tail feathers of a raven. Small heads show up in joints, even in the nostrils of another creature. Reid's distinctive mastery of Haida art forms seems to derive from a fire in himself that began as far back as his late teens, when he started consciously to reach back for the Indian inheritance denied him as a child. His acceptance of the native half of himself is now so profound that sometimes in conversation with him it is almost possible to *see* the European-oriented white man and the mystical Indian struggling for dominance. The latter always wins.

Contemporary life of Northwest Coast natives is a hodgepodge of contrasts. There are the familiar high infant mortality, suicide, unemployment, and alcoholism rates, in the midst of which tremendous positive changes are taking place. Indians are going after labour opportunities, and several fishermen own fleets of boats. A few

Indians are coming out of technical colleges and universities, and more and more native bands have taken over management of their own affairs. The regeneration of Northwest Coast art has paralleled these changes, but Reid believes it could not have taken place without the intervention of anthropologists Harry and Audrey Hawthorn of the University of British Columbia. Perhaps because the Hawthorns came from other places — New Zealand and the United States — they saw the decaying remnants of a great culture with fresh eyes, and in the 1940s began receiving heirlooms at the museum from Indian families and individuals who wanted them preserved from theft, rotting, burning, or disappearance into the commercial market.

"Except for special expeditions to rescue the totems, in every instance among the 25,000 or so items that came to the university, the Indians crated and brought or sent them in," Harry Hawthorn has said. Replicas of some poles were sent back to the reserves that owned the originals. The treasures were stored in a few rooms classified as a museum in the basement of the university library, and became the nucleus of the collection in the stunning new anthropology museum, which also contains the largest assemblage of Bill Reid's work.

A systematic carving programme was organized by the Hawthorns at UBC in 1950, and shortly thereafter at the Provincial Museum by the late Wilson Duff, who was then its curator of ethnology. Among the old pieces sent to the Hawthorns for safekeeping was a decaying sea-lion pole. They discovered that its creator, Mungo Martin, a Kwakiutl fisherman, was still living at Alert Bay. He was about seventy and hadn't carved for years when they brought him to UBC. He began carving again and in 1953 moved to Victoria to become chief carver for the Provincial Museum, where he remained until his death in 1962. He designed a complete Kwakiutl house for Thunderbird Park at that museum, and most of the older generation of carvers worked with him one time or another — among them, very briefly, Bill Reid.

Reid had started carving in his early teens, first a six-inch Viking longship and then a smaller Arab dhow. "I never thought of being an artist," he said recently at his Vancouver apartment. "Then somewhere along the line I developed a unique art, blackboard-chalk carving. I started it in school because I was very bored. Round chalk was such a fine medium that I made little tea sets — cups and saucers — and finished them with nail polish. My sister has the only set left, wrapped in cotton in a little matchbox. It showed me I could do fine work. The first totem pole I ever made was out of blackboard chalk."

On a chrome-and-white draughting table, Reid was working on his annual silk-screen Haida print, the tenth in a series that he began in 1972. He was one of the first Northwest Coast native artists to make silk-screen prints, and they have been very successful. His yearly print is his main source of income; it enables him to subsidize a long-term enterprise he especially wants to do, like the Skidegate pole, or give his art where it would have special meaning. (He has just finished designing the doors for the house of an old friend; Jim Hart will carve them.) Reid usually gives the original hand-painted drawing of each print to a museum. The Children of the Raven Gallery in Vancouver handles his prints and the whole edition of last year's print of a thunderbird sold out at $1,000 each before it was finished. When Reid issues a new print, 195, signed and numbered, make up an edition, along with ten artist's proofs, and ten remarques for which Reid does "a little doodle. I draw a little wolf head, my crest. It's a little different on each one."

"What do you mean by a crest?"

"A crest is the material representation of a mythological creature who played a prominent part in the mythical origin of a kinship group or family," he said. "The images are used as identifying symbols in a heraldic way. The wolf is the subcrest of a larger crest category, or moiety, to which I also belong, the raven. All Haida are either ravens or eagles."

Last year he made a second Haida print, on silk, as a wall-hanging. It is a classic black, red, and blue design which he describes as "Mr. and Mrs. Nanatsinget and their killer whale, who is carrying Mrs. Nanatsinget into the nether world while her husband hides behind the whale's flukes. Actually, Mr. Nanatsinget pursues them and rescues her. You cram all the figures of the legend in arbitrarily, so it *looks* as if he's hiding but he never did that in the story. Northwest Coast drawings illustrate the characters, not the action. Mrs. Nanatsinget *appears* to be in the whale's stomach, but she wasn't. That's where the space was, so I plunked her in."

"Who are the Nanatsingets?"

"Oh, they are the actual characters in the myth. Nanatsinget is the hero, and his wife, as usual, has no name."

The wall-hangings were an experiment for Reid. He is an exacting worker, and it took days to get shades of colour he would approve, though he wasn't quite satisfied. The limited edition of twenty-one, signed and numbered, were sold for $2,500 each before the first was made.

Reid is six feet three inches tall, with hair that is turning white, a large head, broad mouth, and alert hazel eyes behind tortoise-shell glasses. For years he suffered from deep depressions and now he has Parkinson's disease, an illness which, he says with typical dry humour, is "so omnipresent that it has cured my depressions. It's a funny disease. When you're feeling okay you are perfectly normal, but in a downspell, you're not capable of doing much — it cuts your life in half. You're not really normal but you feel normal. I didn't realize how slow I was until I saw myself in the documentary the National Film Board did of me carving the pole at Skidegate. I've had the disease since September, 1973, when I found myself carrying my right hand in a funny position and didn't know why. Then I had a pain in my left shoulder and difficulty turning my head, and began to have tremors. It was diagnosed the following February and I got on the drug levodopa, which partially alleviates tremors and muscular inco-ordination. I keep pace with the development of new drugs but I'm not getting any better. The best thing to do is work. Since the symptoms started, I've carved the Skidegate pole and supervised and did a fair amount of work on the big *Raven* carving, and quite a lot of jewellery. When I'm well organized I get a lot done, averaging four or five hours a day of work that is pretty effective. I'm interested to see if I can still make a complicated piece of jewellery, a big brooch, or a gold box. I haven't made one in a long time."

Reid seems to be comfortable talking to me while he works. He bends over tracing paper, pencilling in lines, holding the paper up, setting it down, erasing, drawing new lines, and then inking in the two-dimensional heavy "form lines." He sets his glasses aside and wears a head loupe, grey goggles that magnify. The radio is a low murmur permanently tuned to the CBC, and a pile of discarded tracings fill the wastebasket and circle the floor around his chair. His hand is completely steady, and his whole body is still as he draws in lines over the eyes with his long-shafted, yellow draughting pencil.

"What is a thunderbird?"

"Somebody's got to make all that thunder," he replied. "I've never seen one. Nobody has, so it comes out looking like an eagle, except that the upper part of its bill curves back into its mouth. We don't know why. That's the way it is." He turned up the radio for a programme of classical music. "I haven't had the total experience in the Indian world and I never could have. Everybody who lives at Skidegate has known everyone else since they were born, and I was born in Victoria. My mother thought it was a good place to live since it was full of English people and she was a life-long ardent anglophile. She is the best example of brainwashing that the Indian residential school system ever turned out.

"I had three peculiar parents: my mother, who broke with Skidegate and rejected the whole Indian association; my father, who came from Scotch-German parents and left his home near Detroit, Michigan, when he was sixteen and married at forty, so he never had a family or knew what families were about; and a French woman named Leah Alfonsine Delcusse Brown, who was our housekeeper-nurse-governess, the archetypal British nanny who alternated between sloppy sentimentality and straight sadism. My mother picked her up in the Queen Charlottes, and Mrs. Brown unlearned any French cooking she knew and became British like my mother, except that my mother was a good cook. She was good at everything."

Reid's mother, Sophie, is now in a nursing home in Vancouver. She is the eldest of six children who survived to adulthood of Charles Gladstone, a top-notch boat-builder. He started carving in his sixties in the local slate or argillite — an art production created by the Haida for sale to white people. He was best known, however, for his silver bracelets, which he probably learned to make from Charles Edenshaw, his uncle. Gladstone was born in Victoria, but lived with Edenshaw until he was twelve. According to family history, they were down the coast at Rivers Inlet when his uncle just told him for no particular reason to go off on his own. Bill's grandmother was born at Tanu on the Queen Charlotte Islands, once the great centre of Northwest Coast art. Reid calls Tanu "the Florence of the North," and he sometimes says he wants his ashes scattered there when he dies. "That way I can keep my friend Charlie company," he said. "There's a little graveyard at Tanu — nobody lives there now — with a marble gravestone with clasped hands and an inscription that reads 'In Memory of Charlie.' Nobody knows who he is."

Reid's mother was born at Port Essington, a West Coast cannery, where her father worked as a carpenter. All six Gladstone children were sent 500 miles down the coast to the Coqualeetza residential school at Sardis. Most spoke only Haida when they arrived; at school they were forced to speak English, and punished if they used their own language.

"My mother quickly learned that in white terms it was sinful to be an Indian," Reid said, slowly sharpening the point of his pencil with sandpaper. "She was an extraordinarily clever woman who spoke beautiful English, dressed well, was very pretty, and had very good manners. I don't think she ever had a religious impulse. She hated every display of emotion, but she loved the Church of England as a symbol."

At Coqualeetza she acquired dressmaking skills and an elementary teacher's certificate. When she left she went north and got a job teaching school at Old Hazelton, where she met Bill's father. William Reid was running a small hotel in the nearby town of Smithers.

"My father was a big blond man, hard as a rock, who wore clothes beautifully and was what we call an 'end of steel' man, who followed the railroad." Reid drew in the curve of a thunderbird wing. "His partner was Black Jack MacDonald, a flamboyant would-be robber baron. I think my father had a lot of interesting stories to tell, but he was weak and blustery, defeated by my mother and Mrs. Brown. I wish I had known him better, under different circumstances."

Shortly after the Reids were married they moved to Hyder, Alaska, a border town that adjoins Stewart, BC. At various times William Reid owned several hotels, but while Sophie was pregnant with her first child, Bill, she moved to Victoria, where he was born. She went back to Hyder soon afterward, and Bill's sister, Margaret, a Vancouver psychologist, was born there a year later. Then Sophie Reid moved back to Victoria with both children. "I went to Alice Carr's private kindergarten, and I remember Emily coming through with a monkey on her shoulder," Reid said. His father visited them occasionally, and when Prohibition forced him to move his business back across the border to Stewart, BC, the family rejoined him. Reid's brother Bob, eight years younger, was born there; he now has his own graphic arts studio in Toronto.

"My father was a wonderful gardener," Reid said. He had been drawing on a piece of tracing paper he had pasted over the talons of the thunderbird. He ripped it off, replacing it with a fresh one. "We had a magnificent flower garden, with a cold frame for vegetables and a berry patch behind our house. My father provided for all of us until the hotel he had bought went broke. We moved back then to Victoria for good, without him. I was twelve, and he died in 1942. I never saw him again."

Bill's mother supported her family by becoming a dressmaker, with the élite of Victoria as her customers. She is still remembered there and in Vancouver for the style and cut of the clothes she designed. She was eighty-two when she stopped sewing.

"The Depression in 1933 only made us poorer, but that wasn't my main problem," Reid said. "The dislocations were just too hard to cope with. At six I had been dumped into a mining camp, Hyder, from a kid-glove private Victoria kindergarten. Anybody who smelled weakness jumped all over me. When I returned to Victoria at thirteen I was just entering adolescence and had a terrible image of myself. I finished high school and took a year out, a year at college, and then another year out when I just stayed home. It was really awful. There were four of us in two rooms — Mrs. Brown lived around the corner by herself — and my mother would go to work in her little office downtown and I'd stay in bed until three. Then I'd rush out and shop and cook supper. I spent a lot of time reading, and the book, *Jurgen*, by James Branch Cabell, was very important to me. It still is. I find a lot of it in me. Jurgen was a monstrous, clever, amusing fellow, urbane and detached, the kind of fellow I would have liked to be."

Reid left home when he was twenty. "I went to work in this funny radio station run by an elderly gentleman who just sent five dollars to the government and got a license. I worked for a year for nothing, and then he raised me to fifty dollars a month. I was supposed to organize a record library. Nobody ever listened to Canadian stations in those days, and he fired me after two months." Reid leaned back in his chair and pushed up the glasses.

"Before I was fired, I was at the station all by myself, and one day this intense little fellow with thick glasses came in and said, 'Here's my card. If you ever hear this station's for sale, call me up.' It was Roy Thomson.

"The war was on and I was now an experienced radio hand, so I got a real job in a radio station in Kelowna, but eventually I went to Toronto and looked up Thomson. He sent me to Jack Kent Cooke, the teleprompter king, who was his manager then, and Cooke made me a general announcer at a small station in Kirkland Lake, Ontario. I wake up every morning now with really terrible pop songs from the Thirties going through my head and can't turn them off until I get the radio going. My anxiety dreams are still about the radio business: I have a quarter of an hour of air time to fill and no script. Then I was drafted. I was an infantry private and I never got any farther than Calgary."

After the war, Reid got a job with CKEY, a Toronto radio station, and moved to the CBC in 1948. He stayed with the CBC eleven years, and became a well-known news announcer. At various times he had music programmes and he wrote two scripts, mainly about North-west Coast Indians. A script he did after he left, *Totems*, has become famous as a television documentary about the 1957 expedition that he accompanied to remove salvageable totem poles from Anthony Island in the Queen Charlottes.

Percy Gladstone, Reid's mother's youngest brother, an economist, is the only other living member of her family from that generation. Gladstone recalls Reid visiting Skidegate as a youngster. "He and his grandfather were great buddies. From the very first they had an obviously strong attachment." Reid was in his teens before he was conscious that he was "anything other than an average Caucasian North American. Being Indian certainly wasn't emphasized in my family, but I used to see my aunts and uncles frequently, and since I never knew my father's family they were my only relatives." He had been drawing steadily, but now he stopped again. I asked why he had drawn a face inside the body of the thunderbird. "You've got to put something in there, and faces turn up everywhere. It wouldn't be a Haida design without faces."

He resumed drawing after tearing off the paper again from the thunderbird's talons and putting a fresh piece over them. He was erasing, sitting back, holding up the drawing, erasing, redrawing. "I don't usually get as hung up as this on a print. I'm having trouble getting the feet to work." He reached down in the wastebasket and brought up the pile of papers; they had nothing but talons on them. "See, the thunderbird looks as though it's walking like Groucho Marx, and it isn't supposed to be walking at all. You just keep on making feet until they look right. I use these sheets on top of my drawing like a dress pattern. I hung around my mother's workshop and I remember her sitting at the sewing machine. It was her most familiar position." He was silent, drawing, and then he tore the sheet off and started the whole process again.

"The first thing I ever wrote for the CBC was a eulogy for my grandfather in 1954 that I broadcast myself, since I was the announcer. My grandfather had fair hair and white skin, but my grandmother looked Haida; that is, Mongolian. The Raven launched the Haida, who were the first people, into the world, and they went out and settled Mongolia and China and Japan and all those places," Reid said, with a little smile.

"I just learned that a boat my grandfather built fifty years ago, the *Joyce*, is still working. When I knew him he was in his seventies. He didn't speak much English and I didn't know any Haida. I still don't. He was the last in the direct tradition of Haida silver workers. He wasn't a particularly good artist but he was a careful engraver. My grandfather inherited all Charles Edenshaw's tools. He walked to Masset, eight miles, and then packed them all the way to Skidegate in a big chest on his back. He engraved using a knife-handled tool with a big heavy blade made out of an old file. Like this." Reid gripped a knife on the drawing board.

"All my aunts and my mother owned gold and silver bracelets. To make them you melted down American silver dollars or twenty-dollar gold pieces and then bent the bracelet into its final form. Gold is nice stuff. In the old days gold jewellery was made from twenty-two karat gold pieces. Several old women at Skidegate still have them. The new ones are never twenty-two karat, except mine and Bob Davidson's. I buy the gold from the refinery or a bank now, and alloy it with copper myself. Absolutely pure would be too soft and would break. We think Charles Edenshaw invented the Northwest Coast bracelet after he saw European engraving. I learned how it was done from looking in books.

"I finally achieved a lifelong objective. I wanted to own an Eden-

Illustration by Susan Reynders

shaw bracelet and now I have one. I bought it from someone who inherited it. It's the beaver theme, and it's quite worn silver, so I've restored it." He laughed. "I've evidently taught all the bracelet-makers on the coast how to make bracelets, indirectly, by showing my cousin, Gordon Cross, the tools and how to use them. Now the European engraving method, through Gordon, has become a new tradition.

"I think it's a shame if people feel they have to re-invent the wheel every time. If you start from scratch you don't get very far. It takes a couple of weeks to make most things, and two or three generations to develop the skills. The trouble I have from young native carvers is that they don't have that tradition and don't want to learn from their elders. They're suspicious of them. One encouraging change is occurring in the function of Northwest Coast art. Originally it was largely ceremonial, but in recent years it was made almost exclusively for sale to non-natives. Now the artists are creating more and more objects to be returned to their communities as potlatch gifts, sold or traded items, or as contributions to community life." He sat back and frowned. "I think I'm going to junk this thunderbird and start over again. The head doesn't fit the body." He sighed and got up. "Let's get out of here."

Reid and I walked into the living room just as the front door opened and an elegant young woman with long blonde hair entered — Reid's wife, Martine, a French anthropologist whom he married a year ago. On a high-necked plain beige dress she wore a large wooden pendant in the shape of a wolf's head. It was made from yew, with green eyes, and ears of abalone shell, and eyebrows and nostrils overlaid with copper. When I remarked on its bold beauty, she smiled. "I love to wear Bill's jewellery more than anything else."

The pendant was hanging from small oblong blue glass beads. "They are early nineteenth-century trade beads from Czechoslovakia that belonged to my grandmother," Reid explained. "She sent a shoebox of them to us in Victoria in the 1930s, just before she died."

The Reids met in 1975 when Martine came to Vancouver to get her doctorate from UBC, and went to see Bill about putting on a show of Northwest Coast art in Paris. She is now a lecturer at the university, and Bill has often shown up at her anthropology of art course to give her students a free hour either of talking about the ovoid and tapered form line — "They are the building blocks of the northern style, and if you get these two forms together in enough variations, you end up with a Northwest Coast design" — or to take them through the anthropology museum or his carving shed, a low, rectangular structure with large factory-type windows in a wooded corner of the campus. It is filled with broken sections of old totems and a canoe or two. Lately, Jim Hart has been carving a massive new pole down the centre of the shed, and Reid has set up a jewellery bench beneath one of the windows, where he works part of almost every day. "Of all the places I've spent time in my life," he says, "the carving shed is the only consistent one, my one real base. I always go back to the carving shed."

Reid has been married twice before. Neither of his former wives was Haida but the first is now married to a Haida in Skidegate. Reid was married first in 1944 and divorced in 1959, and had one daughter, Amanda. She is also married to a Haida and lives on the Queen Charlottes. Reid's son Raymond, who died last year in his late twenties, was adopted by Reid and his first wife at seven months from his mother's cousin, Raymond Cross and his wife. The Cross family and Reid are close friends, and he sees them whenever he visits Skidegate.

Martine remarked on her students' enthusiastic reception of Bill's teaching. "I'm not a teacher at all," Reid said. "I consider myself primarily a goldsmith. Goldsmiths were on a par with painters and sculptors in the Renaissance, but they've slipped to just tradesmen, so that's what I am. It's the same with carving. Since I never went to school I feel more comfortable as somebody who just carves as a trade. I started out to learn the jewellery trade in 1948 when I had just gone to the CBC in Toronto and was working nights. One nice sunny day, taking my usual walk, I passed Ryerson Institute. On an impulse I went in and asked about engraving courses, because I wanted to make bracelets like John Cross did. He was my grandfather's best friend and they used to work together. Ryerson had a course in platinum and diamond jewellery, and I took that. Actually, although I walked in on an impulse, I went with the serious intention of pursuing jewellery-making as a career and leaving the broadcasting business, which I never liked."

He went to the kitchen and came back with a bottle of white wine, poured us each a glass, and sat down again. "I was so lucky, because my CBC night shift fit right in with the course times." He made his first pieces of jewellery at Ryerson. His mother still wears a delicate, white-gold ring from that period with a ruby and two diamonds set into it. "I took that one course and at the end of two years I was offered an apprenticeship at the Platinum Art Company in Toronto," he said. "It was all hand work, from eight to four, in a shop. I could go home by streetcar for dinner and be at the CBC by six."

Reid stayed at the jewellery company for a year and a half. In 1951, when he moved back to Vancouver with his family, he started making jewellery in a basement workshop between CBC working hours. "When I was at school I was very much influenced by the post-war American design of that period and got caught up in it," he said, steadying his right hand with his left while bringing his wine glass to his lips. "My heroine was Margaret Depatta, a famous American contemporary jeweller at that time. But when I got back to the West Coast I got reinfected by the Haida virus and started applying Haida designs to bracelets, earrings, brooches, rings, and decorated boxes."

Reid accompanied British Columbia's Provincial Museum expedition to collect totem poles from the abandoned Queen Charlotte Island villages of Tanu and Skedans in 1955. He went to Anthony Island in 1956 to examine the poles, and the following year was on the expedition that removed them. That same year, 1957, at the invitation of Wilson Duff, who was a good friend, Reid spent two weeks at the Provincial Museum in Victoria working with Mungo Martin.

"Mungo said, 'You carve here and I'll carve there,' and then he said, 'No, we haven't any bandages, you'll have to bleed.' They never cut themselves, those guys. Mungo worked on his part of the pole and I worked on mine, which was a little man I copied from one of the Queen Charlotte poles. The pole we worked on is down at the Peace Arch now in the park between Canada and the state of Washington."

That year Reid also made the documentary for the CBC on the removal of the Anthony Island poles to the safety of the university and provincial museums. Harry Hawthorn obtained a Canada Council grant for the reconstruction of a section of a typical southern Haida village on the UBC campus. It consisted of two houses, five poles, a double mortuary, and a sea-wolf sculpture. Reid was put in charge of the project."

"I was at the CBC when the grant came through, doing the news," Reid remembered. "I read the item about the grant over the air, and after the newscast I phoned Harry. Then I went up to the CBC executive offices and resigned. A glorious day. It was an amazing act of faith on Hawthorn's part. My entire wood-carving career up to then consisted of ten days of partially carving the little man on the pole with Mungo."

"Reid *was* the project," Hawthorn has said since. "I was on the Anthony Island expedition with him and saw his response to the old carvings. He was haunted by them. We had watched his jewellery work for years and had seen his growing knowledge of traditional forms and his genius for creating new forms."

Reid brought in the Kwakiutl carver, Doug Cranmer, to help him, and in the next three years they built the two houses and made the carvings that are now part of the permanent outdoor exhibit at the anthropology museum. When the project ended in 1962, Reid set himself up in a small jewellery business, using mainly Haida designs. He also made wood carvings, notably an eight-foot totem pole for the Shell Oil company's centre in London, England. The company recently gave it to the handsome museum on the Skidegate reserve, where it has become a favourite object to draw in the children's art classes.

Reid had met Doris Shadbolt in the early 1950s, and she is one of the people—another is his artist friend Takao Tanabe—whom he considers among his closest friends. "I like having them around and enjoy their company." When Shadbolt was working at the Vancouver Art Gallery (she eventually became its associate director), Reid was still a CBC announcer. She remembers that he used to phone her whenever a programme contained Mozart sonatas, because he knew she loved Mozart. After Reid left the CBC he moved to the top floor of a two-storey asphalt brick structure across the back lanes from the gallery. He had jewellery benches there and Shadbolt, who often dropped in for lunch, met Bob Davidson and other young carvers Reid put up.

The famous Arts of the Raven centennial exhibition was presented by the Vancouver Art Gallery in the summer of 1967 under Doris Shadbolt's leadership. The gallery sent Reid and Bill Holm all over North America to document works in museums and private collections for the show. It was a landmark in public recognition of Northwest Coast artifacts as great art rather than ethnological material. Reid, Holm, and Wilson Duff, who by then was professor of anthropology at UBC, wrote the text for the catalogue. It was the most comprehensive show of the masterworks of Northwest Coast Indians ever presented. A separate section of the exhibition was devoted to the work of Charles Edenshaw; a gallery for contemporary art contained a number of Reid's pieces.

Reid made his first gold box, a large Haida-style casket surmounted by a three-dimensional sculptured eagle, for the Canadian pavilion at Expo 67 in Montreal. He also carved a seven-foot-square Haida cedar screen as a centennial project for the new building at the Provincial Museum in Victoria. In 1968, he left for Europe on a year's Canada Council grant to study silversmithing and to photograph Northwest Coast art items in European collections. He found the latter task impossible, but the Central School of Design in London let him use its facilities for jewellery-making. He did some of what he considers his best work there: a gold-and-diamond necklace in an intricate contemporary design that he has given to Martine; and a magnificent three-inch-wide gold bracelet in a sculptured formal design of a raven and a wolf, with the figures in half-relief, that he made by the repoussé method, hammering out the design from the inside, and then re-pushing from the front. Repoussé is a rarely practised art, and Reid's repoussé work has been compared to that of such European masters as Cellini and Fabergé. Two of Reid's pieces were resold last fall at a Sotheby Parke Bernet auction in New York for impressive prices: a gold and abalone brooch of a human-hawk face went for $16,000 US, and a gold repoussé bracelet of a thunderbird with a human face for $19,000 US.

After his return from England he stayed in Montreal for three years. While he was there he made the original three-inch-high carving depicting the discovery of the ancestors of the Haida in a clam shell. The massive version, which is seven feet high, is now part of the decor of the anthropology museum at UBC. During this period Reid also created a gold vessel with an engraved beaver-and-human design, surmounted by another three-dimensional figure, which is now at the Provincial Museum; and an exquisite, delicately fashioned gold dish shaped like a bear, and with a three-dimensional mother suckling bear cubs, which was bought by the National Museum of Man in Ottawa.

In the 1960s Reid also illustrated a book, *The Raven's Cry*, by Christie Harris. "The book dealt with the impact of the Anglo-American white man on the life of the Haida, particularly the Edenshaw family," he said. "The designs illustrate narrative episodes in a dynamic way and at the same time wherever possible I employed Haida convention in the black-and-white drawings." Harris included a section about Reid in the narrative, and one of his illustrations—a carver working on a totem pole—is a self-portrait.

In 1971 Reid wrote a remarkably poetic accompaniment to a volume of photographs by Adelaide de Menil of Northwest Coast totem poles, called *Out of the Silence*. A second book, *Form and Freedom*, a dialogue between Reid and Bill Holm, an accomplished carver himself, discussing pieces of Northwest Coast art collected for an exhibition by Rice University in Houston, was published in 1975. Their often humorous comments accompany a photograph of each object, and are a revelation of their different personalities and approach to art: Holm, the cool, analytical intellectual; Reid, the warm, intuitive artist.

Although Reid had only one year of college, he has four honorary degrees, from UBC, Trent, York, and Victoria. In 1977 he was awarded the $20,000 Molson Prize, for his contribution to the arts, and in 1979 he received the diplôme d'honneur from the Canadian Conference of the Arts, for which he himself designed the medal given to recipients. He shrugs off his art as "a nice way to make a living. I don't know how to make money except by working for it. I make a living because I am an honest tradesman and put a lot into it. What I do are pastiches. Bill Holm has invented a word for them: artifakes. They're in the style of the nineteenth-century Haida, but they're more than that. Once you get started there are channels to explore and there is no end of flexibility. A lot of emotional weight goes into them."

Bob Davidson is a handsome man of thirty-five, with a round face, black hair, and a very black moustache. A gifted carver, he is often referred to as "another Bill Reid." He dropped by the Reids' apartment while I was there, and I asked how they had met.

"It was fifteen years ago," Bill Reid said. "Someone told me Bob was demonstrating slate carving in Eaton's store here in Vancouver, and I had heard a lot about his slate carving, so I went in and said hello, and we started talking. Eventually, Bob moved in with me."

Davidson laughed. "It was when I was going to high school in Vancouver. I was advertised in the newspaper, demonstrating slate carving at Eaton's, and a few people came by and took orders. There was this person I didn't see who stood there for a while but didn't look at me, and then a big voice said, 'Hi, I'm Bill Reid.' I wanted to crawl under the table because I didn't think that highly of my work. But he invited me over and I apprenticed to him for about six months and began improving. He showed me a few things, how to improve ovoids, what to look for to balance; everything had to balance. I had been carving since I was thirteen, about six years. My teachers, my dad and two uncles, had very high standards, but Bill really rubbed off on me. His presence is a very strong influence."

Reid shook his head. "In my shop you worked on your jobs and I worked on mine. I learned as much from having you around as you did from me. I helped you on the eyeballs; that was the only place. I showed you a few basics, but you were always your own man and for the most part found your own way."

"I sort of *feel* that it was an apprenticeship," Davidson said, "I gained a lot of insight and knowledge from being with you and working with you. Bill's always fitting everything in, trying to explain. It's a whole way of explaining rather than teaching."

"Well, *protégé* is a better word for our relationship," Reid said. "Everybody was hanging around everybody else. Nothing formal, just the normal course of events."

Audrey Hawthorn took a Northwest Coast art collection to Montreal in 1969 to the summer exhibition area on the site of Expo. Bob Davidson was demonstrating there as a carver, and Reid, who was living in Montreal at the time, spelled him on weekends. At his carving demonstrations, Reid made a little wolf grease dish that is now in the UBC museum collection. Both men are used to carving in public. At the end they gave a little party for the mayor and his staff to celebrate the presentation to the city of Montreal of the totem pole Davidson had been carving. They served sopalala, an Indian dessert made by beating soapberries to a froth, with thirty carved spoons which they had made in the previous two days, and they then gave away. Reid and Davidson appeared wearing Chilkat blankets and ceremonial headdresses made of carved crest frontlets.

Two projects then began to consume Reid's time and energy. The first was instigated by Walter Koerner, a retired Vancouver industrialist who has been Reid's most consistent patron in recent years. Koerner says he never recovered from his first visit to the Queen Charlotte Islands forty-three years ago, when he "came across a magic world that was man-made." He has been collecting Northwest Coast art ever since, with an extremely discerning eye. He and his wife have given their collection to the UBC anthropology museum, and in 1973 he commissioned Reid to make a larger version of the *Raven and the First Men* carving for permanent display there.

Reid was hesitant, but Koerner persisted. Reid finally agreed to supervise the job, bringing in outside help and carving as much as he could himself. It took two years to find the right kind of virgin yellow cedar, which had to be eight or nine feet in diameter. When the log arrived he and Bob Davidson examined it. They found it knotty and twisted inside, and abandoned it. The project lay idle for several years, "but Walter kept nagging me to do something about it," Reid recalled, and finally a four-and-a-half-ton laminated block of wood was devised, made up of 104 small pieces of sawn yellow cedar that would dry without much cracking.

The wood sculpture, completed in the carving shed on the UBC campus, eventually cost more than $100,000. The larger carving may have lost some of the mystery of the original in its sharper lines, but Reid is considered to have carried Haida design an important step further by carving entirely free sculptures that retain the conventional Haida forms. In freeing his bird from the vertical totem, Reid himself appears to have shaken off some of the constraints that bound him to the past.

Much of Reid's time between 1976 and 1978 was spent carving the totem pole at Skidegate. Not long ago, I travelled with the Reids to the Queen Charlotte Islands. They were going to attend the wedding of Bill's daughter, Amanda. We talked on the plane about Reid's future.

"I'm back at the jewellery bench and I'm going to do nothing but gold from now on, with boxwood originals for the castings," he said. "God decided the world needed a good carving material and provided us with boxwood. The original of *The Raven* was done in boxwood. It's completely honest stuff, takes a beautiful finish, and can be as detailed as you want. Most of it comes from France. Martine brought me two sticks, two feet long and four inches in diameter, heavy as lead, that were cut at least fifty years ago for an extinct button factory.

"Right now I'm working on a dogfish lady pendant. I originally made a lyre-shaped dogfish design on a purse for Martine, but it's still unfinished. A friend wanted a pendant, so I started making a dogfish head for that, but a dogfish head is such a funny looking thing; it doesn't really stand on its own. So I changed that head to a dogfish lady. There's a legend I can't find of a lady who changes herself into a dogfish, and in the iconography she had a human face, a funny dogfish forehead, gill slits, a hawk beak, and wears a lip plug or labret.

"I decided to carve it from the boxwood Martine brought from France, and have it cast in gold. I got this idea of doing a larger disc about three-and-a-quarter inches, gluing the little miniature dogfish lady mask in the upper centre and distributing the fish body in the remaining areas. But when I was carving the disc I suddenly realized I was dealing with a transformation myth, a big thing in Northwest Coast mythology. So instead of gluing the mask to the disc, I carved a regular dogfish face in the disc centre in very low relief. The dogfish lady mask will fit over that, hanging on silk or leather cords, and will be removable. The small mask can be worn as a separate pendant, but you'll still have a complete piece of jewellery in the big piece. I'm going to have the whole thing duplicated in gold."

While he was talking he pulled a piece of paper from his pocket and began rapidly drawing the three parts of the pendant, and then added a second set, marking the first one "boxwood" and the second one "gold." Then he started a third drawing in the shape of a lyre with a head in the centre. "The original idea for Martine's purse was lyre-shaped, so we're going back to that for three more pendants. The dogfish body will be split and it will hang from chains to the top of the tail on each side and a dogfish face in the centre. There will be three variations of this," he added, quickly making rough sketches of the three variations. "One in solid gold, not cast, but formed out of sheet metal; the same thing again from gold, but with abalone inlaid in the ovoids, eyes, and other embroidery, with a little bit of ivory in the teeth; and a third of gold, with ivory replacing abalone for accents, and the entire dogfish lady's face carved in ivory.

"I guess that's enough to keep me out of the pool halls," he said, "except for my crusade to repatriate a fifty-seven-foot Haida canoe that's sitting in a warehouse in Ottawa. It was built at Masset by Bob Davidson's grandfather and great-uncle for the Alaska-Yukon-Pacific Exposition in Seattle in 1909, and the design on it was painted by Charles Edenshaw. It's a big canoe, high in the bow and stern, big enough to hold a crew of at least twenty rowers. It's one of only two left in the world; the other is in the Museum of Natural History in New York. The National Museum of Man in Ottawa has it, although it hasn't been displayed in years. In Norway, longships are in palaces. We keep ours in warehouses."

From the air, the Queen Charlotte Islands look uninhabited; a narrow line of beach circles the islands and the sun shines on soft, round contours of green woodland, with blue lakes interspersed and black mountains in the background. A bare, broad, brown gash, with roads, denotes a logged area. The Queen Charlotte Islands are being heavily logged, and Reid has been an eloquent participant in the movement to set aside the unique ecological area on Moresby Island as a park.

On the small ferry across to Graham Island and our destination of Queen Charlotte City, Reid went to the bow. Passing a green, grassy place on our left, Reid said, "That used to be the village of Haina. Nothing's there now but one shaman's grave. There weren't enough people, so they all moved to Skidegate."

The ferry slowly curved and Reid extended a long arm to point out the Skidegate reserve — small buildings scattered at the edge of a beach.

He and Martine attended the marriage in the afternoon. Late that night, after the festivities were over, he said, "I have never seen my Skidegate pole by moonlight. I'd like to do that."

We drove over to the reserve in a borrowed pickup truck. On the way Bill said, "In the smallpox epidemic in the 1860s, two-thirds of the natives on the coast were lost. The Haida lost the most, about ninety-five per cent of their people. There were so many dead they couldn't even bury them, and the house excavations at Skidegate became improvised burial grounds. The Haida who were left felt they had to adjust to the white men, and they became instant Christians. Even so, people of my grandfather's age adapted beautifully, and things might have been all right if the white men hadn't brought in the school system. It took away the children, took away the language, taught them no skills, and then left them without a culture. That's what they have to overcome. They should go out and learn about the rest of the world and appreciate that outer world for what it is. Then they can come back and really appreciate their own culture."

We were entering the reserve, passing low rectangular houses that looked white in the moonlight. Martine stopped the truck at the shoreline beside a house with cedar siding and a glass front overlooking the water and the islands beyond — the new Skidegate band office. In front of it was the stark outline of a tall totem pole.

Reid walked slowly over to the pole, while Martine and I trailed behind. "It was marvellous when he was carving the pole," Martine said. "We were living together, and the pole grew up and we felt part of the whole thing. The pole was finished in the late fall, and when we came back for the raising in the late spring the colour had already changed.

"Bill said, 'The pole is my age now. Sixty years old.'"

We had our backs to the water and I could hear the waves at low tide, lapping at the beach. The pole, smooth, silky grey in the moonlight, broad and deeply incised, with mysterious figures, reached up and up, far above the roof of the building to which it is fastened against the fury of the Queen Charlotte winds.

"Fifty-seven feet high," Reid said softly. He ran his hand gently over the pole's surface and then stood back. "Do you see those three little men at the top? They're watchmen. They are watching either way in the village and out to sea. Just watching. I doubt if they are doing anything more than that.

"The bottom group is the bear family—the mother, father, and two cubs. The mother is a human lady and she's got a labret in her lip, which is a symbol of nobility and the only way of showing a man from a woman in a totem pole. In Haida legend, a human woman was kidnapped by bears and married to a bear prince who sacrificed himself to establish the bear clan. On a totem pole there are primary figures who occupy the whole width of the pole. On this pole they are the bear father, the raven, the killer whale, and the dogfish. The bear father from foot to head goes almost a third of the way up the pole. He's squatting at the bottom, which is the bigger dimension of this red cedar log. The raven is perched on the bear father's head, and his feet are through the bear father's ears. The raven's tail is curled up like a shrimp, and there is a hawk-faced human head in the raven's tail."

"I can't find the raven."

"The raven starts right above the bear father's head," Reid said patiently. "There are no gaps between them. He is sitting right *on* his head. His feet are through the ears of the bear and his wings above. Then comes the killer whale facing us head downwards, with his tail in the air, another main figure. Then we come to the fourth principal figure, the dogfish."

I was looking straight up in the air and said I found it all a bit confusing; there were so many other things going on.

"Oh, you mean the secondary figures," he said. "The bear mother is between the bear father's legs and arms, and on each of his forepaws he's holding a cub. Do you see that?"

"Yes."

"Then comes the raven's tail, and the raven's tail is shown as a little face with feathers on its head and has a pair of hands grasping the bear father's forehead. The little man in the tail has a hawk-human face with a beak-like nose, and in his beak the raven is holding another secondary figure, a frog, by its bum. Then in each of the raven's ears, there is a little man."

"Why?"

"For no reason," Reid replied. "Now, lying on the back of the killer whale is Nanatsinget's wife. She's lying on the whale's back and Nanatsinget's head is showing between the flukes of the killer whale and he's grasping the whale. I can see you're going to ask why again."

"Yes."

"They're just making a pole, and the dogfish at the top is all by himself with his tongue hanging out of his mouth and his tail pointing toward the sky. His dorsal fin is projecting straight through the legs of the little watchman who's facing the water. The other two sit on either side of the pole on the pectoral fins, which point upward. The little men are a method of finishing off the top of the pole."

Several yards away there was one other pole, listing heavily as if only will power kept it from falling. "There's a photograph of Skidegate taken in 1890 with poles lining the beach," Reid said. "This pole that's left is so old and rotten, you can put your hand in it and dig it out." He backed up and looked at his own pole again. "My grandfather's workshop was right here, just a little shake house sitting by the water. It was torn down when they built the band headquarters."

He turned, walking toward the truck. "I've never felt that I was doing something for my people, except what I could to bring the accomplishments of the old ones to the attention of the world," he said. "I think the Northwest Coast style of art is an absolutely unique product, one of the crowning achievements of the whole human experience. I just don't want the whole thing swept under the carpet without someone paying attention to it."

While he was talking, a phrase I had read about Reid—about his having revived a flame that was close to dying—flashed through my mind. It was in the catalogue for Reid's one-man show at the Vancouver Art Gallery in 1974, and I looked it up when I got home. It was by the French anthropologist Claude Lévi-Strauss, who wrote:

"Of all the arts of which traces remain that of the Indians of the Northwest Coast is certainly one of the greatest. But at a time when the statuary of Egypt, Mesopotamia and Greece, those of Soong China and of the European middle ages have irretrievably disappeared along with the men whose dreams they fed, our debt to Bill Reid, an incomparable artist, is that he has tended and revived a flame that was so close to dying. That is not all; for Bill Reid by his example and by his teachings has given rise to a prodigious artistic flowering, the results of which the Indian designers, sculptors and goldsmiths of British Columbia offer today to our wondering eyes."

Published in *Saturday Night*, February 1982.

Bella Coola

◆

THIS PIECE ABOUT BELLA COOLA was originally part of my book, *Fishing with John*. My editor for the whole book was Bill Shawn, who had just resigned from *The New Yorker*. It was a wonderful experience to work with him so directly.

You can tell the difference right away between great editors and the rest of them, because the great ones don't rewrite; they leave your thoughts and phrasing intact, and just clean up around them so that everything is very clear. Bill thought, and I agreed with him, that the Bella Coola chapter carried a story of its own, but it broke the thread of the narrative, so we removed it.

John and I went to Bella Coola because we had the time and were more than halfway there when the 1975 fishermen's strike began. We wanted to see whether we would like to move there. John believed Pender Harbour, with its scenic beauty and proximity to Vancouver, was about to become a tourist mecca and a place where retired people would want to come to live, which is what has happened. He felt that many people would be far more concerned with so-called "development" and the value of their land, than with the quality of the life here. Areas of Pender Harbour could already be mistaken for a city suburb, houses side by side with manicured lawns.

Fortunately for me, it rained almost the whole week we were in Bella Coola: all kinds of rain, from cold drizzles to pelting rainstorms, and once, a hailstorm. I say fortunately for me, because after I drove partway up the only road into or out of Bella Coola, I knew I wasn't going to live there. There are two other ways to depart from Bella Coola: by air, and the weather can make it impossible to fly in or out for weeks; and by boat, and the Trudeau government eliminated the scheduled coastal passenger service that stopped regularly at Bella Coola.

I said to John, "If you want to live in Bella Coola, I will visit you from time to time, but I can't live here." After that week of rain, rain, rain, I never heard another word about moving there.

Our fishing life was put on hold while we were in Bella Coola, but our visit there was quite an experience. I was glad afterward that I had been there. Howard White liked what I wrote as an entity by itself, especially about the Bella Coola Road, and thought it should be part of *Raincoast Chronicles*.

◆

Bella Coola. The name caught my eye on a map of Canada long before I ever dreamed of moving to British Columbia. I saw BELLA COOLA at the end of one section of a jagged waterway called North Bentinck Arm, part of a fjord that made a deep cut in the coastline. The words stood out because they were, I mistakenly thought, so Spanish, so romantic, in among a lot of Indian and Anglo-Saxon place names. I longed, for no logical reason, to go there some day.

When I came to British Columbia for the first time in 1969 with my two young sons, Jay and Richard, we flew out from New York, where we were living, and camped in provincial parks, following a route marked in heavy black ink on a worn road map that I clutched like a security blanket. Bella Coola was not one of the marked stops, but I figured we would make a side trip there if we possibly could.

Our route took us north on Vancouver Island, by ferry boat to Prince Rupert, along the Skeena River and down into the Chilcotin, to Williams Lake. At a crossroads there I saw a sign pointing west that said, BELLA COOLA.

We turned down a bumpy, dusty dirt road and stopped for gas. "How far is it to Bella Coola?" I asked.

The man selling the gas looked us up and down, stopped chewing tobacco long enough to spit accurately into a trash can and said, "How long you got?"

"Only today," I said. "I thought we'd go and take a look."

He shook his head. "It's a couple of hours just to get to the road," he said. "The Bella Coola Road. You driving?"

I said I was, and he shook his head again. "That's a pretty rough road. You better come back when you got more time. Plenty of time."

In 1973 I met my second husband John Daly, a commercial salmon fisherman, and went fishing with him on his forty-one-foot troller, the *MoreKelp*. One season we had to stop work suddenly for a whole month because the fishermen went on strike. We were in Namu, where BC Packers has an upcoast fish-buying installation in summer, when the strike started, so we decided to go on our boat to Eucott Bay and visit two elderly gentlemen, Frenchy and Simpson, who lived there on a rotting fish-camp float. On the way in I looked at the map and saw that we were now inside the same fjord-like waterway system as Bella Coola and said, "I wish we could go there!"

By coincidence, on our way out of Eucott we met Al Perkins, a big man with a large black moustache, who was an old friend of John's. We stopped to admire his handsome new white troller, the *Salmon Stalker*, and he remarked, "I've just been to Bella Coola, where I've been looking for land. I live in Duncan, and that place is getting too crowded for me."

"I know what you mean," John replied. "I've been thinking of doing the same thing myself."

The next morning John said, "I think we ought to explore the idea of moving to Bella Coola ourselves," as he started the boat's motor. We were soon moving along back down from where we had come, and part way he turned left, and right, into new territory; I lost track of our direction in the winding passages. The channel had high rock borders, and as we proceeded, mile after mile, twisting and turning through a steep-sided corridor, snow-capped mountains appeared ahead, above and around us. We must have gone at least fifty miles, deeper and deeper into the fjord, until we were in the narrow reach of North Bentinck Arm.

While we were running, I plucked our reference book, *British Columbia Coast Names*, out from under the mattress on John's bunk and looked up Bella Coola. Spanish origin indeed! According to the book's author, Captain John Walbran, the name Bella Coola is "an adaptation of the name of a tribe of Indians residing in the neighbour-hood," and Bella Coola is "the local spelling used by the postal authorities," and only one of several ways of spelling it; the others being Bela Kula; Bellaghchoolas; and Bel-houla. So much for Spain and romance!

After eight miles, we arrived at an area of mudflats and swamp grass swathed in mist. Low red buildings marked CANADIAN FISH COMPANY were on our left, and to our right were a mass of floats crowded with the boats of other commercial fishermen on strike; plus the usual mix of sailboats and pleasure cruisers. Behind this pictur-esque jumble were the highest mountains I had yet seen on the mountainous BC coast, with snowy tips and the white streaks of glaciers on their slopes. "It's like Switzerland here," I said. "These mountains have that same lofty beauty." I looked at the chart to reassure myself. "Bella Coola! What a surprise!" I exclaimed. "I didn't know it would be so lovely. I guess I didn't know anything about it at all."

John was busy looking for a place on the floats to tie up. He stopped beside a troller about the size of ours, the *Jan-Jac-Ann*. When our ropes were securely fastened to it, he came in and said, "Bella Coola has a big fishing fleet, and a strong union group. I've *always* thought I'd like to live in Bella Coola some day. When Al Perkins talked about moving here, I decided we'd take a look too. I don't know how much longer I can stand the noise of those airplanes flying in and out of Garden Bay, and the crowds. All the things I came to Pender Harbour to get away from are catching up with us. What I like about the people in Port Hardy and the Bella Coola-ites is they don't want to increase the gross national product, they want to garden, and stay as they are. They do get tourists who fly in to hunt or fish, and a few drive in, but coming over that road is a long and hairy trip. I don't think Bella Coola is likely to get the hordes of tourists we get. At least, that's how it seems to me."

It had been raining, but now, at the end of the day, the sun took a notion to shine. I stood on our deck, dazzled by the scenery; fading rays of sun lit up the mountains, their glaciers and their valleys. "Is *this* Bella Coola?" I asked. "I don't see any houses."

"Oh, it's a two-mile walk to 'downtown' Bella Coola," John said. "I hope the telephone on the dock works. Last time I was here, the rain was *pouring* when I went up to phone you in New York, and most of the glass in the kiosk was smashed. All I got was a recorded voice, and I lost the money I had put in, besides. I walked into Bella Coola three or four times and tried to telephone. I reported the phone the first day, and when it wasn't fixed the second night, I put my foot through the last whole piece of glass and you know why? Because I kept getting that bloody recorded voice that said, 'The number you have reached is not in service.' It just enraged me. If I had a human answer I would have been far less mad. Those fiendish recorded voices are an atrocity against all who cannot afford a phone in their own houses; a non-humanity that causes real angry frustration. I certainly understand the violent vandalism that occurs in an inarticulate 'won't answer back' phone booth." With that, he turned and marched up the ramp to telephone.

The telephone must have worked, because he was back shortly to say we had been invited for supper by the local game warden, Tony Karup. He arrived shortly in a yellow government truck; a greying, bald man in a khaki uniform. He drove us along a road bordered by the grassy flats of a river estuary that appeared to be a dumping ground for dilapidated and abandoned boats; and then we were in the main part of the town of Bella Coola. It consisted of a few rectangular streets, a United Church hospital, a library, several churches and stores. He pointed out a large store, famous for its excellent stock of books and handicrafts, that was owned and run by a local author, Cliff Kopas, whose book, *Bella Coola*, has become a standard historical reference. Driving along, it was clear that most of the Indian population in town lived on one side of the main intersection and the white people on the other.

We spent a pleasant evening at the neat, official house of the game warden and his good-looking Danish wife, but our meal was interrupted several times by telephoned reports about a grizzly bear in the area. "It's been killing cattle right in town, and I don't want any vigilante action," Tony said, returning to the table looking concerned. "Everybody's complaining now about all kinds of bears since they heard about this one; about bears that show up at their back doors, or claw marks on the windows, or garbage bags ripped apart. I was talking to one of our best Indian guides this morning, and he said, 'If I want to attract a bear for my clients, I buy new bread and they can smell it for miles around.' He also told me, 'I was at the garbage dump yesterday and I felt the wind of a paw on the back of my neck, and I sure jumped into the cab of my truck in a hurry!'"

The next morning, John and I walked the two miles into town in drizzling rain that shortly turned into a downpour. When we were wandering around in the Cliff Kopas store a tall, cheerful man greeted John. He was walking with the aid of two canes, and his name was Tom Gee. John called to me several counters away and I arrived in time to hear that Gee had jumped off a roof and landed on his heels, breaking them both. The last time John had seen him he was gillnetting.

Tom hustled us into his truck and for the several more days we stayed in Bella Coola he was our guide and transportation. That was fortunate because it never stopped raining. The rain in Bella Coola had a special wetness that gave everything a damp aura, and soaked through my fairly waterproof red windbreaker. Even now, when I am asked my impression of Bella Coola, all I can remember is the rain — and the friendliness of the people.

One morning when Tom arrived to pick us up he said, "I thought we'd go up the Bella Coola Road, oh, just for an hour or so." He explained as we drove away that the local inhabitants had built the road themselves. It was a tremendous effort, over the mountain range that separated Bella Coola by land from any other community. It connected over the top of the range to the town of Anahim Lake, where my sons and I would have landed if we had been foolish enough to keep on driving from Williams Lake.

John said, "I've never been on that road. It's the only land route in and out of Bella Coola. The only other way to go is by boat or plane, and often the weather's so bad planes can't fly. The government wouldn't do anything about a road, so the Bella Coola people built their own. I think they got a little grant for dynamite. Constructing that road over that mountain range was an extraordinary achievement."

"What's the road like?" I asked.

John replied, "I once met the man in charge of roads for the government and he said to me, 'It's really embarrassing. When I make road inspections my wife and daughter sometimes come with me, but when I start down the Bella Coola road, they either insist on staying at Anahim or they drive in with me with a rug over their heads.'"

We turned and started up a gravel road through a valley. Tom stopped once to show us an old water wheel, and again to let cattle cross in front of us. We drove past Indian smokehouses, sheds with rows of deep red salmon hanging on lines, then a federal fisheries counting hut that looked like an outhouse perched over a stream, and then a house shaped like an ark. "Here's hippieville in Noah's Ark," Tom said, and then we were crossing a bridge over rushing water. "A truck went through here when the bridge collapsed, and a little boy drowned," he said. "The fellow driving found the boy pinned under a bunker." We passed a handsome farm. "That belongs to the biggest farmer around here; he also has a house in town," Tom said.

Somewhere along the way, near where Tom said the Bella Coola River joined with the white water of another river, I saw a sign that said, "Closed to bear hunting. Do not feed, tease or molest bears." The road was becoming steeper and below us was spread a vista of beautiful bare green hills and snow slides. Tom was driving in first gear now, very, very slowly. Rocks slid down, rolling around the fenders of the truck.

I saw Tom put his elbows on the wheel, steering with them while he lit a cigarette. It was a horrifying sight. "You'd be surprised at the number of people who come in and don't drive out again," he said casually. "They put their cars on a barge instead and fly home. The road was just a goat trail when I came over it in 1956, and pretty tough here in the beginning; not the way it is now, with lots of turnbacks and turnarounds. Hello there!" he exclaimed, as a boulder hit the truck and rolled over the embankment.

I was sitting between the two men, so I had to stretch my neck to see where the rock had gone. The boulder bounced along down until it disappeared into what looked to me like a bottomless chasm, at least two thousand feet down.

We stopped suddenly. A large truck was just ahead, which shocked me. We could see such a short distance in front of us that I thought we had the road to ourselves. We sat and waited while the truck backed up over the edge. Its rear end hung out over space while it made the sharp turn in the road to go forward again.

Gee said, "Someone asked a trucker friend of mine how he did this in winter, when it's a sheet of ice and he said, 'Nothin' to it. I just drink a gallon of goof at the top of the hill and it smooths out like a prairie.'"

There was a general chuckle, which I joined in weakly. Then we went through the same manoeuvre we had watched the truck make: backing over the edge in a switchback, to go forward. I tried not to think about the back end of our truck hanging out into space while we sat in the front end.

"There's never been a fatal accident on this road," Tom continued cheerfully. "A fellow went over in a Toyota station wagon with a load of sewing machines 'way up past here, and dropped sixty feet onto a switchback below, hit a tree and hung up there. It wrecked the tree, and he was in the hospital for two or three days. That's all. People drive this road at a crawl because they know they have to, even if they are drunk."

We were grinding our way up the road again, catching up to the truck ahead of us, then falling back to wait. We continued to stop and back up at each hairpin turn on what I now viewed as an insane road, admirable as the effort must have been to build it. I was not put at ease by Gee's steering with his elbows again as he lit another cigarette. John was silent, but I must have stirred nervously in my seat between them, because to ease the tension Gee said, "There were four bears on Main Street last night. One about four hundred pounds was seen in the telephone booth, probably phoning to find out where the garbage dump is, and when he came out someone saw him pick up a garbage can and walk off with it. A bear scattered a garbage pail on the back porch of the hotel, and another bear was seen by the beer hall, looking in store windows. I guess they're taking the path of least resistance and not picking berries any more. Tony finally shot one last night."

I was beyond conversation; just hoping, well praying, that Tom wouldn't light another cigarette. When I thought I couldn't stand looking over one more thousand or two thousand or whatever thousand-foot drop on another hairpin switchback turn, I saw a turn-around ahead. John glanced at his watch and cleared his throat. Tom said, "Do you think we'd better go back now? We're having supper with the matron of the hospital, who wants to meet you, and we shouldn't be late."

"I think we'd better," John said. We turned around and headed back. My relief was short-lived. Going down was worse. Looking through the windshield, the short span of road ahead extended only a few feet and disappeared in the vertical drop. Then, over the edge and down we went, to another vanishing point and another steep drop, prefaced by a switchback that left us teetering over the side of the mountain. I tried looking ahead. Glancing over the side, across John, was not a pleasing view either—just emptiness, nothing below as far as I could see from where I sat, except on the switchbacks, where I could unfortunately see exactly how far down it was into the canyons beneath us. I thought about the mother and daughter who drove with a blanket over their heads. I wished I had brought one with me. I would have used it, without shame.

John put his hand over mine. He said, "Tom, I heard you had some sort of an accident with your gillnetter. What happened?"

"It was off Egg Island, and the engine started to miss," Tom said, throwing his cigarette out the window. I took a stick of gum out of my purse and started chewing, bracing myself for the moment when he would light another cigarette. Mercifully, he didn't. "As soon as I turned off the switch she blew, and blew me right out over the drum into the water," he continued. "I think the fire caught in the fuel pump. I didn't have a skiff along, so I swam away from the boat and got mixed up in some kelp. Then I swam back to the boat, got a grip on the tail end of the net, and made a hand hold. With the stabilizer and poles and the mast coming down, I felt pretty small, I can tell you. Everything burning and no skiff; and a hundred and twenty dollars in my pocket that I couldn't use. I was sure I'd be picked up because I had seen the Air Rescue on Egg Island. Somebody finally *did* pick me up, but I've always taken a skiff with me since then. I don't know when I'll get back fishing though. Breaking all those little bones in your heels is *really* painful, and they take a long time to heal."

We were down in the woods, in the valley now, driving through lovely green forests. I sat back with an audible sigh of relief. "If we had gone the whole way to Anahim, how long is that road?" I asked.

"Two hundred and fifty miles," Tom said.

"And that's the *only* way out of Bella Coola by land?" I asked.

"That's right," John said.

Back on the boat that night I said to John, "If you move to Bella Coola, I'll come and visit you. Maybe." He laughed and turned on the news. A few minutes later, the fisherman on the *Jan-Jac-Ann* told us that a strike vote had been called for the next day in Namu.

It was time to leave anyway. The continual rasp of our boat rocking against its neighbour, the rumble of the Gardner being run to prevent the chilly damp from overwhelming us, particularly in my quarters below, and the endless patter of raindrops on the pilothouse roof were getting on our nerves. For the first and only time on the *MoreKelp*, we began to snap at one another.

I packed for travelling; stowing loose items in the sink, ramming a knife in the cupboard door to keep it shut. The sun came out, casting a lovely yellow-white light on the mountains as we moved slowly away from the dock. I had seen Bella Coola, at last. It was beautiful, just as I had imagined, but I had no regrets about leaving.

Published in *Raincoast Chronicles #12*.

Fishing with John

———————— ✦ ————————

I HAVE BEEN AMAZED at the success of my book, *Fishing with John*. I honestly thought while I was writing it that nobody would read it except my family and friends, and I wasn't sure of them.

I started out writing about what it was like to live on a commercial salmon troller owned and operated by my husband, John Daly. It was supposed to be an article, what *The New Yorker* calls a Reporter At Large.

On my first regular fishing trip with John, in 1974, while he was delivering our first load of fish to Seafood Products in Port Hardy, I ran upstairs to the cannery office and called Bill at *The New Yorker*. "I have the most wonderful story!" I said. I explained to him that commercial fishing was not just a job but a way of life that I could not have imagined, and he told me to go ahead and write about it.

The longer I stayed on the boat, the more complicated I could see that it would be to describe this way of life. I just kept on taking notes and hoping I would find a way to write what I had in mind, and meanwhile, I wrote my Profile of Arthur Erickson.

In December 1977, John and I sat down in my study one day, talked about the article, and he gave me a story or two. After he left, I wrote a couple of paragraphs, and then he stuck his head in the door and said, "Let's go get a salmon for supper," which we did. It was late afternoon, and we fished at a place called Fearney Point, where John liked to go because he could look up Jervis Inlet at the snowy mountains while he fished.

John died two months later. I put the article aside, but I kept thinking about it. In 1980, I started writing again. I also started storing a case of sockeye salmon from Seafood Products under my bed, because there was no place else to put it.

At the end of every season, John used to present me with a case of sockeye that was mine to do as I pleased with, and when he died, Don Cruickshank, the manager of Seafood, sent me one. The next year I felt insecure without it, so that's when I started buying a case of my own every year and storing it under my bed. I have more space now, but being a fisherman's wife, I don't meddle with a good omen. I started writing again after John died, when that first gift of sockeye found its home.

It took me eight years to write *Fishing with John*, and it became a book. A year and a half was spent writing Chapter Five, about the gear. I was determined to get it right. After John's death, I turned to his fishermen pals for instruction, and ran up a terrible telephone bill. I guess I finally did get the gear straight because readers, always quick to spot a mistake, have noted only one in the book, and it wasn't about gear. I said "knots per hour" when it should have been just "knots." If I have to have made a mistake, I'll settle for that one.

When I had about forty pages of manuscript, I showed it to Bill and he told me to keep going. I said, "I can't seem to stay within the confines of a piece. It's going to be much too long."

Bill said, "Keep going. We'll take out what we want." Every so often I would bring another section to Bill, and he would say again, "Just keep going." By then I was getting a lot of encouragement also from John's son, Richard and his wife, Liv Mjelde, my sons, a few others to whom I would read sections, and from Howard White, who wanted to publish it as a book.

At the beginning, I thought I was composing a pretty technical piece about salmon trolling. Each day when I sat down to write, I was living again with John, though, and without my realizing what was happening, a subtle change occurred as I dug deeper into my memory.

John and I met quite late in our lives, and as people age I have noticed that they can remember way back but often forget their immediate past. I was afraid that might happen to me, so as I kept writing I thought, I can read about John if my memory fails me. Somewhere along the way, John just moved in and took over. I am told this book is a love story, but that was not my intention.

I get wonderful letters, hundreds of them, from people who enjoy knowing John through my book. He would be amused and, I think, pleased. He would be delighted as I was, with a letter I received the other day from Christchurch, New Zealand. Mr. Dick Georgeson wrote that he had "loved the book and it evoked some vivid memories as I was a cook for John for part of a season." Georgeson turns out to be the unnamed sixteen-year-old lad John hired who had "various viruses" and, in John's words, "got. . . so goddam seasick that when the doctor examined him on his return he was well again."

Dick Georgeson is sixty now. He explained that "because of seasickness I didn't appreciate either John or the environment at the time. However, later it has become one of the most fascinating parts of my life." He enclosed the original telegram, dated 7:04 p.m. on July 2, 1947, that John had sent him from Bull Harbour, near the fishing grounds, offering him "a share and you might make a few dollars" to join him. "Your book has brought alive those far off days and added a new dimension to those memories," Georgeson wrote to me in closing.

The story of young Georgeson, one of my favorites, which appears in the excerpt from *Fishing with John* that follows, was the last story John told me, the Christmas before he died, while we were sitting in his workshop down by the water, having a cup of tea.

◆

I rejoined John in July, at the height of the fishing season, at a place called Namu. The serious business of fishing terrified me. I wasn't worried about living on a boat or being seasick; I was afraid of being a nuisance by getting in the way or falling overboard. I didn't think about the actual process of fishing; I didn't know enough about it to do that. Permission to join John on his boat during the commercial fishing season came from Ottawa in June, but I had to pick up the formal document in the regional office of the Federal Department of Fisheries in Vancouver before I could proceed north. Without that, John would risk losing his commercial salmon-fishing license, in the unlikely but still possible event that a Federal Fisheries officer boarded the *MoreKelp* while we were fishing and asked to see my papers. I arrived in Vancouver with barely enough time to do some shopping for John and go to the Fisheries office to pick up the paper. TO WHOM IT MAY CONCERN, it read, and went on to grant me permission "to act as an observer, along the British Columbia coast, aboard the troller *MoreKelp* owned by Mr. J. Daly of Garden Bay, BC . . . and possibly other Canadian fishing vessels . . . for the purpose of writing . . . and research for a book which she intends publishing."

Running around Vancouver on my errands, I nervously calculated the three-hour time difference between the East and West Coasts and reset my watch one hour short. I missed by that hour the departure of my plane and had to wait overnight in a Vancouver airport hotel for another aircraft going north. In addition to my two small pieces of luggage — a duffel bag and a soft black leather case — I was carrying a large shopping bag of fresh fruit and greens John had requested: raspberries, strawberries, peaches, grapes, lettuce, water-cress, eight or nine avocados in varying stages of ripeness, and a half pint of heavy cream. In my luggage I also had two globe artichokes and a jar of preserved kumquats as a surprise. I handed the bag of fresh groceries to the desk clerk to put in the refrigerator overnight, and the next morning, when I took back the bag, it was a solid block of ice. He had put it in the freezer by mistake. During the three-hun-dred-mile trip north, with a two-hour wait at a halfway point for a small coastal float plane that could land on the water at Namu, the bag sat at my feet, defrosting moistly on the various floors.

On the map John had sent me during the winter, Namu was a name on the mainland surrounded by empty land, almost halfway up the BC coast — an indentation in a large body of water called Fitz Hugh Sound. He had explained that during the summer it was a fishing center owned and operated by the dominant fish-processing company on the British Columbia coast, BC Packers, where fishermen could sell their fish, make necessary repairs to their boats, mend nets, and take on fresh ice and supplies for the next trip out. In the winter, he wrote, it was deserted, except for a crew of eight men with their families, to maintain the buildings.

From the air, skimming above the trees, I could see waterfalls and streams and the raw scars made by logging — huge strips of exposed rock as if the bearded mountainside had been shaved. Namu came into sight as a clump of white buildings covering several acres of waterfront, with NAMU painted in large letters on the biggest roof. There were substantial dock structures, and a flotilla of fishing vessels appeared to be tied up or moving about. Little figures scurried around as we descended and our plane's floats skimmed the water. All I could see was John, arms folded across his chest, a head taller than anyone else, in faded bluejeans, looking thinner than I remembered him. His beard and mustache were as white as the T-shirt he was wearing, bleached by the same sun that had burned his face and arms so brown. Our eyes met for a second time as the pilot climbed down on the plane's float and opened the cabin door, and then I turned around facing the ladder, descending backwards, and stepped off a pontoon onto the dock. A clean-shaven man with glasses, about John's age, was standing beside him, eyeing me curiously, and John hastily introduced us. "Meet my old fishing pal, John Chambers," he said.

John brusquely refused Chambers's invitation to join him for lunch at the commissary, and hurried me and my luggage to a white wooden dinghy (painted green inside), which was tied to the dock. Sitting upright in the rowboat facing him, I noticed he was facing forward, rowing with short, rapid strokes. "I don't think I have ever seen anyone row any way but backwards," I said, "although rowing backwards really doesn't make sense."

"Most of us feel it's a good thing to be able to see what's ahead," John replied.

The *MoreKelp* was riding at anchor, its poles pointing skyward, in their running position. From where I sat, watching the boat rock in the light wind, its deck looked unattainable—as high above me as an ocean liner, although it was about three and a half feet. John threw my luggage over the gunwale; and, with John pushing from behind and my feet desperately groping for a foothold, I managed to scramble over the rail and roll like a sack of salt onto the deck.

I looked around hastily. John was busy pulling up the dinghy, and there was nobody else in sight. I thought, I hope nobody was watching us through binoculars. By the time I had collected my purse and shopping bag, John was attaching the dinghy to a pulley that held it upright on the port side of the open deck, and was moving my luggage to my quarters in the fo'c'sle, below the main space of the pilothouse in the bow. To get there, I slid down backwards from the floor of the pilothouse, since there was no step, to a narrow white bench on the starboard side where John had put my bag.

The port side, my sleeping quarters, was fully occupied by two bunks; the lower one was filled with fishing gear, but the upper had been freshly made with flannel sheets, gray wool blankets, and a pillow with a bright blue pillowcase. John called down that lunch was ready. I had put on jeans, red windbreaker, and sneakers for the plane ride, so I was dressed for the boat. Without unpacking, I climbed right back up to the pilothouse proper, where he was serving the special lunch of abalone he had prepared for my arrival—a coast delicacy I had never seen. He had gone out before dawn and pried a dozen or so of these tough shellfish off the rocks, pounding them into tenderness and half cooking them before I came. He finished frying them, in butter, and we ate them on the deck in the sunshine, listening to Bach on the CBC concert hour, washing them down with cool beer that John had stored in the cockpit. We had soggy raspberries for dessert, and John threw nine black avocados overboard, one by one. As the last avocado disappeared over the side, I clapped my hand to my head and said, "I forgot! I've brought you something that'll make up for the disaster of those frozen avocados." I dashed down below, opened my bag, and pulled out the two globe artichokes in their brown paper bag, and the jar of preserved kumquats from the sock in which I had wrapped it. I brought them up on deck and handed the artichokes to John. "A treat especially for you," I said.

He opened the bag and looked inside. "What *are* these?" he asked.

"Artichokes," I said.

"Those things you eat leaf by leaf that have nothing on them?" he said. "Certainly not!" He pitched them into the sea, bag and all. He wheeled around, peered down at me with a worried look, and gave me a quick hug. "Never eat the damned things. Too much trouble for what you get." I was still holding the jar of kumquats, so I backed up into the pilothouse and tucked them into the low cupboard, never to be mentioned again.

While I was washing the lunch dishes, John appeared with a box of my favorite Bourbon Creme biscuits — an English chocolate cookie with chocolate filling. "Don't eat the whole box at once," he said. John started the motor and hauled the anchor up. We began running out of Fitz Hugh Sound toward the fishing grounds. The three o'clock marine weather report had issued a small-crafts warning and we were coming out into the vast open water of Queen Charlotte Sound when he began looking anxiously at the sky. "I've been traveling along this coast so long, I could probably find my way blindfolded, but I like to check each anchorage," he said, pulling down a chart and examining it. Before we could find shelter, the wind rose and the rain came down — not gently but in huge, pelting drops that the gale washed wildly across our windows, so that we couldn't see even our bow. The gale wind shrieked through the rigging, and although we were snug inside the warm pilothouse, John was alternately looking at the compass and peering ahead for some physical sign, between gusts of rain, of the safe anchorage he was aiming for. We rocked and pitched in the enormous groundswell. This is what a following sea is all about, I thought, as I gripped the edge of the compass shelf to keep from falling off the stool.

The wind died down as swiftly as it had come up. Although the rain continued, we could at last see landmarks familiar to John. He slowed down when we were in the lee of a small island, and, with the bow pointing toward shore, put the clutch into neutral. He was standing inside at the wheel, and he reached over and opened one of the starboard windows. Then he turned and dashed for the door, reaching down before he went through it to pull a chain that engaged the hydraulic motor that powered the anchor winch, and pushing the clutch of the anchor winch just outside the door with his foot as he passed.

Through the starboard windows, I watched him edge his way slowly forward along the narrow foot-wide space between the pilothouse and the gunwale toward the bow. Arriving on the bow deck, he crouched next to the bow hatch cover directly in front of me, with one hand on a steering wheel mounted on the outside wall of the pilothouse. Reaching in through the open window with the other, he pushed the clutch to reverse. Then he gently moved the throttle so that we backed up a little, continuing to maneuver with throttle and clutch back a little, then forward, until he was satisfied with our position. He stood up and shoved the heavy galvanized anchor that I could see hanging, poised at the bow over the roller, into the water, giving the heavy chain an encouraging tug. With a deep-throated groan, the anchor chain clattered over the bow for a dozen or so fathoms, pulled by the weight of the anchor. John gave it a couple of kicks, and it continued to travel down until the sound changed as the shackle joining chain to rope went over the bow roller with a rumpelty-clunk, down the narrow footpath on the port side, unwinding steadily from the winch. The end of the chain went over the side with what seemed to me like a sigh of relief, followed by the smooth-sliding rope, which ran along quietly until it halted, abruptly. The anchor had touched bottom.

The motor had been idling, and again John pushed the clutch, from neutral to astern, the boat moving almost imperceptibly, tugging at the anchor, until he was satisfied that the anchor was holding.

"How far down is it?" I asked.

"Twelve fathoms," John replied.

He came into the pilothouse then and shifted the clutch to move the boat forward and back once more, to make absolutely sure that the anchor had caught and would not drag during the night, and said, "Stop the Gardner."

"What? Where? Where?" I cried. I didn't know what he was talking about.

"Stop the engine. Pull that green rope behind you to the right of the pilothouse door," he said. "It's beside the exhaust pipe."

I ran to the back. An implausibly slim vertical green rope came up through a small hole in the floor there and was attached to a spring on the exhaust pipe at the ceiling. I would never have guessed it had anything to do with stopping a motor. I pulled hard. Nothing happened. I pulled harder, and the motor stopped. Enormously relieved, I let go. The motor instantly started again. I looked wildly around. Where was John?

He was just coming into the pilothouse. "Pull harder and hold on until the buzzer sounds," he said. "That will tell you that the oil pressure is down, and you can let go then."

I pulled on the rope this time until the motor stopped and a buzzer, a piercing, drill-like tocsin, had replaced the low rumble of the Gardner engine. Then I let go. The buzzer persisted.

"Now push the button that stops that buzzer," John said patiently.

"Where? Where?" I cried again.

"I thought you had seen me do that," he said. "Push that little silver knob on the bulkhead to the right of the steering wheel."

"Where? Where?" was my recurrent cry, especially when instructions were shouted at me in emergencies. Then I forgot the little I knew. It was not until some time during the second year that all the *MoreKelp*'s systems came together for me as if I had been living on her all my life. The rope-and-buzzer routine for shutting off the motor continued to perplex me, because, despite all John's explaining, it remained hazy in my mind. I crawled back behind John into the engine room one day, and he showed me the connections between the big complicated Gardner diesel motor and the mechanical parts above us in the pilothouse, and that helped. I could then visualize what was happening.

At anchor, it was wonderfully quiet. No shrieking wind, no rumbling motor, no buzzers! Quiet. All quiet. John poured himself a Scotch, looked questioningly at me, and, when I held out my mug, poured a smaller one for me. He settled down on the pilothouse seat with his mug, and I sat on the stool beside him, nursing mine with both hands. "Nothing that has to be done on this boat comes naturally to me," I said unhappily. "I don't think I can do any of the things you really need."

"Like what?"

"Oh, cleaning fish, or making up gear, or jumping off the boat and tying it up to docks when you bring it in, and I'm not very good at steering. I don't understand compasses and charts, and I can't do *anything* mechanical."

"You'll learn. You'll learn," he said. He leaned over and took one of my hands in both of his. "All my fishing life, I've dreamed of having someone like you with mental protein between the ears as a permanent partner on my boat. I've fished alone most of my life, so I don't need help there. Besides, with our difference in height, I can't see how you and I both could fish from the stern. The gear is set up too high for you now, and would be too low for me if it was correct for you; and if you stood on a box it would get in the way. No, no, don't worry about any of that! If you cook, and wash our clothes, and tidy up from time to time—because I'm such a messer—and steer when I ask you to and learn to look ahead *all the time* instead of at me, so you can watch out for kelp patches and logs, you'll be a real help. Later on, you might like to ice the fish and turn a hand at making up gear, but the important thing for you to do is write, and you'll have plenty of time for that. We'll each have our own work. Frankly, I think it's better that way."

He sat back in his seat, and his smile made the small pilothouse sunny, even though it was raining. It was lovely to sit there and watch the pale yellow of the fading sun in the soft rain shimmer along the treetops on the nearby shore and slip away. John said, "I used to dream of having a partner your size who could monkey-wrench that engine in that bloody small engine room that I have to crawl into on my hands and knees. What do you think?" I shook my head, and we both laughed.

"I've had fishing partners—both my boys, principally, whom I took with me one at a time when they were at school, from the age of about eleven, and later when they were working their way through university," John went on. "The eldest one, Dick, used to make wonderful faces out of kelp; he would jab a knife into the globe to make a nose and eyes, and the kelp strings would become hair. He'd put the head over the top of one of the gurdy handles when he was back working with me. The first time, I was a little surprised, but I liked it. It amused me a lot. My younger son, Sean, used to draw, always sketching and painting everything with pen and pencil: sunrises and sunsets, other boats. He was also a good experimental cook; he mixed grapefruit and ham, I remember, and one summer, when it didn't stop raining for more than three hours twice in three months, he did two or three hours of mathematics every day with his back against the exhaust pipe, which is behind the wall now. The boat was very uncomfortable then. It's palatial now, by comparison. As for other partners, I'd rather slave at chores than have to be bad-tempered with youths raised on moron TV and rock radio. When my forty-six-year-old pal from Port Hardy, Peter Spencer, comes for ten days, it's a complete rest for me, because I trust him to take over one hundred percent. All I can do he can do better, and he knows the coast like a book. Most of the modern youth smoke, and I can't stand butts stinking up the place and I worry about fire, which is B-A-D on a boat. The very *worst* is when they talk above the engine, and the younger ones *must* talk. I can only put up with one trip of that stuff. My friend Charlie Walcott, dead now, always took along two deckhands, because they could amuse each other, but you need to make a lot more money to do that and I didn't want to. On the occasions when I have hired a deckhand, however, I had a very simple test for finding out whether he would be a good worker. I found it to be practically infallible. What do you think it was?"

"I can't even guess," I said.

"I gave him a cup of coffee, and if he picked up his mug and put it in the sink when we were done talking, or even better, if he rinsed it out, I would hire him. If he left it wherever we had been sitting, I wouldn't."

John reached up to a small, round, wooden-based barometer that was hanging between two pilothouse windows and casually moved the top needle on its old-fashioned china face from the Gothic print of STORMY to RAIN and said, "Years ago, I was in Winter Harbour on the west coast of Vancouver Island, tied up to a great big beautiful troller who was making really big money at that time. I just couldn't understand having to support such a huge boat. As long as I could pay all my expenses and educate my kids and save a little money, I just wanted to go on fishing, because I loved it. Another friend told me he wanted to extract a certain number of dollars from the ocean by a certain age and then quit, but I have never had any idea of ending fishing so long as I'm healthy. It's a way of life for me. I just want to take things a little easier as I go along. The people and the sea life of the coast and all its rain and fog and beautiful sunrises and sunsets become part of you and you part of it. It's indivisible. That was quite a squall we went through. On the water, you have to keep in mind all the time that *the sea is out to get you.* Treat the sea as if it is *always*

Illustration by Edith Iglauer Daly

trying to get you. It's the only way to survive. You can never really relax. Never!"

He got up and poured himself another drink and turned around to face me, holding his mug in midair. "Say, do you get seasick?" he asked. "Peter went out with me the trip before you and left his seasick pills for you, in case you do."

"I've never been seasick, but I've never been on a fishing boat, either," I said. "I'm glad those pills are here, just in case."

John resumed his seat. "Am I ever lucky you don't get seasick!" he said. "But if you *do* happen to get seasick, enjoy it. Don't worry over being a nuisance if it happens. It can be very constructive physically, because it cleans out the system. A doctor friend of mine who lives in Crumpet Town — that's Victoria — says I cured his New Zealand nephew of various viruses because I took him trolling and got him so goddam seasick that when the doctor examined him on his return he was well again. The doctor said, 'The ocean completely cleaned him out!'"

"I don't plan to stay if I get seasick," I said.

"Nobody knows how they'll feel in this terrible groundswell until they try it, but chances are if you didn't get sick today you're probably all right," John said. "It's one of the reasons I mostly fish alone. Of the several partners I've had for short periods, the younger they are, the more seasick they seem to get, and the worse it is for me, because I suffer so for them. You have to break up a twelve-day trip and run some poor seasick man fifteen hours to an airplane."

I had made myself a cup of tea by this time and moved to the bunk to sit against the wall, and John stretched his long legs across the stool I had vacated. "I had this huge husky sixteen-year-old from Prince Rupert with me," he continued. "I had used him in the harbor there to unload fish and wash down the hold: a wonderful worker in the quiet waters at the float. But the poor devil started off the first evening out being seasick, and the following morning, with a northwesterly blowing twenty-five miles an hour and a boat running on either side of us, he lay across the door with his feet in the cabin and his head on the deck, wishing he could die. All I could do was to dash over from the wheel and move him to one side of the door, where I walked across him like a wet sack of spuds for a couple of hours. The next day, he managed to get down a piece of dry toast and sat on the hatch cover swaying back and forth. I was so afraid he might fall overboard in a big swell that the third day, when he didn't improve, I went to quieter waters, into Port Hardy, and put him on a Co-op fish packer and sent him back to Prince Rupert. Peter Spencer was on holiday just then, so he went fishing with me for the next ten days. I had so much grub on board for that seasick kid that Peter *had* to come along to help me eat it! Peter had fished all his life—he was gillnetting briefly with a boat of his own at thirteen—but never commercially after that. We fished that first day until the tide changed and I went to bed. Peter was pulling up the gear and the boat rolled and dumped me out of the bunk. He says I just grabbed the blankets and kept sleeping on the floor. You've already seen how the *MoreKelp* can roll when we're running."

"I wonder whether my cats would have gotten seasick," I said. I had wanted to bring my two cats, Saskia and her son, Angel, with me from New York, but John had vetoed their presence on the boat, so I had found a new home for them back East; but I missed them. In the squall we had just gone through, they would have been terrified. "You were right about those cats of mine," I said.

"If you start a cat on a boat when it's a kitten, it can be quite useful," he said. "I had a Norwegian fishing pal who used his cat as a barometer. Joe was a real tough fisherman, with this very small boat, who trolled a long way offshore. He told me, 'I used to watch my cat, and whenever the cat spat at me and ran up the mast and clawed hell out of it, I knew it was really going to blow and I'd better head for shelter. Then someone gave me a barometer, and every time it dropped a long way down I started running in. Often the wind didn't come, and I lost money. So I got fed up and threw the barometer overboard and said, "Yaw, I go back to the cat.""

Late in the afternoon, the rain stopped and the sun came out long enough to create the kind of sunset I had seen on the slide screen in John's kitchen. The dark clouds parted to reveal a red ball that slowly sank in the darkening sky below the horizon, casting silvery and yellow threads on the black ripples of water surrounding us. The boat swung gently at the anchor John had cast over the bow earlier. Ahead were the rocks and trees of the apparently uninhabited shore, an unbroken strip of shadowy darkness; behind us, the open, black, glistening sea.

"Time for supper. Come see where the fresh food is kept, so you'll be able to get it from now on," John said. He bent his head low at the pilothouse door, and I followed him outside to the large box under the boom. The four-by-four-foot lid had a smaller lid in the near corner, which he lifted off and set aside. He reached in and removed a three-by-five clear plastic mat filled with a green, quiltlike material, that he laid on the deck. "This is an ice blanket, made of glass-fiber insulation material," he said. "Very useful for preserving ice."

I knelt and looked in. The hold was filled to the brim with sparkling snowy particles of crystalline ice. Two neat fillets of red salmon were laid out on a board on top of the ice, beside an open white box filled with groceries. A rope attached to it was hooked to the wall at the top of the hatch opening.

"I ice my fish and put them down in the hold as I catch them, starting at the bottom, until I bring them in to sell," John said. "I sold two thousand pounds of salmon at Namu just before you came, and took on three tons of new ice there. I keep all my groceries on top of the ice, except milk and meat, which I bury along the edge." He lifted out the board with the salmon fillets on it and pulled the box up by the rope, set it on deck, and picked out a head of lettuce, new potatoes, broccoli, and fresh peaches, then dropped the box, which contained several egg cartons, cheese, bread, and more fresh vegetables and fruit, back on the ice. He dug the half pint of heavy cream out of the ice, replaced the ice blanket, and put the lid back on the hatch. "Never leave the hatch cover off longer than absolutely necessary," he said. "That's good Namu ice and holds up the best of any I get, but it has to last us ten or twelve days, until we deliver fish again."

Back in the pilothouse, John pulled a seasoned, black cast-iron skillet from one of the shallow shelves under the stove, put it on the hot burner, rolled the fillets in cornmeal, and while he waited for the safflower oil he poured into the skillet to heat, dropped the potatoes into another pot, pumped water into it from the sink, and set the potatoes on the stove to boil. He had already brought down the table across the bunk to get at the salt and pepper behind it, so I set the two plates—his worn tin one and the glass pie plate that became my regular dish—on the nonskid mesh mat inside the table rim. I was beginning to see that every detail on this rocking horse of a boat was designed to utilize every inch of space and to keep everything in place.

The stove interested me. The top, which was not quite two feet wide and a foot and a half deep, with a trough an inch in from the edge to catch fat if it was used as a griddle, was surrounded on four sides by a brass-rod rim an inch or so above it, with vertical fastenings at the corners. A spring hooked from the front to the back rim divided the top in half—a movable barrier that prevented pots from sliding and crashing into one another or onto the floor. There was a black stovepipe at the rear, and right in front of it, embedded in the stove top, was a lever. When you pulled the lever up, it closed an opening in the pipe and sent heat around the minuscule oven instead. The word SEACOOK was stamped in black letters across the white enamel door. John had added color by painting the oven handles a bright marine-paint blue. The stove sat on a little metal apron, and three shallow shelves below held, in addition to the skillet, a saucepan, our red stewpot, a stainless-steel lidded pan with two handles, the old Brown Betty earthenware teapot when it wasn't in use, and two shallow dishpans, one of which served as our bathtub.

The rest of our equipment consisted of a double boiler stowed over the sink, together with a variety of loose items, reasonably secure behind two-inch-high shelf edges. In a storm or a continuing deep swell, the more dangerous movables were stored below the sink behind sliding doors in the cupboard. A fish knife rammed into the crack there kept the doors from popping open and spilling the contents onto the floor, from which, with every deep roll of the boat, they would otherwise have taken off, as if on skids.

John sautéed the salmon until it had a light-brown crust, and at the last minute he dropped dried mint from the garden at home into the pot of boiling potatoes, while I sat on the bunk with my legs curled under me out of his way, and watched him cook. This was different from Christmas, when we had brought prepared food onto the boat in pots from the house. For a refrigerator then we had used the deck corner right outside the pilothouse, in the winter cold. I hadn't even known there was a fish hold, although I had tripped several times over the corner of the large blue hatch lid. After the dirt of New York and the limitations of apartment-house living, the beauty of the rocky coast, thickly covered with trees that extended far into crevasses and over mountaintops that became higher and snowier in the distance, had so dazzled me I could hardly absorb anything else. On my first trip, except for the wall sayings, I had scarcely noticed my immediate surroundings, taking even the stove and its cozy heat for granted.

Now I was alive to everything: the smallness of the boat and the largeness of the rolling sea around us, whose only perimeter was the single black line of coast on one side; the primitive character of the space that confined us — one hundred and forty square feet for working, sleeping, walking, sitting, and eating. I thought, I am floating on the ocean with John, in a ten-by-forty-one-foot wooden box that contains sleeping bunks, cooking and storage areas for food, clothing, towels, sheets, and spare engine parts; a hand pump that produces fresh water at the sink from two one-hundred-gallon tanks that I cannot see below deck, where there is also a chugging motor I can hear, fed by fuel tanks also mysteriously hidden whose diesel fumes I can smell; radios, fishing gear, beer, Scotch, wine, even one small split of Mumm's French champagne — but no bathroom. All the other fishing boats I have been on that were the size of the *MoreKelp* have contained a toilet, or head. The only facility on ours was a beat-up galvanized iron pail, which was flushed out by hand at sea on the end of a long, heavy blue rope tied to its handle and then returned to the deck half-filled with fresh seawater: a movable bathroom that could be set down on the deck facing wherever the view was best, or taken inside the pilothouse. I hadn't even noticed the lack of a head the previous Christmas until we were well out of Pender Harbour. John had nervously brought up the subject as we started up Jervis Inlet. "I am six feet four inches tall, and when I built this new pilothouse I had a choice between putting the floor down far enough so that I could stand up straight when I steer or walk inside, or making room for a head," he had explained. "The one thing I couldn't do was add to the height of the pilothouse, because that would have made the boat top-heavy, and a vessel this narrow can sink in the kind of storms we get on this coast. Not having a head is a protection, too. It's a good excuse for not taking passengers."

I was remembering now the telephone call I had received late one night in New York from John in Pender Harbour a month or so after that first winter visit. It was 2 a.m. — 11 p.m. his time — and it began with his usual husky-voiced shout, "Hello!"

"Hello," I said, anxious. "What's wrong?"

"I've just bought a wooden toilet seat that I think will fit very well on top of that pail on the boat," he said. "It's sky-blue, and I paid eight dollars and fifty-six cents for it."

"Lovely," I remember saying. "But it's two o'clock in the morning here. What about it?"

"What about it?" he had shouted back. "Marriage! That's what!"

What a proposal! How could I resist him, and why should I? I laughed myself to sleep.

Frequently over the years, despite the extra height John had given to the pilothouse, he was to complain about the *MoreKelp*'s space limitations. He claimed that his chronic leg cramps were due to lack of walking area, and he jogged regularly in place in the cockpit while he waited for the fish to bite. Two idiosyncratic characteristics of the *MoreKelp* really bothered me. There was no comfortable place to sit, anywhere, and no solid barrier outside on the deck between me and the sea. I dreamed about upholstered easy chairs, and carried a square of green foam rubber John cut from a larger piece, which I sat against or on whenever I sat out on deck. A folding beach chair would have done, and we had one on board, but it could only be set up outside when we were at anchor in calm weather.

My real concern was the absence of guardrails on the *MoreKelp*. As a piece of unwanted baggage, I carried a mental picture of myself making a misstep on the slippery deck or losing my balance in rough weather and going over the side. Only a foot-high gunwale separated me out on deck from the water, except in the stern. There the deck dropped several feet behind the fish box where John spent most of his time, making the gunwale hip height for John but chest high for me, and, to my way of thinking, "safe." On the port side, the stern space behind the pilothouse was filled by the dinghy that all commercial fishing vessels are required to have, so I never went there. Ours, pointed toward the sky, hung from a pulley and was lashed to the rigging above the boom. Starboard was the frightening side. I was constantly traveling from pilothouse to stern, carrying food or equipment to John, moving around for exercise, or just being sociable. It was the only cleared walking space we had. John strung up a heavy iron chain along my path at waist height, which was a convenient drying line for dish towels and clothes, but I was always conscious that the yawning space between the chain and the gunwale was large enough for a body (mine) to fall through. I was often asked after that first trip how I had spent my time. "I concentrated on not falling overboard," I said.

Paradoxically, my only serious accident on the boat occurred when it was safely tied at our dock in Pender Harbour in the fall. I was cleaning out the cupboards, and I walked off the boat with a Mason glass jar in each hand and slipped, catching my leg between the boat and the scow, badly twisting my knee, breaking both jars, and cutting my hands. John had given me credit for more common sense than I possessed. His observant troller friend, Reg Payne, at a rendezvous at sea the next season, watching me move around on the *MoreKelp* and then step from our boat to his larger troller, the *Saturnina*, said, "I can see you are not a boat person. A few minutes ago, you told me you were going 'downstairs' to get your jacket. It's *down below*, Edith, *down below*! And by the way, for your own safety, you must always hold on to something solid when you are standing or moving on a boat; never let go with one hand until you are holding on to something else with the other." It was the best piece of boat advice I was ever given.

◆

One night, there was a full moon, followed by a spell of rainy, chilling cold weather and westerly winds, so John was careful to anchor in a protected harbor under the lee of the land. Early the next morning, the weather was so stormy that we stayed in the harbor, and, after the news, John turned the dial of the Wesco to the international radio band. An American fishing boat running to Alaska was asking permission to go into Winter Harbour, a settlement with a government dock, a general store, and a post office, on the west coast of Vancouver Island. John always listened attentively to any news about Winter Harbor, because he had fished off there for so many years and owned a lot on the waterfront, where he occasionally suggested we should move.

Canada's Federal Fisheries patrol boat, the *Tanu*, answered the call and gave the boat permission to go into the much closer but uninhabited anchorage at Cox Island off Cape Scott, north of Winter Harbour. When the American boat's skipper said he didn't know where Cox Island was and that his splashboards had all been washed loose, the *Tanu*, with obvious reluctance, permitted the vessel to go to Winter Harbour. "You can come in for repairs if it is absolutely necessary, but you can only stay long enough to make them and must leave again immediately," the voice on the *Tanu* said sternly. "You know the regulations: keep your poles up and your gurdies off and in your fishhold, and be out again by twelve noon tomorrow, or get further permission."

"All those American guys want to do is get in and sleep, but if an issue is made of it the *Tanu* has to have a proper reason for letting them — maybe a broken shaft or mast," John said. "If you want to do something that's not exactly right, you should know the other guy's law and give a reason that will cover it. Your American fish-patrol boats do the same — especially in Alaska, with its hundred-mile winds — and when some of our fishermen have asked, your Coast Guard has said no, if there was any American boat still to come in. In a real blow, coming in can take nine, ten, or eleven hours, making maybe two miles an hour for forty-five miles."

Shortly after, another American boat called in and the *Tanu* read them the regulations again, giving them permission as well, with the same strict limitations. John switched back to the Mickey Mouse in time to hear someone describe a birthday cake he was making for a party he and a friend were planning in the harbor. Later, he went out and waved at another boat, a red troller, as it came past to anchor. "That's Walt Nygren and his two sons," John said. "He's only got one arm, and he's one of our best fishermen."

That day, since it was too rough to fish, I cleaned out the cupboard — John called it the locker — under the sink, a half shelf at a time, setting the bottles and bags, pots, and jars that contained staples like brown Demerara sugar, flour, coffee, tea, oil, vinegar, and numerous condiments over on the bunk while I wiped off the shelves. Especially in rough weather, the locker's contents shifted, no matter how tightly I had packed them against one another. After a week or so, the shelves would be in a terrible mess and need tidying again.

During the cleanup, the floor had to be kept clear as a passage for John. Each container had to be laid carefully on the bunk canvas so that it wouldn't roll when the boat heaved, which was all the time in the groundswell. I enjoyed fitting things back into the cupboard again, closely packed to brace one another in niches that were now as familiar to me as they were to John: the coffee can, far left front, bracing the Scotch whiskey bottle directly where the doors slid open, kept in place by the wide jar that held pieces of Britl-Tak, both supported by the battered big rectangular blue-and-white painted tin decorated with pretty pink flowers which held the pancake mix, next to the round can containing sugar, next to another of flour, and so on, right along the two shelves, upper and lower, into the far corners where we kept seldom-used items, like chopped nuts for baking and unopened jars of preserves and pickles. It was important not to change the location of any item; everything on the boat had its own special place. "It could be a matter of life and death to find something in a hurry just by reaching in for it," John warned, one day when he found I had used a screwdriver and thoughtlessly dropped it back on the tool shelf instead of in its proper slot in the wrench box. "Besides, looking for things is a huge waste of time."

The storm abated, the weather turned sunny, and we were fishing again. I could no longer bear to stay inside at my typewriter, and to justify abandoning it I washed the *MoreKelp*'s windows. Mary Gunderson's daughter, Vera, had told me in Port Hardy about washing windows with newspaper as the scrubber, and warm vinegar water in place of soap, so I put warm water and vinegar in the laundry pail, and shoved it and a newspaper through the wheelhouse window. Then I went out and crawled along the narrow deck on the starboard side to the bow, holding fast to the roof, and washed the front windows. (I later discovered that the vinegar-and-newspaper process was as common as using commercial Windex, but it was all new to me.) I was delighted with the results, which made me daring enough to wash the side windows, too, although the boat was moving, slowly. I crouched on the narrow planking, my rear half over the gunwale, feeling the wind in the empty space between me and the sea, seeing the foamy water rush by out of the corner of my eye, while I gripped the wall with one hand and washed each window with the other.

It was such a lovely, clear day that after lunch, and an extended nap that began during the Music Hour when he pulled up the gear and flopped down outside in the sun, John decided to take a bath on deck. He filled the kettle and the bucket with water at the sink, put them both on the stove, turned it up, and while he was waiting for the water to warm, stripped all his clothes off. He leaned out of the pilothouse door and looked around. "All clear," he announced. "We've got the whole ocean to ourselves. I am going to celebrate this day by showing you how to have a *real* bath at sea."

He soaped himself from the top of his head to the soles of his feet, grabbed the bucket, and stalked out on deck, where he dumped the whole bucket of water enthusiastically over his head. I hastily took up a position on the far corner of the hatch lid to escape being splashed. Standing on the deck naked, with water dripping from his head and beard, he had a kind of walrus look, and I began to laugh. "I've never seen anybody look so *wet!*" I said. I was going to offer to get rinse-water when he rushed back into the pilothouse, poured the contents of the kettle into the pail, hurriedly pumped water in from the sink to fill it up, ran back out on deck, and dumped the contents over his head again with the same abandon.

We had had such a pleasant day and John had such a long nap in the afternoon that I announced a cocktail hour when we anchored, and put on the one long dress I had brought with me in the bottom of my pack. Before I came, I had the idea that from time to time we would go into charming little seaports like the ones I had seen at Cape Cod in Massachusetts, or around Chesapeake Bay in Maryland, and step out for dinner to the small, chic kind of restaurant one finds in summer along the Eastern seaboard of the United States. It was already clear to me that, living with John, I would be saying goodbye to all restaurants except those that were practical, cheap, and preferably Chinese, and that there was nothing I needed less than a long, low-necked dinner gown. The dress was bright-red cotton—made specially for me from cloth sent by friends working for the Canadian government in Lesotho, Africa—and I was determined to wear it just once. To my surprise, John was delighted with the idea, put on a clean blue shirt, and opened a split of champagne that he had hidden under my bunk. I was curled up on the bunk, laughing, my bare feet tucked beneath me, when John suddenly swooped from his perch on the steering seat, seized the square mirror from its slot behind the sink, and held it up to my face. "Look at yourself!" he exclaimed. "Look at yourself in the mirror and tell me whether you think this fishing life with me agrees with you or not."

I looked from his beaming face into the mirror and saw, as if for the first time, the sunburned face, brown eyes, white hair, and freckles of a woman I was familiar with, all right, but the glowing look was new. I turned back with astonishment to John, who was still holding the mirror up to my face. "Is that really me?" I said, and covered my face with my hands. He took my hands away and looked at me.

"I guess I've come to stay," I said.

Published in *Fishing with John*, 1987.